Hold on please, Emily

LIFE HAPPENS. CANCER HURTS.

LOVE HEALS. COFFEE HELPS.

DORIS SIU

HOLD ON PLEASE, EMILY

FIRST EDITION

Cover design by Cutting-Edge-Studio.com.

ISBN (e-book): 978-1-7775609-2-8

ISBN (paperback): 978-1-7775609-0-4

ISBN (hardcover): 978-1-7775609-1-1

dorissiu.com

For my son, Lucas,
who gave me the courage to start
my authorship career.

Author Note

Dear readers,

Words cannot 'espresso' how thankful I am for all your support. This book is a part of my #HoldOnPleaseEmily Campaign to raise awareness for glioblastoma (GBM), a terminal cancer with no cure.

Words build connections, educate, and empower us to take action. As a cancer advocate and author, I was compelled to produce a medium to connect with patients and families impacted by cancer by helping them feel validated, less afraid, and more motivated in their journey. Knowledge is a powerful tool in the fight against cancer and for inspiring hope. #HoldOnToHope and together we can #EndBrainTumours.

Illness and death are tough topics to discuss. I hope my novel could inspire my readers to find their voice, be brave, and be hopeful. My mission is to use realistic fiction, songs, and videos as a medium to educate, advocate, and inspire. Check out my website at dorissiu.com for more details about how you can join my #HoldOnPleaseEmily Campaign. To learn more about GBM, visit braintumour.ca.

Although Emily McGregor is a fictional character in my novel, she embodies every person whose lives have been impacted by brain cancer. Emily symbolizes the struggles and fears that come with a cancer diagnosis, and the hope and strength in the face of adversity. Her empowering story shared in *Hold on please, Emily* can inspire us to never give up.

As you enter the world of Emily McGregor, let me remind you that *Hold on please, Emily* is a fictional book. Any recognizable names of songs, movies, TV shows and celebrities I mention are purely to highlight some of my personal favourites.

To celebrate the launch of my debut novel, I teamed up with musician Matthew Isaacs (also known as *Kromatix_*) to transform my lyrics, from *Hold on please, Emily,* into inspirational songs. Where there is music, there is hope. Where there is hope, there is love. Now accompanying this novel is a mini music album (EP), *Hold on please, Emily: Songs of Hope*, featuring the singles of some of Emily's songs. Check out my latest music on Spotify and subscribe to my YouTube channel.

Although the path we follow in our lives may be unknown, always remember to seek comfort from the stars that fill the night sky. Trust that with patience, hope will find us, and music will follow.

As I embark on my authorship career, your feedback is invaluable. Please leave me a review on Amazon or Goodreads to share your thoughts. If you have a story to share, I would love to hear from you. Perhaps you may even inspire me for my next book.

Love my music? Want to collaborate on a song? Connect with me to become a part of my songwriting journey of building an inspirational soundtrack to raise cancer awareness.

Hold on to hope. *Hold on please, Emily.* Help Emily spread her message about hope by supporting the Brain Tumour Foundation of Canada or your local cancer charities.

Grab a cup of coffee and follow me on Instagram (@doris.siu.writes), Facebook (@doris.siu.writes), Twitter (@DorisSiuWrites), YouTube, or online at dorissiu.com.

Happy reading,

Doris

Doris Siu

Free Thank You Gift

Thank you for purchasing my book to support my work and for joining the #HoldOnPleaseEmily Campaign. As an author and songwriter, your support goes a long way. Thank you for helping me continue my mission of using realistic fiction and songs as a medium to connect with patients and families impacted by cancer. The power of words in novels and music can inspire hope.

Please visit my website at dorissiu.com to sign up for my newsletter and receive a free thank you gift. Download a limited-edition printable *Hold on to Hope Gratitude Journal* for free featuring inspirational quotes from *Hold on please, Emily.* This gratitude journal outlines a seven-day challenge to help boost your attitude towards gratitude. It is an excellent resource to help anyone cope with life challenges. As you personalize your gratitude journal, you will bring your stories to life. Your appreciation for all the little things will grow. Think big, start small. #HoldOnToHope. #HoldOnPleaseEmily.

Chapter One

Christmas morning. 20 degrees below freezing. I stood alone, surrounded by a sea of tombstones covered by a dusting of freshly fallen snow. Though I wasn't *really* alone.

My nose was half frozen, so I took a nice long sip of coffee to try to warm up. Coffee. My sweetest companion. As long as coffee was within my reach, how bad can life be? I fiddled with my coffee cup as I meticulously cleared the snow from my parents' tombstone. It had become an odd tradition, spending every Christmas morning singing songs to the dead. Okay, maybe not *every* Christmas. But *every* single one since my fourteenth birthday.

My parents' most favourite holiday was definitely Christmas. The two of them used to wake me up on Christmas morning through song. Mom and Dad would always pick a different Michael Bublé duet to sing together, but "White Christmas" was their ultimate favourite.

Each visit to the cemetery served as a reminder of some of life's medley of fears. I used to fear old people. Their eyes. The way they looked at the young. It was like they knew death was near, and they hoped the youth could spare them some time. As we aged, we were flagged with milestones—50th, 60th, 70th—almost like we were trying to extend the finish line of a race. Life's race. And when we eventually stopped reaching our milestones, we would vanish beyond our senses, leaving only scars on the hearts of those we touched.

Our time was always too much at the mercy of our health and karma. Those lucky souls who were blessed with old age, or those who were touched by some sort of *medical miracle*, often spoke of a perpetual black hole as the gateway to the birth of stars. I wondered if we really did vanish that beautifully.

But death doesn't discriminate. And whether we faded from this world in our infancy or endured until we were 95, time was a journey to unknown territory, and how much we had was never sufficient enough.

As for my parents, well, they *almost* kissed the 50 mark. Almost. Dad's dream to solo at the *Place des Arts* in Montréal was a dud. Sometimes life can be cruel. We often don't realize the significance of someone until they're suddenly removed from our lives. I only wished I told them more often about how much I loved them. After the accident, I never looked at old people the same way ever again.

•••

When our fears impaled our dreams, we created this nasty concoction known as nightmares. Almost everyone had a dose of these concoctions at some point in their lifetime. But the truly unsettling nightmares were the ones that returned every night, over and over again. The product of my overactive imagination tormented me. The traumatic experience of my parents' car crash had pushed me beyond my boundaries to forever remain in a world of deep slumber. Clearly, the genesis of my recurring nightmares was the unspeakable pileup on Hwy-5.

Exactly three years ago, I'd been living within the shadows of my unpleasant dreams. My nightmares. I wished so badly to wake up and erase this agony. But people weren't built like machines. We had no reset button, and there was no such controller in this world that could rewind time. My nightmares consumed me. It infested my brain and left deep scars in my heart. Every morning, I pinched myself to wake up. But I never did.

My parents were returning from Paris after celebrating their 25th wedding anniversary. Mom dreamed of seeing the stunning panoramic views from atop the Eiffel Tower. The French were always so romantic. The melodious flow of Français was enough to make my heart sing. And Paris deservingly held the honourable title of the 'City of Love.' Dad worked extra shifts at the studio to surprise Mom with her dream vacation. They set off to Paris in mid-December but promised to be home in time to celebrate Christmas together. Yet another promise that they couldn't keep.

A special weather alert was on for the town of Glenwood. ETA was originally noon, Christmas Eve. But their flight was delayed, and Aunt Brenna, who was caring for me at the time, had an early morning shift at the hospital on Christmas morning.

So, by the time their flight landed at Lethbridge Airport, Aunt Brenna was already asleep. Rule number one: *never* wake a sleeping Aunt Brenna if you valued your ears. I foolishly broke rule number one on April Fools when I was eight. As a joke, I thought it would be hilarious setting her alarm clock for a 3 a.m.

wake-up call. It was a bit cruel, but she always occupied my room whenever she visited, and I hated sleeping on the living room couch. She screamed my name so loud that even the deaf could hear *Emily McGregor* ringing in their ears. I was stupid. Just a tad evil. But *really* stupid.

I remembered waiting for Mom and Dad in Aunt Brenna's living room. I dozed off a couple of times before hearing the telephone ring. Dad wanted to sort out pickup logistics with Aunt Brenna before entering the dreaded line to pass through customs. I bickered over having to wake her up and refused to attempt such an atrocious crime.

Mom eventually compromised by calling Uber; she texted a smile emoji with the message, "See you in under 2 hours." I anxiously waited at the front door for their arrival, like the obedient dog waiting for its owner to return home from work. Uber ETA was a quarter past one in the morning, Christmas day. It was the first time Uber was wrong.

Mom and Dad died at the scene of the crash, along with their Uber driver, when their blue Hyundai collided head-on with a red pickup truck. The culprit: Mother Nature in a bad mood. I wondered if this was her form of cruel punishment for all those times I littered at the beach. The human body was remarkably resilient to most forms of trauma, but going from 100 km/h to zero in seconds flat would cause blood vessels to pop and internal organs to shatter. Humans were tough, but we were not unbreakable. Only Superman could have survived that collision.

On Christmas day, the unspeakable happened. I became an

orphan, and the worst part was that I slept through it all. I was asleep at the front door when it all happened. And when I woke, I thought I died inside. I fell back to the floor in a dishevelled heap as my grief poured out in a cosmic cataclysm of tears. My body went numb. My gut-wrenching sobs filled the silence in the room. I literally cried until I had no more tears left in me. My heart felt heavy yet empty. I was alone. From that moment, I promised myself to never cry like *that* ever again. I was only fourteen. It was perhaps the most difficult thing in the world to face at the time, but when tragedy struck, my life had to go on.

The photo published on the front page of *Glenwood News* encapsulated my nightmare best. The remains of a crushed Gibson that was supposed to be my Christmas gift from Jolly Old Saint Nick (a.k.a. my Dad) covered in blood and shards of broken glass. Broken dreams. Broken promises. Broken hearts.

•••

Being surrounded by a labyrinth of tombstones on probably the most anticipated holiday of the year was truly satisfying. I found their melancholy inviting, and I appreciated their lonely world. There was a pleasant, yet eerie, comfort of being at the cemetery with my two biggest fans. The protective tenderness of these moments helped to put my heart at ease. After all, the silence at the cemetery was my perfect lullaby for peace of mind. So, while every other kid in Glenwood was still asleep in the comfort of their homes, wondering if Kris Kringle would be kind this year, I somehow felt right at home.

I dedicated my next song to my parents. I turned to face the sea of tombstones and bowed to my adoring lifeless crowd. I felt obligated to continue my parents' tradition, albeit at a cemetery, because music was the only way for me to express my emotions.

Music, at its essence, was what gave me strength and possibly what cured my loneliness. It was a collective emotional experience shared between the singer and their audience simultaneously. And that commonality was a very powerful thing. To know that in that *one* moment, we were *alike*.

Life was seemingly effortless when it was filled with music. It was a language that everyone understood. And it was everywhere. So, I held my head up high and sang about my darkest and deepest thoughts until my voice was as hoarse as Bryan Adams.

♪♫♪♫♪♫♪

Every day, there are moments, when I give into fear
Close my eyes, hoping, the pain could disappear
If something, as beautiful as a rose can have thorns
The struggle is real, living in the eye of the storm

All is dark, I'm alone, struggling to survive
Memories, fading, nothing left to thrive
Like a stubborn old stain, grief brings forever pain
Frozen in time, trapped within these walls I can't climb

Save me from drowning

Catch me from falling

I know you're still here with me

Give me a sign

Gotta believe

I know you're still here with me

♪♫♪♫♪♫♪

I paused my musical rendition of a Christmas carol extravaganza and squeezed my eyes shut to compose myself. Crying was not on my to-do list today. And I absolutely had no time, or desire, to make any unnecessary changes.

So, I forced myself to think of something. Anything. Just something that would momentarily plaster a smile on my face or muster even the slightest giggle.

I thought back to a time when I was five. The kids at school told me that Santa was a childish thing to believe in, and Jolly Old Saint Nicholas fell in the same category of make-believe fairy tales and the Easter Bunny. I remembered coming home quite upset because my classmates crushed any hope of stirring up the 'magic of Christmas' that year. Boy, kids can be so cruel!

Mom and Dad did what any parent would do when their child's dreams were crushed—they tried to fix it. Dad actually bought a horse just to glue on a blinking red nose and a fake pair of antlers. He claimed that Santa lent him Rudolph for the day because I was such a good little girl. Then, Mom intentionally left 'Santa evidence'—a long trail of cookie crumbs from my gift to the chimney—for me to discover Christmas morning.

A hint of a self-satisfied smirk started to pull up across my lips. Although Christmas had now lost its magical spark, and Santa, to me, was nothing more than an omnipresent behaviour patrol guard, those were still the good old days. I could not help but smile at the thought of Christmas through a young child's eyes.

Suddenly, my mind was overwhelmed with a sea of emotions that overpowered the emptiness I felt inside. Love. Comfort. Joy. I may have lost my parents many years ago, but I have yet to lose all my memories. No broken promise could ever erase those warm fuzzy feelings I treasured inside.

"Merry Christmas, Mom and Dad. Thanks for not calling me out when I sang off-key during that last performance. I better get going before Nate the Great and Ramona the Pest over there arrest me for breaking the peace," I said, pointing to the right.

I'd come to know the names of the tombstones at the cemetery by heart. I cursed at myself for having such a good memory. I had more *dead* friends than *living* ones. I even gave nicknames to a few.

I hushed, "I'll come back to visit you again, I promise." I turned my back momentarily to wipe away a tear. I didn't want my parents to see me cry. I wasn't sure if I believed in an afterlife, but just in case they really *were* watching, I had to be strong and smile. No parent ever wanted to see their children cry.

I turned back to face them. "Dad, how was my first live performance on Grandpa's guitar?" I asked, proudly placing my hand on the guitar strap that hung over my left shoulder. "It's just like yours. The Maestro by Gibson. It's a beaut." I stared deeply at my guitar and whispered, "I got a lot to learn if I want to be as good as you and Grandpa. And I have even more to learn if I want to be the next Jimi Hendrix. I'll make you proud. Promise."

School took up most of my free time, but I was determined to get straight A's and have a full repertoire of songs I'd mastered. We are the promises that we keep. And I had every intention to keep all my promises. I was nothing like my parents.

My parents rarely kept their word, so their promises were nothing more than sweet lies. It happened enough times for me to figure it out. But it didn't mean that they loved me any less. I never saw it that way.

As a child, I frequently demanded their undivided attention, so they often responded with hasty assurances to keep up with my demands. A vow to read a bedtime story or make my favourite dessert were inconsequential in the grand scheme of things. Although I was grateful for all the good things they'd done for me when they were around, my heart refused to forgive them for not returning home.

I knelt by their tombstone and closed my eyes. I hummed a tune my Dad used to sing to me and let out a loud sigh. Music was one of the most important things in my life. A life without melodies would be empty and meaningless. Just like how every river needed water, I needed music. I actually needed music just as much as I needed to breathe. Whether I was in the car, the house, or just walking down the street, there was always music continually playing somewhere in the background.

"There's always time for music, right?" I chimed.

I was certain that Dad grew up in the stockroom of Yamaha Central. He held a ukulele at two, mastered the grand piano by the age of nine, and composed his own tunes on his guitar before adolescence. I mean, there was absolutely no way one person could learn *that* many instruments (fifteen to be exact), have a voice like Michael Jackson, *and* have the moves like Mick Jagger. My Dad was my hero, music guru, and legend.

My parents' death came on the one holiday that would shut 95% of a normally bustling city, like Calgary, down. It was a Christmas that I would *never* forget. But the music world was reprieved of grief until the following day when the news finally went viral. Music fans from around the world then grieved with me, but I still felt alone.

I actually never went back to my childhood home after my parents died. I just hid in the guest room at Aunt Brenna's, behind closed doors, for weeks. I even refused to attend my parents' memorial service at my Dad's studio. Aunt Brenna made her way down to Calgary for the service and insisted that I come. But I told her that I did not want to return to a place that I used to call home if everything I looked at reminded me of them. It was too painful, even just thinking about it.

She arranged for my neighbour to watch me so she could pay her respects to her brother and sister-in-law. I, however, forfeited that opportunity to say goodbye properly. And to this day, it is something I still regret deeply. Sometimes, the truth was nowhere near as deadly as silence.

Their memorial service was beautiful. Well, at least from what I inferred from the pictures in *Glenwood News*. It was a shame to have missed it. Dad's studio was filled with hundreds of flowers from his millions of adoring fans that came to pay their respects. White lilies. Red roses. Blue forget-me-nots. It was like a carpet of hope.

Shock. Disbelief. Grief. These emotions epitomized my silence. I was not ready to be a part of a world that did not include them. But a life of no regrets was a life without lessons learned. And no matter how long I remained silent, the pain still burned inside.

Days turned to nights. Nights turned to days. Life went on.

Although the rabbit hole of regret still lived within me, sharing my music with the dead had blessed me with an oasis of serenity. Though my silence did more harm than good. I missed them terribly.

•••

We would often describe happiness as being *contagious*, like an infectious smile. But what about the opposite side of the spectrum? Frankly, death was contagious too. With death comes grief and despair. Like the Great Plague, I'd shared my sad tales and ravaged face to the world.

My life would never be the same without my parents. I longed for Dad to complain again about how my clothing choice revealed too much of my midriff. Surprisingly, I even yearned for Mom to pester me about my male friends.

Teenage years were supposed to be about independence and rebellion with, of course, the loving guidance of our parents watching from the corner of their eyes. I was destined to struggle. To fail. To have heartache. It was inevitable. My parents were my safety net, a constant reminder that no matter how much I messed up in life, they would love me endlessly and always have my back regardless of how much trouble I ever was in. I was certain that was what parents do.

But who was I supposed to turn to now? Oh, how I wished they could have just taken me with them so I wouldn't have to face the world alone.

A hot tear trickled down my frozen nose and dripped off the lid of my coffee cup. I crouched down in front of my parents' tombstone and nestled my coffee cup against a fallen branch. I tucked two paper airplanes—one red and one green—into the rose bush by their grave. Carefully, I placed two peppermint candy canes in the shape of a heart in the snow and stepped back.

"I know you're still here with me. I just wished I could see you again," I whispered as I tightly squeezed my eyes to fight back the tears. "I love you both so much."

I pulled back further from their tombstone and took a deep breath. Goodbyes always made my throat hurt. I hated goodbyes.

Chapter Two

What goes up, must come down. And whether I truly believed in Sir Isaac's Laws of Physics, I believed in this. Life required us to be both a mountaineer and a marathon runner. We never spend too long at ground level, and we always had to keep moving.

Unfortunately, I was never the athletic type, so I constantly felt that life forced me to exercise a little bit *too* often. Sadly, surfing the Internet never qualified as an Olympic sport. If not, I could have won Canada a gold medal.

I always felt so out of place at the gym. It was such an intimidating environment. Each motion on the elliptical was accompanied by this tingling sensation. This eerie feeling started at the back of my neck and eventually crept down my spine. Most of us had experienced this 'sixth sense' feeling at some point in our lifetime. It was like my brain sensed something was out of place, but my conscience didn't register it. This paranormal experience raised several uncertainties that lurked deep in my subconscious whenever I entered a gym. Was I wearing the wrong clothes? Was everyone laughing at my exercising technique?

Although I'd tried to convince myself that being self-conscious about those things was only the figment of my imagination, the gym was a place of unwanted attention, and I felt imprisoned for doing my body a favour. So, I repeatedly made up a million excuses not to go there.

I was in my room listening to Alan Walker's single, *Faded*, before being interrupted by a knock.

"Em, why don't you change and come with me to the gym?" Aunt Brenna asked as she opened the door to let herself in. "You've been studying all day. Your AP Physics midterm isn't for another two weeks."

She closed my textbook and pulled off my headphones to take a listen. "Alan Walker again, eh? I still don't understand how teenagers can study with music on full blast. Some things just don't make sense," she sighed.

"The simplest explanation is that it doesn't *have to* make sense," I huffed as I refused to budge or show interest. "Walker and I are on a date, okay? Do you mind?"

It was either Aunt Brenna was playing dumb with me, or she was tired of hearing my excuses.

She continued to babble, "You could use a bit of sunshine. You know, it's okay to gain some muscles in those flimsy arms of yours. They say exercising reduces the risk of heart disease and osteoporosis, and we all know—"

I interrupted her. "You have to want those things, Aunt Brenna! And I don't want them." I grabbed back my headphones and folded my arms. "You're not at work today, so you don't need to make a patient out of me. I need to study. Do you mind?" I yelled rudely.

Aunt Brenna looked hurt. Deep down, I knew she just wanted to get me out of the house. After my parents passed, I drowned my sorrows with school and music. I even limited my interactions with friends, apart from study group sessions, and confined myself to my room on most weekends. Aunt Brenna probably thought I was depressed or something. But I wasn't depressed. I still woke up every morning motivated to get through my day. I was just *unhappy*.

My head started pounding, and I felt nauseous. There was this strange lump in my throat that I could not swallow. Was it guilt? As luck would have it, I could not for the life of me think of a good excuse today, and it was absolutely frustrating. I loved Aunt Brenna, but I hated the gym. We'd both been so loving and kind to each other since we moved in together, so it was a pretty big deal if either one of us ever yelled at each other. I excused the outburst as stress, but something just didn't feel right today.

Tears trickled down my cheek. I could not control them. I was upset at myself. It was wrong to take out my frustration on the one person who'd been there for me since the passing. My shoulders tensed. I turned my back away from my Aunt and hesitated to say anything else to make matters worse.

Aunt Brenna put a hand on my shoulder to comfort me. She pulled me into a super tight hug as I apologized profusely. She wiped away my tears with her sleeve and kissed the top of my forehead.

After several long minutes that felt like hours, she broke the silence. "Em, I'm sorry that I'd upset you. I just want to see you happy again. If you're not at school, then you're in your room. You are always studying or strumming your guitar. Life goes beyond these four walls, Emily. Where's the Emily McGregor that lights up the world with her beautiful smile? The fun-loving girl that would simply dance around life's problems regardless of what was in her way. I miss that girl," Aunt Brenna said softly.

I tried smiling to please my Aunt, but I wasn't one to smile on demand. "I still am that girl. Just without the smile," I said sadly.

Aunt Brenna continued, "Em, I'm really sorry to be so pushy today. But I came up to talk with you. I'd realized that I'd failed you. All this time, I'd been so worried about providing for you that I lost perspective. I shouldn't have picked up so many extra shifts at the hospital. I created 'Emily the Hermit Crab.' I did this to you. If I were home more, you wouldn't feel so lonely. And you definitely wouldn't have trapped yourself within these walls. I'm here for you, Em. You know that."

Aunt Brenna nudged me to speak. But I remained silent.

"You know, my colleague lost her mother this week to cancer," Aunt Brenna blurted out. I was unsure why she changed topics, but I turned to face her this time. "She told me how much she regretted not making an effort to spend more time with her mother. Also, she realized that family should always be our top priority. It was a wake-up call for me. I don't want to be her mirror image. To build a better life for us, I need to be in it. You're right to be angry. But, please don't shut me out. I want you to be happy again, Emily. This is what your Mom and Dad would have wanted. Let's start over and make things work."

The room was awkwardly silent again. I was dumbfounded by Aunt Brenna's confession. She apologized for *my* outburst.

That just didn't seem right. Though, I understood where she was coming from.

We should never live our life full of regrets. But I was guilty of this too. My head shouldn't have always been stuck in a book. Aunt Brenna deserved my time too. It was times like these that I wished Earth's rotation was slower, so we would have more than 24 hours in a day. Though science never worked to our advantage.

I was at a loss for words. The mix of emotions that overwhelmed me swirled in my mind like some overpriced cocktail. I just stood there and fought back the tears. I felt so fortunate to have Aunt Brenna in my life, but also so miserable that I said all those mean things in the first place. I should have just agreed to go to the gym with her. It would have definitely saved us both from mental breakdowns.

"I'm sorry," I finally whispered.

"I'm sorry, too," she replied softly. "You know, Em, we can never get back time, but we do have time to make changes. I want to make this work. For us. You know, the kids at the hospital call me a fairy godmother because I can make them feel better with the push of some buttons. But, I'm no magical fairy."

"You're pretty amazing with the kids there. No wonder you've chosen to work in pediatrics," I said, smiling.

Her eyes perked up as she raised her eyebrows. "I do own a very sparkly golden pen that you could mistake as a magical wand, but nil on the fairy wings," she joked, pointing to her back. "Oh my, that would be terrible. Me with wings," she shuttered. "I'll need to buy a whole new wardrobe and say goodbye to all my cute tops. Unless a shopping spree could convince you to get out of the house," she winked.

I lightly chuckled and winked back. "If your definition of a shopping spree includes a stop at the music store, then I'm all yours."

"So, I'm forgiven?" she asked sheepishly.

"As long as you pick up a big bucket of some finger-lickin' goodness after your workout," I proposed. "Rain check on our shopping spree, okay?"

Aunt Brenna was always so good at making light of any situation, and I was always so good at negotiating. We were a good match.

"You bet! And when I get back, we can either binge watch some romantic comedies on Netflix or re-watch *Aquaman* for the hundredth time just to drool over Jason Momoa's body," Aunt Brenna exclaimed excitedly.

I glared at her before we both burst out in full laughter.

"If you need me, call. Okay, hun?" Aunt Brenna said as she started inching closer to the door.

"Okay," I responded quietly.

She already had one foot out the door when I shouted, "Aunt Brenna?"

"Em, just because I'd opened up about how we need to spend more time together doesn't mean you need to change your mind and come. I won't force you. Unless someone wants to be my workout buddy!" Aunt Brenna hinted with a hopeful look on her face.

"It's not what you're thinking. And no. No workout buddies," I said. Aunt Brenna didn't pressure me to continue, but I did. "Actually, I was thinking. Isn't life an oxymoron? It's bittersweet."

Aunt Brenna thought for a moment before responding. "Well, I'm not sure about *that*, but I am sure that going to the gym and bringing home a bucket of grease afterward is definitely a paradox." She waved goodbye and closed the door before whispering, "Love you. I'll be back by six."

•••

I was certain that everyone had been asked, 'what do you want to be when you grow up?' at some point in their childhood. It was one of those default questions all adults asked kids, but it was hardly an innocent question.

Dad first asked me at my kindergarten graduation. I responded with, "I don't know. Maybe a musician like you." Dad was ecstatic.

Obviously, Dad approved of my juvenile aspirations. The truth was, I remembered almost nothing about why I said what I said. I loved listening to music, but *listening* was not the same as *performing*. Was I trying to please my father? I idolized the man. But I wasn't sure if *this* was me.

I was positive that I possessed some sort of music gene in my DNA. Like a hidden talent that just needed nurturing. How else would music have survived so many generations in our family line? But I wasn't like the other McGregors. They relished in the media spotlight while I enjoyed my private solitaire world.

Frankly, it wasn't fair to be held accountable for an answer I gave when I was *only* six.

But my answer *did* dictate my future. My response started a ripple effect of musical opportunities deliberately organized by my Dad. All of which pushed me in the *right* direction. Music lessons. Concert tickets. Songwriting retreats. One-on-one meets with some of the world's greatest musicians still alive. Each opportunity got me closer to my *dream. His* dream. And I was too far along to find a new path. It would be a pity to throw in the towel now and change directions. Truthfully, my only goal in life was to stay in bed until three in the afternoon with a good cup of coffee and a lightly buttered croissant, listening to music. I would have loved to live a life of simplicity. But simple was not my middle name.

When I moved to Glenwood to live with Aunt Brenna, I never left *this* musical dream behind. I owed it to my parents to keep music alive in our family. I even told the school's guidance counsellor, Miss Penny, that I wanted early acceptance to the *Académie de Musique de Paris*. She told me not to be so ambitious, and that only one *Glenwood High* graduate ever accomplished that feat.

Clearly, my odds were against me. But I knew that I had to believe in myself even if no one else did. It was my parents' dying wish before they passed. And I intended to keep *that* promise. I'd fantasized about continuing my father's legacy to make my parents proud. Although I was determined, accomplishing such a feat meant that I somehow had to get over my stage fright. I just had to.

Dad had millions of followers, but he proved that it was possible to be famous yet discreet. Ultimately, I took that to my advantage. I was never too fond of the limelight, and Dad was always careful about keeping his family life private. He was highly selective about the family moments he shared on Instagram. He never tweeted about family. Plus, not many even knew he had a daughter. So any pressure I'd put upon myself was purely dictated by me.

AMP was Paris's top music academy and Europe's oldest school of music. It was perhaps one of the finest in the world. So, to be accepted by the best meant my grades needed to be the best. But, was I foolish enough to make such a bold statement? I was my Dad's daughter, but I wasn't him.

Staying at the top of my class was no easy feat. I used the 'let's prove Miss Penny wrong' motto to motivate me to work harder. And I did. Naturally, I thrived whenever anyone doubted me. I took every naysayer's comments to heart because I felt a very special responsibility to work harder just to prove them wrong. I dreamed of the day when I could wipe my early acceptance letter in Miss Penny's face. It would definitely be one of life's sweetest revenge.

•••

Like the weather, life was unpredictable. On good days, the sun would be out. On bad days, it would rain like cats and dogs. And rarely, but not impossibly, we would see rainbows.

It was a snowy Sunday morning, late January. I was, of course, studying, and Aunt Brenna was home baking my favourite triple chocolate chunk chewie chocolate chip cookies. Try to say that three times fast! I'd simply call these delectable morsels of goodness Aunt Brenna's extraordinary triple six. I had a weakness for chocolate chip cookies, and Aunt Brenna's recipe was the ultimate best.

"Emily dear, can you help me in the kitchen?" Aunt Brenna called out from below.

"In a minute! I'm FaceTiming Clara," I shouted. "We're doing our weekly study group session. Want to join our intimate discussion on Chemistry?"

"Sounds like fun, Em. But I got a hot date with milk and cookies," Aunt Brenna joked teasingly. "You girls have fun!"

•••

Life seemed to enjoy playing with my emotions. Things were running smoothly before my parents passed. Well, I'd always encountered rough patches along the way, but they were brief, and in the grand scheme of things, quite manageable. If I told you the world would end because I got detention a couple of times for being late for school, I would admit that I was melodramatic. To be frank, the pre-trauma Emily McGregor was undeniably a "drama queen," but the post-trauma Emily McGregor was nothing more than a wandering ghost. A lost soul, trying to find its purpose in life. Honestly, I would gladly accept some blemishes on my school's permanent record if it could give my life more direction.

Grief was like an active volcano because, just like how nature doesn't follow black and white rules, I could not predict when my emotions would erupt. The unpredictability of magma resembled the unpredictability of how my mind coped with grief. I was often stuck in this unpleasant state of fatigue and irritableness that made my chest and heart feel heavy. Sometimes I could control my tears, while other times, I could do nothing to stop them. Somehow, I had to figure out how to become fire-resistant or burn whenever lava erupted.

Adolescence can be quite daunting, and the addition of a myriad of life-changing circumstances made matters even worse. I was forced to switch schools once Aunt Brenna took custody. Friends? What *friends*? And because I was a stranger to the outside world, I could disappear off the face of the Earth today, and nobody would notice. Okay, maybe Aunt Brenna. She was the *only* family I had left. Truthfully, it would have been hard living in a place where every nook and cranny made me think of Mom and Dad. So, moving in with Aunt Brenna wasn't really an option, but a necessity, for both of us. Their deaths were really hard on me. Us.

Even after all these years, I haven't had the nerve to return to my childhood home or my Dad's studio. I'd only visited Calgary in passing, on my way to the cemetery, where my parents rested. I used to love the busyness of the city. Calgary was home to some of the best Motown, and they had a vibrant stretch of live music venues in the heart of the city. Studio Bell. Music Mile. Festival Hall. It was the perfect place for any Canadian music lover to live in.

Aunt Brenna lived in Glenwood, a small little village on the south side of Alberta. Honestly, I never knew this village even existed until I officially moved here. Aunt Brenna typically came to visit us, rarely the other way around. Well, we did visit Aunt Brenna once or twice in grade school, but I had no recollection of that portion of my childhood.

To be frank, Aunt Brenna took me in with open arms. She loved me as her own. The guest room became my bedroom, and she never fussed once about her new responsibilities. To be fair, I was the one who raided her life.

She was gloriously single. Brunette. With a beautiful hourglass figure. Long legs. Smart. Super smart. Like the top of the class smart. But absolutely not musically inclined. She was sharp-witted and youthful. Adventurous and passionate about her occupation.

Aunt Brenna was a senior registered nurse for the pediatric dialysis unit at *G&C*, Glenwood's busiest children's hospital. That meant long shifts and absolutely zero time for a love life. So, I guess I made matters worse when I popped into the picture. Trust me. I totally made her *look* like a single Mom even though she was actually *my* Aunt. I knew the situation wasn't very attractive for any potential suitors.

In our busy lives, we are inevitably pulled into a never-ending cycle of work, stress, and more work. Ultimately, this inevitability would get the best of us. But if we acknowledged that things could only get better even in the worst of times, the sooner we would be in a happier place. Bad things were still going to be terrible.

And good things were still going to be golden. But, if the poop emoji could gain such popularity, it only meant one thing. That not all things are as bad as they may seem. Sometimes we needed storms before we could reach our destination. After all, without the rain, there would be no rainbows.

Aunt Brenna turned out to be my *rainbow*. I mean, she insisted we start spending more time together, and I enjoyed her company. I missed family time with my parents, so this was the next best thing. I liked the *new* Aunt Brenna. And I actually felt happier getting out of the house more, even if it was just a walk around the block. Life, finally, seemed easier as the days turned to nights, and nights turned to days. Perhaps I was beginning to wake up from my living nightmare.

Maybe I was selfish for hogging all of Aunt Brenna's free time. But life never promised to be fair. I wanted my little happiness to last forever, even though I knew things were bound to be tainted with time. Nothing good ever lasted forever.

Aunt Brenna did what most could not do. She was listed as my next to kin. And she had kept her promise to take care of me ever since my parents passed. Even though it would have been totally awkward to call Aunt Brenna 'Mom,' she was like a *Mom* to me. She took an interest in *my* interests, even though she only pretended to be interested. To my surprise, she attended *every* single school concert even though she claimed to *dislike music extremely*. Even my own parents never had such perfect attendance! And whenever I wanted to visit Mom and Dad, she would always find someone to cover her shifts. Even if it meant bribing her entire team with coffee for a whole week to make up for the favour.

•••

Suddenly, I heard a loud crashing sound beneath me. I panicked. Quickly, I closed my laptop, grabbed my baseball bat, and raced down the stairs towards the cloud of white smoke coming from the kitchen.

"Aunt Brenna! Aunt Brenna! Are you okay?" I coughed as I inhaled the mysterious white powder into my lungs.

"Emily dear, I'm fine. I think winter has come *inside* this year," she chuckled as she dusted white powder from her hair and straightened her apron.

"That's not snow!" I exclaimed.

"You're right, indeed! Just an explosion of gluten-free goodness," Aunt Brenna laughed as a small mischievous smirk crossed her face. "Explosive all-purpose flour, to be exact," she said while reading the package on the kitchen floor. "I was calling for help to grab the flour on the top shelf. You know how much I hate using stools." At which point, she pointed to her feet. "I can never balance on my two left feet," she laughed and shook her head slowly as she observed the mess.

I paused for a moment to take in the white powdered kitchen. I was kind of scared to say something. Listening to people complain about their imperfections was not on my list of favourite conversation topics. Plus, I also felt slightly responsible for the mess.

"Sorry, Aunt Brenna! I should have come down earlier," I said apologetically.

Clearly, the baseball bat was of no use in this situation, so I put down my bat and walked back towards the doorway. I sighed and said, "Let me get the vacuum and—"

Aunt Brenna interrupted me. "Forget the vacuum, Em! Let's make some snow angels!"

"Seriously?" I asked, unsure if the idea was too wild for serious consideration. Sometimes it was hard to tell with Aunt Brenna because she was so good at being both serious and sarcastic.

"Yes, seriously, mademoiselle Emily! Why waste this perfectly fresh layer of *snow*!" she winked and pointed to the remaining flour still left in the fallen bag.

"Oh, you're so on!" I challenged as I darted towards the avalanche and grabbed a huge handful of powder.

The sounds of joyous laughter filled the kitchen and echoed throughout the house. Aunt Brenna and I spent the next hour having an indoor snowball fight. We finally settled down and made a couple of snow angels before calling it quits to clean up the now *bigger* mess.

•••

It was a beautiful winter morning in February. The heat of the sun warmed my chest as I laid on a patch of exposed grass in the backyard. I breathed in the herbaceous aroma of soil and bobbed my head to the beats of Roy Orbison's "Oh, Pretty Woman." I loved that song.

Both Aunt Brenna and I were hard at work. Medical paperwork for her. Calculus and Algebra for me. Mathematics was boring, so I decided to start a conversation.

"Aunt Brenna, why are you single?" I asked.

Although surprised with the sudden questioning, she calmly replied, "Life is not a simple arithmetic formula. It's derivatives and integrals. It's long division and improper fractions. Simply put, singularity equates to feeling forever young, freedom from marital responsibilities, and minimal Prince Charming encounters."

I tapped my pencil on my notebook and scribbled some numbers on the page while unintentionally thinking out loud. "But *I* am your responsibility," I blurted out.

My eyes widened in horror as I quickly covered my mouth. But the damage was already done. There was an awkward silence, and I regretted being responsible for starting the conversation in the first place.

Aunt Brenna finally spoke. "When your Dad, my brother, asked me to be your next of kin, I agreed without hesitation." She pulled me in for a tight hug before pulling back to look me in the eye. "Do you know why?"

I shrugged my shoulders to avoid saying anything else stupid.

She gently smiled and continued, "That's because you're family. My family. We may not have everyone here today, but together we have it all."

My eyes felt heavy, but I refused to cry. Not today. I took a deep breath to compose myself before speaking. "Thank you,

Aunt Brenna. I don't go by a day thinking about how life would have been if you hadn't kept your end of the bargain. I still miss them, though. But I'm so glad I have you. I'm happy that we're spending more time together too. I really am."

"I'm glad too," Aunt Brenna whispered.

The rest of the afternoon was quiet. We both finished all our paperwork and indulged in a 2 L tub of mint chocolate chip ice cream while re-watching *Aquaman* for the hundredth-and-one time.

I first fell in love with Jason Momoa after he played Khal Drogo in HBO's *Game of Thrones*. Man, if all Hawaiian men were *that* hot, then I should have convinced Aunt Brenna to relocate to Honolulu so we could feast our eyes on nature's beauty daily. And for the record, my infatuation with Momoa's rock-hard abs was almost as strong as my love for music. *Almost.*

Chapter Three

Aunt Brenna once told me that there was something called seasonal affective disorder, or SAD for short, which I thought was a completely appropriate acronym. SAD was a mood disorder, a type of depression that was related to changes in seasons. Watching seasons change can be, well, rather *depressing*.

Spring was the start of new beginnings. *Life*. Beauty. Excitement. And in summer. Well, everything was green, so it was just lovely. But in autumn, leaves fell. They rotted. Come winter, the trees were naked and exposed. And everything looked slightly *dead*.

Those who suffered from SAD started to feel moody in the fall and continued feeling down into the winter months. So, the arrival of spring was most welcomed for everyone, whether you suffered from SAD or not.

•••

Winter had come and gone. Spring break was due to start in T-minus two days. This year, Aunt Brenna managed to convince me that I needed a life outside of the house. After our blowout that sparked the new Aunt Brenna, we both made a New Year's resolution to do something for ourselves and to spend more quality time together. Well, technically, they weren't New Year's resolutions since they were made well after New Year's, but it was the thought that counted.

I challenged my Aunt to improve her cooking skills so she could melt her future hubby's heart *and* stomach. She challenged me to make some friends outside of *Glenwood High* because I desperately needed to improve my social life.

We always had room for improvement; the human potential was limitless, so it was merely impossible ever to reach a plateau. The extent of our imaginations only limited us. If we believed that all the power we needed to succeed was already within us, then nothing would be impossible. We simply just had to awaken that untapped potential and channel it to our advantage to make what was seemingly *impossible* possible. Well, any grade-schooler would insist that we can't spell 'impossible' without the word 'possible.'

Our journey to self-improvement required us to keep the promises we made to ourselves. Commitment, no matter how small, goes a long way. It was exactly how we got the most out of our lives.

The thing about New Year's resolutions was that many don't see the light of day. But Aunt Brenna made quick on her pact by signing up for Tuesday night cooking classes at our local community centre. Although she'd been religiously attending, I started to believe that some people just sucked at things no matter how hard they tried. Chef Peters, who clearly had a crush on her, almost scarred his taste buds from weeks of sampling

Aunt Brenna's creations. It was almost ironic that Aunt Brenna could be such an exceptional *baker* but such a terrible *cook*. Though, I had to commend her persistence.

Aunt Brenna's resolution wasn't an unreasonable one. Lots of people signed up for cooking classes. I mean, we weren't talking about a seven-course dinner for an entire banquet hall involving a soufflé and bacon-wrapped prawns. Think big, start small. It was more about classic comfort foods like spaghetti and meatballs, sloppy Joes, and split pea soup.

Aunt Brenna dreamed of one day cooking her own three-course meal without the help of Ronald McDonald or Colonel Sanders. I had total faith in her. Except that it would require *a lot* more practice and patience. Good thing Aunt Brenna was so persistent and very patient. This combination of persistence and patience was like her superpower. And although absolutely essential for success, it was what kept her going whenever things didn't work out on the first try.

Unfortunately, I was never one to be committed to things that were deemed low on my priority list. I thought my resolution was very unreasonable. I was aware of our finite lifespan once my parents passed, and I chose to spend the unknown time I had left with only a select few.

Dad probably had one of the largest social circles in the world, but what good did that do for him? Social adequacies did not equate to a longer and healthier life. I was reluctant to make progress on my resolution despite my Aunt's constant nagging to do *something*. But I did promise her. After all, we are the promises that we keep.

We were three months into the New Year, and I still haven't made any new friends. I thought about the flyer pinned on the bulletin board of my favourite coffee shop, *Espresso Amore*. It advertised a week-long guitar camp during spring break at *Glenwood's Music Conservatory*, better known to us locales as *GMC*. Music was like our own secret language. The musical population of Glenwood would never dare mistaken *GMC* for General Motors trucks and SUVs.

Convinced that the camp was at full capacity, I decided not to call to inquire. But that evening, I reached some sort of freakish epiphany and decided to see if I was destined to be attending this musical venture. The greatest enigma of life was perhaps destiny. There was just *one* spot left, and it was now mine.

Surprisingly, I actually felt excited about the whole thing. I hadn't felt this way since my sixteenth birthday, which was over a year ago, so the feeling felt almost foreign to me.

•••

I was sitting in the cafeteria with my friends Clara Osgoode and Rachel Moore. My food was cold, my pork chop was rougher than sandpaper, and I was half asleep from staying up all night reading five chapters ahead for Biology. So, I decided to do a little daydreaming to wake myself up.

Rather than my normal fantasy of a hot summer day at a secluded beach, laying beside Jason Momoa, gawping at the exposed upper half of his body, my mind was on someone else today. Jimi G.

Jimi followed me everywhere; he was my confidant. I told him everything without reservation. We even collaborated on songs together. He was an excellent listener who rarely spoke. But if he did, only I knew how to decipher his symphonic melody. He was the first thing I saw every morning and the last thing I laid my eyes on every night. Just the thought of spending my entire week intimately with him, fiddling with his strings, totally made my heart skip a beat.

Suddenly, the cafeteria filled with smog, and I started floating towards the clouds. Higher. Higher. Higher. Until I collided with a paraglider who gently pushed me into a mysterious door that dangled freely in the sky. I entered the doorway and was swooshed into a world that appeared to be some sort of white-on-black augmented reality. My hands faded in and out until Jimi appeared by my side. I intuitively picked Jimi up and moved deeper into the mysterious room.

Although it was cold and dark, I relished the silence. But as though on cue, the silence was immediately replaced by a loud chatter. The fog thickened, and I hesitated to proceed forward as if remaining outside would absolve me of responsibility from what laid beyond the midst. The fog dissipated. I was now centre stage, in front of a crowd of probably thousands of squealing—piglets? They chanted my name, "Emily! Emily! Emily!" I anxiously stepped forward; the crowd hushed. It was impossible to hide the slight quaver in my voice.

I was still under a magical spell until Clara snapped me back to reality.

"Emily? Earth to Emily? Emily?" Clara interrupted, lightly shaking my shoulders.

She waved her tiny arms frantically in front of my face, but I did not respond. Her movements were hypnotizing, and I preferred to prolong my daydream to avoid talking during the lunch hour.

Clara had wavy blonde locks that bounced off her shoulders. Her smile was radiant, and she could make any outfit look cute. Next to her, I looked plain, even in my Sunday clothes.

Clara was probably Glenwood's top social media expert. Instagram. Facebook. Twitter. She managed her own YouTube channel, *Clarabella the Good*, with over ten thousand subscribers. Her road to fame was all thanks to a viral video she posted of herself making fishy faces with Rachel's pet fish. Clara had been posting daily vlogs ever since to keep her adoring fans up to date with her personal life. So much that a psychopath could easily stalk her if they wanted to. I was fortunate that Dad was never *that* open to his fans. I was always wary of telling Clara things because I worried that my secrets would be just another one of her tweets.

Rachel was Clara's best friend. They'd been besties since kindergarten. Grew up together. They even lived on the same street. Rachel had dark brown puffy hair that looked exactly like Chewbacca's, though I never had the guts to say that to her face. She was the complete opposite of Clara; she was a reserved, almost taciturn gal. But I guess opposites *do* attract. They were basically like an old married couple. The two would constantly bicker at each other, but in a weird, lovingly way that was *almost* too disgusting to watch. Wherever Clara was, Rachel would never be too far behind. I never had a bestie, so I only assumed that it was normal.

Clara was the first person I met at *Glenwood High*, apart from Miss Penny and my homeroom teacher, Mr. Robinson. She sat next to me in Geometry class. I was doodling a picture of Jimi Hendrix on grid paper when she tapped my shoulder and said, "Purple Haze?" Instantly, we hit it off. I was so relieved that another student at *Glenwood High* spoke music.

"What are you daydreaming about?" Clara asked.

"Nothing!" I exclaimed as I buried my face into my lunch to hide the blush on my cheeks.

"Doesn't seem like nothing. Rachel, say something. I'm going to go live on Instagram," Clara directed as she rummaged through her purse to grab her iPhone.

"So, spring break plans?" Rachel asked.

"Rach, seriously? Don't change the topic! Get Em to talk about her daydream!" Clara insisted as she pointed her phone in my direction. "I'm rolling in 5, 4, 3, 2, 1 ... Hi, world! It's Clara Osgoode here live at *Glenwood High* with my bestie Rachel and sleepyhead Emily."

Rachel shrugged her shoulders and whispered, "You said to say something, so I did. You never said what." Rachel peered directly into the camera and dabbed on another coat of lip gloss. She turned to me and asked, "Oh, Em, how does my hair look?"

I shifted uncomfortably in my seat and huffed, "Guys, just leave me alone, okay?"

"But Em. Come on! You know I'm just trying to take some interest in *your* life," Clara retorted frustratingly.

I grabbed my lunch bag and bolted out of the cafeteria without another word. Sometimes I wondered why I continued to put up with Clara and Rachel. I mean, they were both good friends, and we had similar interests. Clara loved music almost as much as I did. And Rachel loved Jason Momoa. We all knew how to play the piano and equally agreed that true love only existed in Disney movies. But Clara and Rachel were sometimes too annoying to be of good company. No one frustrated me quite as much as they did. Though everybody had at least one annoying friend in their lives. So, if Clara and Rachel weren't one of them, then the annoying one would be me.

•••

Although my most recent daydream caused so much grief, Jimi was the closest thing I had to a father after Dad died. Aunt Brenna *never* once complained about me spending the night with Jimi. That was probably because it was her gift to me on my sweet sixteen—a customized Gibson she inherited from Grandpa George on her sixteenth birthday. I was hesitant to accept such a valuable family heirloom at the time, but Jimi was the best thing that happened to me since the accident.

Apparently, Dad and Aunt Brenna both received matching guitars on their sixteenths. On my sixteenth, Aunt Brenna gifted me her Gibson and assured me that she had no use for such a *complicated* instrument. She admitted that the Gibson was simply collecting dust in her attic as it never saw daylight since she received it. When I held that Gibson in my hand for the very first time, I instantly felt a bond with the instrument; I was in love.

"It's definitely a Jimi," I exclaimed with excitement. Jimi Hendrix was Dad's most favourite guitarist, and I admired him just as much as he did.

"Jimi?" Aunt Brenna questioned inquisitively.

I responded, "Jimi Hendrix. The Great Jimi Hendrix. He's probably the greatest instrumentalist in the history of rock and roll. Purple Haze?" I sounded more disappointed than frustrated. It was like I was talking to a brick wall, but I continued. "Wild Thing? Hey Joe?"

I was now on the brink of a mental meltdown. "I still can't believe how little musical knowledge you have compared to Dad. Didn't you guys used to play instruments together?" I asked as I nudged her shoulder. "Didn't Grandpa George ever enlighten you with stories from his rock and roll past?"

I turned away as Aunt Brenna's smile hardened, and I could feel her eyes burn on the back of my head like kryptonite.

I decided to stop pestering before I really got on her nerves. There were only two simple rules in Aunt Brenna's house, and I was about to break rule number two. Rule number one: never wake her up if she was sleeping. Rule number two: never mention Grandpa George unless she brought it up.

She composed herself before she spoke. "The closest Grandpa George ever came to share with me his musical career was giving me this guitar. However, I disappointed him when I told him that music was a foreign language to me. No one wants to disappoint their parents, but I find disposable bed sheets more attractive than staff paper. Grandpa wanted me to evolve into a global superstar, just like your father, who successfully evolved from his humble beginnings as a musical prodigy. But I couldn't help myself from feeling the way I did."

I nodded and said, "Sometimes, you can't fight destiny. That's just the way the cookie crumbles."

Suddenly, Aunt Brenna grabbed Jimi out of my hands and hugged him tightly. Her lips perched, and a mischievous smirk grew on her face. She carefully laid the guitar back on my lap and victoriously clapped her hands. "So, it's settled. Jimi G."

And that was the start of a year-long relationship (and counting) with Jimi G. And might I add that there was absolutely nothing wrong with naming an inanimate object of such great importance. Throughout history, we've named swords and cars to raise the social status of our most prized possessions. Or rather, we simply named our instruments to avoid feeling embarrassed whenever we spoke fondly of them. It was better than admitting to others that I had no real friends. Hey, even BB King named all his guitars Lucille. There was absolutely nothing wrong with that.

Jimi was more than an acoustic guitar to me. It was a part of me. A piece left from Grandpa that reminded me of Dad. The one piece in my life that was constant. We'd had some wonderful times together, and he'd been my anchor when I needed something solid to hold on to. And just to clarify, simply naming my guitar "the brown Gibson" or "Triple G" (for Grandpa's Gibson Guitar) just wouldn't do justice to the relationship and history we had together.

Chapter Four

It was finally spring break, and I couldn't wait for my class to start at *GMC*. I was a bit nervous when Aunt Brenna dropped me off two hours before the start of lessons. She had an early shift at work but refused to let me take the bus by myself for my first class. I guess it was one of those 'proud mother moments' that she secretly wanted to be a part of but refused to admit so that things wouldn't be 'awkward.'

"I'm so proud of you, Em. Don't forget to introduce Jimi to everyone. Make friends!" Aunt Brenna cheered before I filed out of her white Mazda. "Call me if you need anything. Okay? I finish late tonight, so if you don't mind waiting, I can pick you up after work."

"I'll be fine, Aunt Brenna. Stop being such a worrywart. I've taken extracurriculars before, and it's not like I haven't taken the bus on my own. I won't get lost," I reassured before she rolled back up the passenger window and headed off to work.

I had never been two hours early for a class before. Luckily no one saw me waiting outside, or they would have labelled me as an obsequious person. And I refused to go down that path. I had plenty of time to kill, and I felt idiotic standing outside a closed shop, so I walked to *Espresso Amore* just three blocks west of *GMC*. I hadn't been outside *this* early in the morning before—5 a.m. was for snooty businessmen and hockey moms.

My parents were neither, and I followed my own schedule that mirrored freshmen college students. So, obviously, I was walking into unknown territory.

Mornings were beautiful. The air was fresher. The wondrous sounds of nature weren't overshadowed by the chatter of people and the buzz of transportation. Though there was only one drawback. Mornings came at such an inconvenient time of the day. We've heard of the saying, 'snooze you lose.' Well, that was absolute baloney. I gained more sleep hitting the snooze button, so what exactly made me the *loser* anyway.

But today, no snooze button was required. I was awake and feeling *alive*. Maybe all I ever needed *was* a morning wake-up call. The thrill of being outside under the morning sunshine with Jimi was like no other. The only thing missing was coffee.

Espresso Amore had the best coffee in town. Nestled in the corner of Allen Glen Way and Baker Street, it was my go-to place for everything. Aunt Brenna and I discovered it a year ago when we turned the wrong way on Baker Street. I wasn't a coffee addict at the time, but with just one sip of *Amore*'s signature blend, I was hooked. We became regulars, and I was certain Aunt Brenna caught the eye of André, *Amore*'s owner, after our first visit. Especially since André would often treat us to a slice of carrot cake and occasionally raved about us being one of his best customers. *That* was enough of a hint for me, and the rest was history.

Well, not *really* history. About three months ago, I told my Aunt that André was totally head over heels in love with her.

Obviously, she denied it and pleaded for me to stop turning her life into the next season of *The Bachelorette*. Eventually, my Aunt stopped visiting *Amore*, but their secret love affair did not stop me from satisfying my taste buds. I wasn't going to let some lover's spat stop me from getting my share of delicious coffee. Clearly, Aunt Brenna was in denial, and André was too shy to make a move. They were both doomed to live a lonely life if neither one of them was willing to overcome their emotional blockage.

"Miss Emily! My most favourite customer. What brings you here so early in the morning? Picking up coffee for two? How's your Aunt?" André questioned nervously.

"Guitar lessons at *GMC*," I said and tapped Jimi. "No, just for one today. Aunt Brenna already left for work. You know, André, you could just call her to let her know you've been thinking about her. She would find that *sweet*. It's a very attractive trait, André. You should use it more often."

André let out a loud sigh. "Mademoiselle Emily, I wished love was that simple." He raised his eyebrow and asked curiously, "But maybe you speak from experience. Yes?"

I laughed, "No, André, I'm still single. The guys at *Glenwood High* are not my type. They just don't understand music at the same wavelength. I don't have time for dating anyway, especially if I got to keep my grades up."

"Still dreaming big?" André asked.

"Definitely," I said, smiling.

I got my usual order of a double-shot espresso with a touch

of cocoa and cinnamon spice. André smiled back and told me to send his regards to my Aunt. He then quickly snuck a small piece of carrot cake onto my tray and winked. I warmly smiled back and quietly whispered, "Thank you." I didn't want the other patrons to know that I received special treatment.

I occupied one of the corner booths by the window, placed Jimi beside me, and spent the next hour indulging in life's simple pleasures—silence, coffee, and music.

The silent hum of the espresso machine in the background was surprisingly very soothing. *Amore* was my sanctuary from the reality that I called my life. The very same reality that I'm totally *not* impressed with.

Coffee was my sweet escape. Unfortunately, caffeine only temporarily numbed my mind from whatever annoying thing I was thinking about. Our bodies needed this escape. Our realities are inherently laced with madness, melancholia, and fear. And coffee was nature's medicine. Plus, I'd been told that coffee was a whole lot cheaper than champagne. And I would never need an ID to purchase it. Life was good with coffee.

As kids, we'd experienced the 'sugar rush' sensation. The satisfaction of indulging in pastries with high levels of sugars and simple carbohydrates was exhilarating. The only flaw was the extremely high risk of excruciating toothaches or cavities the size of Manhattan.

As a child, I was inevitably cursed with cavities. *All* my baby teeth experienced this horrible misfortune. Obviously, my parents blamed my cavities on candy. My sugar rushes were then kept to a minimum. No more desserts. No more lollipops at the doctor's office. And definitely no more *unhealthy* snacks in my lunchbox. That was when I learned how so many of my edible pleasures had sugar listed as the top three ingredients. Ugh.

Life was so cruel! At least my life was. Fortunately, I found coffee just before I turned sixteen. That very first sip of coffee in the mornings was to die for. I had never missed my daily dose of adrenaline ever since.

•••

It was almost time to walk back to *GMC* for the start of class. I finished scribbling some lyrics into my pocket-sized black Moleskine notebook and tucked it beneath Jimi before I cleared the table.

Writing was a form of therapy for me. I started songwriting once I picked up guitar in my earlier years. They kind of went hand in hand. Dad got me my very first Moleskine, but it wasn't until after the accident that I started writing songs more frequently. I scribbled everything in my Moleskine. Song ideas. Poetry. Lyrics. Even doodles whenever I got writer's block. Eventually, those scribbles became songs that I could hum to with a melody. And whenever I finished writing a song, I would randomly select a coloured piece of paper and copy out my lyrics onto the sheet. Then, I would fold a paper airplane with it and pin it to the bulletin board that hung in my room.

As I wrote more, I eventually ran out of space on my bulletin board. I began taping my paper airplanes to the walls of my bedroom. It became my *Wall of Hope*. One day, I would let my music soar through the sky and touch the hearts of random strangers. One day my voice would be heard. But not today. And probably not tomorrow.

It was a bit ironic that I wanted to be a musical star but feared performing in front of a large audience. Music was meant to be shared. But I was too scared even to show the world who I really was. I was too scared to find my voice.

There was something magical when words joined in tune with a melody. I felt that magical feeling whenever my mind met with paper. It was like the birth of something. Something beautiful.

•••

I gathered my belongings and quickly bolted to the door. Suddenly, a sharp, throbbing pain on the left side of my head temporarily incapacitated me. I fell to the ground, crouched forward with my hands tightly cradling my head.

At that same moment, a mysterious well-dressed *Amore* patron entered and *literally* tripped over me. The contents of my backpack were scattered across the floor. My Moleskine flew to the opposite end of the shop. And Jimi fell out of my grasp, landing awkwardly by the front door.

"Woah! I'm not sure why you've decided to take a seat on the floor in the middle of the entryway, but Miss, you may not want to do this at a busy coffee shop," said the mysterious man.

He chuckled as he got up and dusted his suit. Then, he offered his hand to help me up onto my feet. "You okay there? Sorry about that. I didn't expect to run over anyone this morning," he said apologetically.

He walked back to the doorway and picked up Jimi. He stared at Jimi wide-eyed, and his eyebrows tensed. It was almost like he saw a ghost or something. It was rather strange for someone to have such a reaction from the sight of a guitar. My guitar.

The man finally spoke. "Wow, Maestro. Gibson. It's—"

I quickly snatched Jimi out of his hands and glared at the mysterious stranger. "I think you had enough time ogling my guitar. I never said you could touch it."

"Oh, sorry. Umm, where did you get this guitar of yours? And you are Miss—"

"Late. I'm late!" I screamed.

I had no time for small talk. And I felt agitated about how fashionably late I was for my very first class. I was never one to be tardy. Without another word, I quickly stuffed everything sprawled on the floor into my bag and zoomed out the door. I ran so fast that several onlookers probably thought I was a madwoman on rollerblades fueled by mass hysteria.

•••

I was obviously late for class. As fate would have it, I was out of breath after thirty seconds of sprinting. I ran as fast as I could, stopping when my legs demanded a break, which was actually quite often. Even the pedestrian signs operated against me. It was only moments like these where I wished I was more athletic. I ended up arriving fifteen minutes late, despite sprinting more than half of the way. I felt so embarrassed about my tardiness because I *was* technically the first person to arrive at *GMC* this morning. But, given that this was my life, I wasn't really surprised. After all, life only promised to make things difficult.

We had to work in pairs for the rest of the week, and my late arrival meant everyone else already made acquaintances. There was an odd number, so I was left to work independently. Or so I thought.

"Emily, since we are short a student today, I'm going to pair you up with one of our volunteers. Ava Scott should be here tomorrow. She had an urgent dental appointment that couldn't wait," Mr. Thompson explained.

"I'm fine with working alone," I replied.

"No. It'll be hard to teach a lesson about guitar duet playing without having a partner. Let me just see who's in this morning," Mr. Thompson said as he buzzed his administrative assistant. "Ah, yes. Max Miller," he said as he spoke to the lady on the other line.

Mr. Thompson hung up the phone and looked at me, satisfied that he resolved the situation. So, I patiently waited for this *Max Miller* to show up. Five minutes passed. Still nothing.

"Um, is this M&M guy imaginary?" I scoffed, pointing to the empty seat next to me. "Can I just get started on my own? I really don't know who you're talking about, Mr. Thompson, and I would like to make good use of my time," I exclaimed impatiently.

"He's referring to me," a voice boldly responded from behind me.

I turned my head and saw *him*. The guy at *Amore him*. The guy who tripped over me *him*. That *him*. Ugh *him*. I muttered under my breath, "Not *him*."

Max walked up and plopped himself onto the empty chair beside me. He smiled and held out his hand to exchange pleasantries. I refused his hand and said, "No, thanks, I don't shake hands with strangers."

"But we aren't strangers. We've met before. Today actually. I must have hit your head really hard during that pileup for you to have such terrible short-term memory. Sorry about that. Really," Max said with a chuckle.

"Oh, good. You two know each other. Now class, let's warm-up for ten minutes before we start playing," Mr. Thompson said happily.

"But—" I said before being interrupted.

"So, Miss Late. How should we warm up?" Max asked innocently.

I was flabbergasted at the turn of events. I held my breath until my face turned blue. This couldn't have been happening. Just one day. Just one day. I kept reminding myself.

Finally, I turned to Max to speak. "First off, tripping over me does not mean that we've met. Plus, you don't have to poke fun at the fact that I was fifteen minutes late for class today. And the thing is, it was all because of you!" I fumed and fidgeted uncomfortably in my chair as he playfully draped his arm around my shoulder.

Max removed his charcoal heather wool coat and smirked.

"For the record, I was late too. But with all seriousness, I'm not making fun of you. I really thought that 'Late' was your last name. I'm also flattered that you'd been thinking of me. My face really is hard to forget."

"You are just impossible!" I muttered under my breath before asking, "Mr. Thompson, can I switch partners?"

"No, Emily," Mr. Thompson said bluntly.

"Fine. I'll just have to deal with you. Just like every other horrible thing in my life," I huffed before settling back down in my chair.

Max chuckled, "It must mean we're friends now, Emily. Now that I'm a *thing* in your life, what's in it for me?" He laughed as he held out his hand again. "It's Max Miller, by the way. So, Emily. Emily—"

"McGregor," I said. I figured that if I told him my *real* last name, he would stop calling me Miss Late.

Max smiled and winked. "I have a gift for you, Emily McGregor."

I sighed and continued to ignore his flirty banter. I turned to look at him right in the eyes and spoke. "Okay, we got to set some ground rules here. Number one. Can you stop flirting with me? Number two. I'm not going to accept a gift from a complete stranger. And number three. My head hurts, so stop making me think of so many rules."

My head started to throb uncomfortably again, but I was certain that Max was the cause of this headache.

"Just so you know, I like to keep things simple. Rules are like promises. I don't promise. So, I don't follow the rules. Not worth the effort of remembering. I'm not flirting with you, but I can if you like. I'm not a stranger; we're classmates. And did anyone ever tell you that you're quite attractive when you're angry," Max responded with a clever smirk.

At that very moment, I questioned my decision to sign up for lessons at *GMC*. If it meant being stuck with some 'know-it-all monster' who constantly padded his ego, then I wished there was an 'off switch' on him so I could be at peace. I truly hoped that Ava would attend class tomorrow, or I would be stuck with this guy for longer than I could handle.

I'd joked with Aunt Brenna before about having OCD, but it's really no picnic for those who truly struggled with it. She assured me that although I was obsessed with being organized, it did not necessarily mean that I was suffering from a mental illness. True OCD sufferers had symptoms that went well beyond being neat and orderly. But I truly felt like I was about to snap and then be stuck with the consequences afterward. I hated the uncertainty. It made me feel very uncomfortable.

•••

After a day that seemed like forever, class finished, and I was ready to go home. Unfortunately, Aunt Brenna wasn't done for another three hours, and I desperately wanted to leave *GMC*. My bus pass was inside a small pocket of my Moleskine notebook, but I must've dropped it at *Amore*. I was stuck *here*. Normally I would be thrilled about spending more time at *GMC*, but today, with Max still around working with the guitars on the lower level, I wanted to be elsewhere.

GMC was the ultimate one-stop-shop full of everything musical. It was home to a wide variety of instruments and had the largest selection of sheet music in town. There was a private garden at the back of *GMC* filled with sculptures of famous artists like Elvis Presley, Elton John, and Stevie Wonder. Dad knew the owners of all the music stores across Canada. And it had its perks. I loved exploring the private garden whenever I had to wait for Aunt Brenna, but it was raining now, and I preferred to keep Jimi dry. Poor Jimi already suffered enough from today's fall. Awkwardly, I stood in the foyer and hovered by the main entrance to appear as though I was waiting for someone.

As though Max was reading my mind, he suddenly approached me from behind and tapped my shoulder. "Waiting for someone?" Max asked.

I turned to face him. "Yes," I said bluntly.

"Your ex-boyfriend?" he guessed.

"What? Class already finished and I'm really tired. Do you have to be this annoying still?" I pleaded.

"I just thought that the 'I know you're still here with me' in your song was about your ex dumping you. I guess I shouldn't have jumped to conclusions. Sorry," Max laughed.

"Ok, listen up, mister. I have only two friends that aren't textbooks. And with all the schoolwork, dating has never even crossed my mind," I pouted, almost embarrassed that I admitted how small my circle of friends was to a guy I just met. Then, it dawned on me. "Wait, how do you know about one of the lines from a song I wrote?"

Max sheepishly stuck his hands into his pockets, and after a couple of seconds of awkward staring, he took out my missing Moleskine notebook. "Sorry. I just had to read it. I found it on the floor at *Amore*. I meant to give it back, I swear. I tried to return it in class, but you got all nasty towards me. You were like the mean witch of the wicked west. I just never had the chance afterward," Max apologized profusely.

I stood there in a loss of words, steaming like a kettle on the stove about to reach its boiling point. I wasn't sure if it was because no one I knew had ever read the contents of my Moleskine notebook before. Or was it the fact that some *stranger* from my favourite coffee shop was relentlessly ruining my day? Plus, this guy just said I was a witch! How rude! Are all guys this insensitive?

One thing was certain. Emily McGregor was NOT an open book. I had a very high threshold on things I deemed private and would never, in a million years, let some lunatic touch *my* personal notebook. My Moleskine was like my diary, a creative exploration of my thoughts, a kaleidoscope of my identity. It was a mess of notes. But they were my notes. My thoughts. My secrets. Everyone had secrets. Clearly, Max had absolutely no respect for the word "private."

Max knew I was steaming; he avoided my glance as if I might bestow on him the evil eye. I promptly took that as an opportunity to retrieve my Moleskine from his grasp. Roughly grabbing it out of his hands, I screamed in anger, "Max Miller, how could you!"

There was a momentary awkward silence. Then, suddenly, Max lunged at me, grabbed my arm, and jerked on it. He blurted out regretfully, "I'm really sorry, Emily, really. I only opened it to see if your name was written inside to figure out who it belonged to. I didn't see your name on the first page, so I flipped, and—"

"Save it, Max. We're done here," I shouted, pushing his hand off my arm. I turned away to face the window again. I frantically searched through my Moleskine for my bus pass, but it was missing. It was probably still under one of the tables at *Amore*. I was stuck here unless I was desperate enough to walk in the rain. Oh, how I wished Aunt Brenna could come right away so I could wallow in my room.

Fortunately, Max backed off, but I sensed that he wasn't lying about regretting it. I knew he was waiting behind me at a *safe* distance. Normally, I wouldn't snap at someone like that, but inwardly, I was seething. The rage I felt from my privacy being invaded nearly consumed me, and all I could do was stand there as I swallowed down my frustration.

After some time, my shoulders eased, and I let out a loud sigh. When I spun around to see if Max was still watching over me in the corner of the foyer, I was surprised to be standing directly face-to-face. I stared into his eyes. Max had amazing green emerald eyes that reminded me of the jade mermaid statue on the tip of the boardwalk from a beach that my parents used to take me to every summer. *Sunrise Beach* was the best in town, and we'd always visited every Labour Day long weekend before school started.

It was strange. I no longer felt angry at Max. I stifled the urge to speak. Then suddenly, we both burst out laughing.

"Emily, I really am sorry about looking through your notebook. I know we started off on the wrong foot, but I promise to never look through your belongings again without your permission," Max apologized. "Let's start off again. Hi, I'm Max Miller. Nice to meet you," he said sheepishly, holding out his hand as a peace offering.

I bit my lip, unsure of how to respond. I took a deep breath, hesitated, then accepted his apology by shaking his hand. I forced a smile and replied, "Hi, I'm Emily McGregor. Nice to meet you too." I knew Max was really trying to make things right. Didn't he say in class that he'd never make promises?

Max and I spent the next few minutes talking like two normal teenagers. Well, two normal people. I assumed Max was at least five years older than me, so I doubted he was still a teenager. He had facial hair that was much more prominent compared to the guys at *Glenwood High*.

We laughed at jokes, gave each other movie recommendations, and critiqued the performances from the latest episode of *America's Got Talent*. Surprisingly, I felt absolutely comfortable talking to Max once we had overcome the bitterness from our initial interaction at *Amore* and the misunderstanding in the classroom.

"So, tell me about yourself," Max asked.

"Me? Why me? I'm quite boring, you know. I would put you to

sleep if I told you my whole life story," I hesitated.

"Humour me," Max insisted and smirked.

I was not trying to impress Max, but talking about my dead parents and my almost invisible social circle was not very appealing. So, I invited Max to speak instead.

"No, you go first," I insisted.

The beauty of those four magical words was that it switched the hot seat to the opposition. Max became the focal point of the conversation. Plus, it helped me avoid potential awkwardness without pigeonholing myself into a conversation about something too personal or sensitive. I had no plans to cry in front of a stranger that I just met.

I'd experienced an epiphany of sorts a couple of months ago when I was flipping through an old photo album that Mom put together. Aunt Brenna came into the room to ask how I was feeling. That was when my emotions got the better of me, and I cried like a broken faucet. Nope. Not today. Not in front of Max. That would just be awkward and embarrassing.

Max smiled and nodded. "Ok," he said, accepting my invitation to start. "I enjoy a good song over a book, a cup of coffee over tea, and a good friend over a bad one. My father left when I was ten, and I'd been living with my mother ever since. I have no siblings, but I once owned a pet fish that eventually ended up on someone's dish. I went to *Glenwood High* before entering med school. My mother wants me to be a doctor. Though, don't be fooled by my well-tailored outfit. I'm actually a rebel in disguise. I am destined to give my mother grief because I enjoy skipping class to volunteer here at *GMC*."

"So, you're a med student. That explains the sophistication. I was thinking of a lawyer when I saw how well-dressed you were. But with the baseball cap, I couldn't be certain. Umm, why med school? I mean, you're pretty talented in music from what I saw in the classroom," I asked.

"I like music. But I failed to convince my Mom that music could be a profession. The small price I have to pay," Max said as he adjusted his baseball cap.

"Oh, umm. Like? It doesn't seem like you just *like* music. Frankly, I don't think I ever met someone who would skip practicum to volunteer at a music store. I mean, it takes about ten years of education and residency before you can become a doctor, so few would actually risk delaying the whole process. I'm starting to get the feeling that you play hooky quite often, don't you," I said, trying to make sense of the whole situation.

"Okay, you caught me red-handed. Guilty as charged," Max exclaimed, putting his arms up. "So, what's your story?"

"Oh, me?" I said surprisingly. For a moment, I thought I caught him off guard and that he forgot about my side of the bargain. I bit the bottom of my lip and took a deep breath. Finally, I spoke. "I also enjoy a good song over a book, a cup of coffee over tea, and a good friend over a bad one. I live with my Aunt. She's a nurse. No siblings. No pets. I want to be a platinum artist and songwriter. I dream of getting into *AMP*. Since you're into music, you should know exactly what I'm talking about. I'm still a year and a half away from graduation at *Glenwood High*. I spend my weekends in my room studying and have an otherwise pretty boring life."

"*AMP,* eh? You know, not all celebrities went to *AMP* to make it to the big leagues. If you're as talented as I think you are, all you need is an audience. Good songs are about your feelings, your fears, or what you care about. And it's the *words* that matter more than the actual music," Max said with a wink. "And you said your life was boring, Emily McGregor. I'm starting to not believe in half the things you say negatively about yourself."

"I'm not a pessimist! I'm just hopelessly realistic. The unfortunate side effect of growing up," I said defensively.

Max chuckled and smiled. "Three. You have three now," Max said.

"Huh?" I responded. Then I smiled too. I turned to Max and asked, "Do you write your own songs?"

"Sometimes. But it's more like a hobby, and I haven't done so in years," Max replied. Then, Max pointed at my guitar. "Do you mind if I ask you about your guitar?" he questioned.

"What about it?" I asked.

"Where did you get it from?" Max asked.

"It's my Aunt's guitar. She inherited it on her sixteenth birthday from my Grandpa. And then she passed it onto me on my sixteenth birthday," I explained.

"Oh," Max said, slightly disappointed, "you don't mind if I take a look at it again?"

"Sure," I replied, shrugging my shoulders. I couldn't help but wonder why Max was so interested in my guitar. But I complied and slowly handed Jimi over. Max carefully inspected my guitar. Every curve. Every string. Almost as though he was looking for something. But what? I smiled at how mysterious Max was acting.

But before I could inquire about his curiosity with Jimi, Max muttered quietly under his breath, “It’s not the same.” Then his brow furrowed as he let out a heavy sigh.

“Huh?” I asked, unsure if I heard him correctly.

Max grinned before he turned towards me and said, “Smile more, Emily McGregor. It looks good on you.” Max handed Jimi back with a nod and waved goodbye to the receptionist at the counter of *GMC*’s main entrance. “I’m done my shift. I’ll see you around,” he said as he headed towards the door.

“Ya, I’ll see you around,” I said just before he exited the building.

We meet new people all the time. At school. On the street. At the doctor’s office. And most of those people we never saw again. But some of those people actually became our friends. No matter how long we spent getting to know someone new, the first encounter with that stranger was the most memorable and exhilarating. There was an undeniable thrill about meeting a stranger and sharing tidbits of each other’s lives.

One of the first few questions we would ask a stranger was usually along the lines of ‘what do you do?’ Which was the perfect icebreaker. And I’d heard some fascinating answers because everyone had a different story to tell. But the enthusiasm with which they answer was a good indication of whether they liked what they did or not. And although a conversation with a stranger might begin with that question, we could tell within minutes of meeting someone which of those fates the new relationship might have. Most of my strangers have remained *strangers*, but not all. Often, when we expressed an interest in their interests, it was a telltale sign that we were bound to meet again at some point in our lifetime. I called that a home run, and today, I scored one.

Meeting Max had opened up the opportunity to create a bond that could maybe even transform into a friendship. Maybe. Though, I knew I was getting ahead of myself. I only wondered when the opportunity would come again.

Chapter Five

I never did see Max Miller again that week. Although I knew that not every person I met was going to be my best friend. And not every guy I met was going to be my soulmate. My gut instinct about Max was that he wasn't *just* some random stranger.

I truly believed that every person I end up meeting in my life served a purpose. I just haven't figured it out for Max yet. Glenwood wasn't *that* small of a village, and with my guitar lessons now over, the likelihood of running into Max again was quite slim.

I sat in *Amore*, enjoying a double-shot espresso with cocoa and cinnamon spice when André approached me.

"Mademoiselle Emily, may I ask you how your guitar class went last week?" André asked as he shuffled into the empty side of my booth.

"It was better than I expected. I made a couple of friends, I think. But more importantly, I learned so many new things on the guitar," I replied.

Although my lessons at *GMC* ended, I started to spend more time at *Amore* post-spring break. A part of me wanted to see Max again, and *Amore* was where we first met. But a part of me wanted to hide back in the comfort of my room. Over the past few years, self-isolating had made being around the company of others even more intimidating than before. I was conflicted, and unfortunately, coffee didn't have the answers I required.

I pulled my laptop from my bag and opened Google for a quick search on 'Max Miller.' But before I could hit the search button, I thought to myself. Is it okay that I Google everything that I questioned in life? I reassured myself by recalling the words of my Grade 8 principal from my convocation, "the thirst for knowledge is a great gift, don't let anybody tell you otherwise." Frankly, if Internet access was ubiquitous, why not take advantage of the technology within our reach.

I nodded and hit the search button confidently. Lesson learned. Google doesn't always have the answers. Seriously! Search results for 'Max Miller' returned 22,800,000 results! And the majority of them were about Britain's top stand-up comedian from the 1930s to 1950s. Oh my! What are the odds that Max would share the exact same name as a successful celebrity? Why was life so unfair?

I took a long sip of coffee before turning back to my computer. I wondered if Max was a regular at *Amore*. Though I would feel embarrassed if I asked André, and I was certain he would tell my Aunt. He had her number. There was no way I was going to risk it.

I thought of Clara. She knew *everything* about *everyone*. If Max was from around here, Clara ought to know. But, whether or not Clara had juicy details about Max, she could be quite vicious once she had a taste of a potential Instagram story. I thought twice about texting Clara. Eventually, I put down my phone, closed my laptop, and returned to my notes to study.

•••

With my midterms fast approaching, my social life should have been placed on the backburner. Needless to say, keeping my grades up was top of my priority list, but my mind was elsewhere all week. I probably spent the last three hours chatting with André or thinking about Max.

It was almost ten in the evening. I was exhausted from a full day of studying, so I decided to rest my head for a quick power nap. Suddenly, I felt a tap on my shoulder.

A familiar voice whispered into my ear, "Sleeping on the job, Emily McGregor!" I jolted up, startled, and spilled the last bit of espresso all over my papers.

"My notes!" I exclaimed, frantically dabbing the spilled coffee from my sheets. I looked up and saw a smiling Max Miller looking down at me.

"Fancy seeing you here this evening. Do you come here often?" Max asked. "Seems like I made a mess of things again. Sorry about startling you."

I quickly sat up in my seat and shoved my notes under my backpack. Max slid his to-go coffee cup across the table and plopped into the booth, sitting across from me. He peered at the mess on the table and smiled.

"Looks like you're studying for midterms. I got one tomorrow too. But shh. Don't tell anyone that I don't plan on studying," Max chuckled as he picked up one of my sheets to take a look.

I was only half-awake from my nap. My head ached, and I looked like an absolute mess. Why does every encounter with Max Miller have to be so embarrassing? I hesitated with my response. My brain refused to function after mindlessly feeding it facts over the past few hours. I just sat there, staring at Max in silence.

"So, cat got your tongue? Don't tell me you forgot about me already," Max said with a sigh. "Goodnight, Emily McGregor. May we meet again someday."

Max got up from the booth and exited *Amore* before I could muster out a response. My heart pounded rapidly. I was deeply fascinated to learn more about him. Though it seemed more like wishful thinking. I had my doubts that our paths would ever cross again because we didn't even go to the same school. So, unless he was a regular, like me, at *Amore*, then today was our goodbye. I cursed at myself for missing the opportunity to exchanged numbers back at *GMC*.

Medical school was a time-suck that often left even the strongest students emotionally drained and exhausted most nights. I'd heard stories about med school being way worse than grad school because MD students would literally be studying *all* the time. Though Max didn't seem like the typical med school student. So, maybe I still had a chance.

Thoughts of Max clouded my mind once again, and all I could think about was him. It didn't seem like I would get any more hours of studying done tonight, even if I forced myself to focus. So, I started to clean up the booth and collect my belongings to go home. That was when I noticed the empty coffee cup on the table. It was Max's. I picked up the to-go cup and saw something scribbled on the lid in blue. I pulled it closer in front of my face and squinted to get a better look. It was a phone number. His cellular? I studied the rest of the coffee cup and noticed a brief message scrawled on the side, "For studying emergencies," he wrote. Were those digits intended for me?

Here's the deal: We could read all the dating and relationship advice online—and there was a great deal of stuff out there, I know—but there was just one thing that didn't compute. Don't guys usually ask for the girl's number rather than freely handing them out on coffee cups? It felt strange to have control of the situation. I mean, it cut out all the uneasiness, in my opinion, which was great. This approach was much friendlier, almost like, 'Here, I trust that you'll call. If not, no biggie.'

I remembered back in ninth grade when a guy at *Glenwood High* kept hassling Clara for her number every day in the cafeteria. Eventually, all that pressure-filled interrogation got to Clara, and she just gave him her number to shut him up. But Max was nothing like that. And although he did run the risk of me never calling him, I liked how he respected my boundaries while still showing interest in becoming my friend. Max's intentions seemed genuine, but I was unsure about my next course of action. I'd never been in this situation before and was torn between curiosity and staying focused. I clutched the coffee cup in my hands as I left *Amore* that evening. I felt my curiosity overpowering me. I closed my eyes and grinned. Who was Max Miller anyway?

•••

After a week since our second encounter, I decided to give Max a chance. I actually spent most of the week writing out the pros and cons of contacting Max. I felt stupid doing that, but it painted a clearer picture of everything on my mind. I convinced myself that this was purely for friendship and that it would be nice to have some friends outside of *Glenwood High*.

I'd been friends with Clara and Rachel for three years, which wasn't really that long. Fun memories. Inside jokes. Girly advice. Those were the days. And although I genuinely appreciated their shoulders to cry on, I was certain that we'd started to grow apart the past year.

We had a lot of history together, and a fair share of my life happened alongside Clara and Rachel. In our ninth grade, when we met, we spent countless nights together engaging in questionable debauchery. It was their method to help me overcome my grief, and I wouldn't be where I was today without their constant *bickering*. Well, *love and care*, if I were to put it nicely. But now, I found their wild evenings out repetitive, immature, and even somewhat annoying. There was nothing wrong with partying, but it was all Clara and Rachel could talk about. And some of their YouTube vlogs were as arrogant and obnoxious as ever.

We could no longer relate to one another. I was more interested in building a career and being anti-social. I would rather spend quality time with Netflix on a Friday night than to be pulled into their shenanigans. I often found myself judging them for being immature and then immediately feeling guilty about it. In the past year, it was harder and harder to connect with them. And it wasn't because one of us did something unforgivable, but rather because we'd simply changed.

Not all friendships were destined to last forever. And that was okay. Outgrowing our friendships did not mean that we disliked each other. Or even that we stopped caring. Nor did it mean we would never speak again. It just meant that right now, they deserved a friend who wasn't silently judging them. I felt that we would be doing us all a favour by creating some distance.

I punched in Max's number on my keypad but couldn't muster the courage to hit the call button. I stared blankly at my phone, wondering how to approach the situation. I decided to send a text instead.

I sent a text message, which said, "What's your deal with Physics and Calculus?"

Max replied almost instantly, "Does graduating with straight A's count for something?"

I smiled and continued to text, "Okay, smarty pants. Want to help?"

This time, Max did not reply instantly. I hoped for his response, but to no avail. I laid in my bed and stared at my colourful collection of paper airplanes. Finally, after ten gruelling minutes, Max replied, "What's in it for me?"

I thought for a moment and wrote, "Meet me at *Amore* in an hour, and we can discuss details."

"See you there!" Max replied with a smiley face emoji.

•••

Our texts turned into FaceTime calls. Our minutes turned into hours. Our days turned into weeks. But soon enough, our hangouts at *Amore* transformed into something beyond *just studying*. And Aunt Brenna couldn't stop smiling ear to ear about the whole thing. I was having the time of my life.

I started to feel like my old self again. But I refused to call it my *old* self because the *old* me had Mom and Dad, and this *new* me didn't.

Studying with Max at the coffee shop was so enjoyable that I actually missed him whenever we didn't study together. I was still baffled at how much fun I had spending time with Max.

For a guy who started off as a jerk, he ended up being a pretty awesome *friend* once I got to know him. Max was still cocky and flirtatious, but perhaps they were just some of those deeply ingrained character traits that made him Max Miller. It was hard to tell if those traits really were hardwired into his DNA, but I liked them anyway. I liked him. My friendship with Max truly superseded my expectations.

Mom always told me that our perspectives shape us and the lives we live in. I never really understood that statement until now. I guess I shouldn't have judged Max until I got to know him. And I'm happier knowing that I gave his friendship a chance. There really was at least one positive in every situation and at least one drop of goodness in every single person.

Mom was a book of wisdom; everything that came out of her mouth was disgustingly quoteworthy. Like "it's okay to be out of tune in life's melodies," or "once you discover your own beat, you will have a symphony," or Mom's favourite, "we cannot live life playing the same note." It was a lot of junk. And I never believed in any of that inspirational stuff. I always thought they were just sentimental statements to make others feel better about themselves. But I was wrong. Mom was a wise woman.

•••

Over the next few months, we were literally joined by the hip. *Three*. Max was right. I guess you could call him my *bestie*. We spent our evenings and weekends together studying, chatting, or jamming at *Amore*. And might I add, Max was a natural when it came to teaching. He could talk endlessly about any subject; Max was a walking encyclopedia. It was quite impressive. What amazed me the most was how he was actually able to make Mathematics and Science *make sense* to me. I honestly thought that comprehending Calculus and Physics would be impossible. We also never ran out of things to talk about. And Max was always ready to just jam whenever either one of us needed some inspiration.

Surprisingly, Aunt Brenna never complained if I was out with Max during her day-offs. She must have been so happy to see me *happy* (and sociable) that she even lifted my normal 10 p.m. curfew so I could stay out later to study with Max. Everyone just seemed *happier*. I was happier.

I finally felt like a *normal* teenager, a feeling that was completely foreign to me throughout my adolescence. I no longer felt like I didn't belong. Max turned out to be my saviour. Once I looked past his flirtatious nature, I'd realized that he was much more of a friend to me than Clara and Rachel had ever been. I was glad that I took a chance on him.

Max was smart. Funny. Really funny. Friendly and kind-hearted. He even named his guitar, a beautiful Seagull Entourage, El, in honour of his favourite guitarist Elvis Presley. Though Max rarely carried El around, and his guitar was quite worn. I'd always wondered why he wouldn't play El more if he were *that* talented. He played his guitar effortlessly like the guitar was just an extension to his arm. It was hard finding friends around my age with *that* sort of musical talent. Max was unlike any other guy I met before too. In a village that seemed to have no one who understood me, I finally found someone, other than my Aunt, who I could share Jimi with. Our common ground was music, coffee, and chocolate chip cookies. For the first time in a long time, I felt *alive* again. And although I'd only known him for a couple of months, it seemed like we knew each other for much longer.

•••

It was exam week, and Max had me running on a full-fledged caffeine diet. I called for another round of espresso shots at midnight. André nodded to acknowledge our pleads for more caffeine and started to prepare the deliciously addictive elixir.

"I'm starting to think all this coffee was a bad idea," I said, rubbing my temples.

"Nonsense! We still got Newton's laws and differential equations to cover. Let's keep going! The night is still young, and we got two more hours before closing," Max exclaimed as he proudly pumped his fists into the air to boost my confidence.

His enthusiasm was infectious. But I'd been overly tired lately, so it was getting harder and harder to stay up past midnight without the migraines. My headaches intensified since our first meeting at *Amore*. But I'd been so busy with studying for my finals that I never had a chance to tell Aunt Brenna about it. I thought of the time Aunt Brenna joked about prototyping a caffeine pill because it was the ultimate neuroenhancement supplement. So, I was certain it was just a side effect of being highly caffeinated. After all, I'd been drinking coffee like water the past few months to ward off tiredness.

Back when I first inquired about Max's emergency studying services, I mentioned to Max about my struggles with differential equations and Physics. Math always got the best of me, and at the time, I never thought much about it. The crux of the problem with math was that it required a lot of patience and persistence to understand it, two traits that were not fundamental in my character. I was a creative artist, a right-brain thinker, and slightly impatient. So, I was easily frustrated with Mathematics. And by the time I finally 'got it,' the teacher would have already moved onto the next unit.

Since I was blessed with impeccable memory, I got around this hurdle by simply memorizing the textbook. That was the panacea for all mathematical problems in school. But this solution was only temporary. Textbooks became thicker, and my brain ceased to comprehend such complicated material. So, technically it was a major *emergency*.

I used to remember everything to the tee, but lately, it'd been more difficult to recall even what was on my weekly grocery list. I could have sworn that my normal YouTube playlist of Alan Walker's greatest hits was perfect for studying. I even went old school and started a playlist with hits from the 1990s featuring the likes of the Backstreet Boys, Céline Dion, and the Barenaked Ladies, but to no avail. Lately, it seemed impossible to concentrate when studying with music playing in the background. I just felt out of sync, but it was probably nothing. Just stress.

"I'm not sure if you drank too much coffee or if you're normally this enthusiastic about Mathematics. How on earth do you have *this* much energy at 1 a.m.?" I asked.

Max simply just shrugged his shoulders and flashed me one of those devilish grins that would make any girl's heart melt.

"Must be my lucky hat," Max said as he removed his baseball cap to expose his messy side-swept textured haircut. He ran his fingers through his dirty blonde hair and adjusted his hat back on his head.

After one more hour of studying, Max's stomach grumbled. "The leftover pizza in my fridge is calling my name right now, and unless you can give me a really good excuse to stay, it'll be taking priority."

Max looked tired. He sported heavy dark circles under his emerald green eyes. His stomach grumbled again like it was begging for mercy, so I decided to call it a night.

I closed my textbook and finished my last sip of coffee. I looked at Max and spoke. “I think that’s enough studying for today. My head is going to explode if I try to cram any more in there. I should be fine with Biology and Chemistry tomorrow. Calculus and Physics aren’t until Friday, so I still got a couple more days to sort things out. Thanks for helping, Max. I really appreciate it.”

“When’s your last exam tomorrow?” Max asked.

“Oh, 2 p.m.,” I said.

“I have a meeting with my practicum supervisor at three tomorrow that I can’t bail. But the rest, I could care less. So, *Amore* around 4?” Max asked as he pulled out his iPhone, pretending to check his calendar app.

I knew Max was skipping classes to hang out with me, and it was wrong for me to support his behaviour. Absenteeism was not something to be proud of, especially if I was the cause of it. But I craved his companionship and desperately needed help with my studying. Plus, I was fortunate that his buddies always had his back. Max was lucky to have that type of brotherhood at school.

“You shouldn’t skip so many classes. Wouldn’t your Mom be angry if she found out?” I asked.

“Nah, I’m careful,” Max said reassuringly. “Anyway, the atmosphere here is much more welcoming than a stuffy classroom or being surrounded by old people. You worry too much, Emily.

Don't *Mother* me, okay? Just enjoy," he said with a smirk.

"Okay, but are you sure you want to spend another night here at a coffee shop with me and not with one of your hot girlfriends?" I asked, curious to learn about his relationship status.

"Well, how could I say no to another round of free coffee? Anyway, Emily, reading the works of Marie Curie, Lise Meitner, and Sally Ride can be totally hot too," Max joked. He tapped my textbook and then smirked, "But really, no hot dates tomorrow. Just you, me, and lots of coffee. I must be either too good looking, or my study partner is just too attractive for anyone to approach me. If it's fine with you, I already made reservations with André for this table until Friday."

"So, we're on for the whole week?" I asked, trying to hide my excitement.

"Didn't I agree to ditch classes so I could help you all week for your finals?" Max exclaimed.

"Well, you make it sound horrible if you put it that way," I said, feeling guilty.

"Okay, didn't I promise to study with you every day this week?" Max said as he leaned in and raised his eyebrows.

"Promise? Max Miller, what have I done to you? Making promises on the whim now, aren't we?" I chuckled.

"What can I say? You have my word," Max whispered, tilting his baseball cap to acknowledge our arrangement.

"But, Friday? I'll be done with all my exams by then. We don't need to meet up to study. I'm actually looking forward to summer break. Two months before I get back to the grind again. I'll still be reading ahead, but I can do that on my own. I wouldn't want to waste any more of your valuable time," I exclaimed.

"Emily, don't be such a party pooper. I thought you could use a day to celebrate after finishing all your exams. And don't ever think you're wasting my time. I quite enjoy hanging out with you, even if we're normally studying."

I couldn't help but smile. Max was truly the *perfectly imperfect* best friend.

•••

When I got home that night, I felt an inkling of another severe migraine. So, I quickly tucked myself into bed, closed my eyes, and collapsed into a deep slumber. That night, I dreamt of my parents.

We were sitting in the living room watching the JUNO Awards, laughing and having a good time. Then, the television flickered, the telephone rang, and the room dimmed. Suddenly, two menacing dark shadows appeared from behind the sofa, and the room started to fill with ice-cold water. The shadows engulfed my parents as I struggled to keep my head above the watery grave that waited to swallow me whole. I reached for my parents, but they were gone. I kicked viciously through the water, trying to escape to the door. My throat burned as if a thousand needles had been plunged into it. The shadows returned, and my leaden lungs suppressed any efforts I made to inhale. I was suffocating. An intense pain ripped through the back of my head and down my spine. My panic faded into numbness. And a raging wave barrelled towards me, throwing my body underneath the water. I gave in to the darkness and let the water take me.

My eyes flashed open, and I gasped for air, my mind reeling as a powerful splintering scream escaped from within. My screams echoed down the hallway to Aunt Brenna's room. My body trembled uncontrollably. I panted heavily; my chest felt tight, and my sheets were drenched with sweat. I felt dizzy as I sat up. My hands clutched my blanket; I tried to forget all about my nightmare.

Then, Aunt Brenna busted into my room, holding a baseball bat. She sprinted towards my bed; her knee caught the corner of my desk hard. She winced in pain and hobbled to my bedside.

Frantically, she scanned my room for a burglar or ax murderer of some sort. When she saw all the windows still closed, she let out a huge sigh of relief and gently placed the baseball bat down before resting her hand on my shoulder.

"Emily! Are you okay?" she asked, concerned.

I shook my head and tried to control my breathing. I wasn't ready to talk about what just happened. Not yet.

She seemed a bit upset about my silence. After all, I did wake her up at 3 a.m.

"This better be something serious 'cause I totally need my beauty rest after a ten-hour shift tonight," Aunt Brenna huffed frustratedly.

I thought I would be able to tell Aunt Brenna, but I became so choked up that I couldn't do it. After a long awkward silence, I admitted in a whisper, "I had a nightmare."

Aunt Brenna took a deep breath and put on a warm smile. "You know, Emily. There is nothing scary about final exams. Calculus and Physics are not worth crying over unless you're talking about Chemistry. Now that can sometimes make you scream," Aunt Brenna laughed.

I didn't say anything. Instead, I just rolled my eyes at her terrible joke and dried my face with my sleeve.

"Just so you know, Emily, puffy red eyes are hard to hide even with the most expensive concealer. This look is not very attractive for your hot date with Maximus tomorrow, honey," Aunt Brenna teased.

"Aunt Brenna! For the hundredth time, his name is Max, and studying does not qualify as a date. He's just a friend, Aunt Brenna. You know, f-r-i-e-n-d. *Friend.* It's actually quite simple. I bribe him with André's coffee. He helps me with the material for my finals. Nothing more. Nothing less," I said defensively.

"You don't need to get so worked up about it, Em. Anyway, isn't *studying* a synonym for *dating*? Check the thesaurus. If it's not in there, then write it in sweetie, okay?" Aunt Brenna laughed as I blushed.

"Huh?" I said, confused.

"And for the record, Maximus sounds so much more mysterious than just Max. Maximus. Don't you love how it just rolls off your tongue? Now get rid of that baseball cap and add some spandex, and you got a hot ticket to La La land," Aunt Brenna said with a glimmer in her eye.

I buried my face into my pillow. I wondered what was more

embarrassing. The fact that my Aunt was trying to hook me up with my best friend, or the fact that I imagined Max in something other than his normal suit combo.

My cheeks blushed bright red with the thought of Max being even remotely mysterious and attractive. I quickly thought of something else before my brain went haywire. I crossed my arms firmly across my chest. There was no way I was going to let Aunt Brenna win this battle.

"André has told me that the two of you are getting close," Aunt Brenna winked.

"Huh? How did you? What? No, are you kidding me?" I said flustered. "André isn't even always around when we're at *Amore* studying," I said defensively before I'd realized something was up. "Wait, you're talking with André again?" I asked.

"That's beyond the point, Emily. Max seems like a great guy. I just thought I give you some relationship advice, that's all," Aunt Brenna said, nudging my shoulder.

"Something is fishy here. You don't all of a sudden start talking with André again," I pestered.

"I'm just making sure I have a watchful eye over you. It's nothing more," Aunt Brenna said with a smile.

Max was a really sweet guy, but I'd never considered the possibility of anything more than just friends. We lived in two different worlds. I was still in high school. He was in college. I was positive he already had a love interest, though we never talked about anything other than schoolwork and music. And if he didn't, I was positive he was into college girls.

One thing was certain. Max was one of those guys that would give up his dessert for you just so you could have seconds. Any girl would be lucky to have him as their soulmate. I was just lucky to have him as a friend.

"Aunt Brenna!" I exclaimed, shocked that she could exploit André as her secret spy.

"Fine, I'll stop asking you about Max if you can tell me why I'm here in your room this early in the morning in the first place. You know, some people actually need their beauty rest to stay beautiful," Aunt Brenna said.

"It happened again. The same nightmare. The one I had every day for two years after Mom and Dad left. I hadn't had these nightmares since. But today, it came back. I don't understand why life must be so cruel. Always invading my dreams just to mess with my sleep. I'm sorry, Aunt Brenna. I know I thought we got past this, but it's back again. What if it never stops Aunt Brenna?" I said, concerned.

Aunt Brenna gave me a reassuring smile. She let out a loud sigh and then spoke, "I miss them too, but no matter how much we try to dream them back into our lives, it's not happening, honey. You just got to learn to let go. It doesn't mean you'll forget about them. And it doesn't mean you love them any less. Rather, it only means that you love them even more. You're Emily 2.0. You've got your whole life ahead of you after high school. You can't let your mind control you. Show your brain, who's boss! You just got to change your perspective. Stop flooding your mind with the sad moments and remember the good ones instead.

Anyway, you can't even swim, Emily!"

"I know. I know," I replied.

Aunt Brenna continued, "When life gives you lemons, don't just make lemonade. You got to—"

"Squeeze back those lemons into life's eyes," I interrupted, finishing off her sentence.

"Exactly!" Aunt Brenna squealed with excitement. "No matter what hurdle is in your way, run up to it, push it over, and keep going."

"But I don't want to let go. Not yet," I said, killing whatever excitement Aunt Brenna had.

"Let go of the weight on your shoulders that is stopping you from living your life to its fullest. You cannot change your past, but you can change your unwritten future," Aunt Brenna said as she gave my shoulders a light squeeze before getting up to leave my room.

"Just think about what I said, okay, sweetie. You got a big day ahead of you. Try to get some rest," Aunt Brenna said softly. I gave her a nod, and she disappeared out the door.

I thought deeply about my Aunt's words. Mom's wisdom had definitely rubbed off on her. It was hard to believe that the same woman who once duck taped me to my bed on April Fools while I was sleeping could transform into someone so wise. I chuckled as I tried my very best to fall back asleep.

Chapter Six

My alarm buzzed. I probably hit the snooze button three times before I was ready to get out of bed. It was morning, and I felt like I had a hangover despite zero alcohol consumption last night. My AP Chemistry exam was scheduled for ten o'clock sharp, followed by Biology at half past noon.

After wolfing down an entire bowl of lucky charms cereal in a record time of five minutes, I was out the door. I had an exam day ritual of eating a bowl of lucky charms for good luck. I know I may have been too old to believe in Lucky the Leprechaun, but the sugar rush from those tiny marshmallows was so 'magically delicious.'

On the bus ride to *Glenwood High*, I finished skimming through my review sheets one last time. My eyes felt heavy as I exited the bus. I was exhausted, and my head felt like it was a volcano about to explode. I regretted pressing snooze so many times this morning; I should have substituted coffee for breakfast instead.

I was literally ten steps away from the main entrance when my heel caught on the asphalt. I started to plunge forward towards the ground. But strong, welcoming arms cushioned my fall. Although my notes scattered everywhere, I was lucky to have avoided hitting something hard and injuring myself. There was a strange familiarity to this stranger's grasp. But I just couldn't put my finger on it. My eyes fluttered open to a wide-eyed, smiling Max Miller.

"Woah there, Emily! Fancy bumping into you again. Looks like I got here in the nick of time," Max laughed with a smirk.

"Max?" I replied.

"Don't tell me all that coffee got to your head. Why do you have that goofy smile on your face? Surprised I'm here, aren't you?" Max joked as he took off his baseball cap and flashed a smug look before running his fingers through his hair. "You got to watch where you're going, or you'll get yourself hurt. My Dad used to tell me, 'keep your head up and your eyes wide.' Oh, and this is for you."

Max steadied me back onto my feet and handed over a steaming cup of coffee before picking up my notes. "You're lucky I didn't spill this on you when I rushed over to catch your fall," Max exclaimed.

"Thanks, Max. But why are you here? I thought we weren't meeting until four," I questioned.

"So, someone needs to keep tabs on my whereabouts now, eh?" Max said, raising his eyebrows.

"Huh? No. But. I thought," I said, flustered.

"Just kidding. Can't a guy just do something nice for his best friend? Thought you'd be in the library already doing last-minute studying. I wanted to wish you good luck before heading to the clinic. Plus, I figured you'll be a hot mess this morning anyway. And boy, was I totally right. Luckily, there's nothing coffee can't fix. Looks like you really need one this morning," Max said confidently, pointing to the cup of coffee in my hands.

Surprised that Max somehow read my mind, I responded, "How did you—"

Max interrupted, "Know you wanted a cup of coffee? Well, you can thank me later. Now no time for small talk. You got an exam to get to. See you later at four. You got this, Emily! Remember, head up and eyes wide," Max said enthusiastically, giving me the thumbs-up as he headed back to his car.

"Thanks, Max. I don't know what to say," I yelled out, taking a sip of my cup of joe.

"You don't have to say anything. Just ace that exam!" Max shouted.

Just like that, Max disappeared. I breathed in the aromatic scent of coffee before indulging in another sip. Sometimes I wondered if I'd mistaken Max's confidence as cockiness because he had his own *joie de vivre*. Despite his personal hardships, he always remained calm and collected, and genuinely wanted everyone around him to succeed. Max had a much better understanding of his strengths and emotions than I did; his positive attitude towards life was infectious.

The thought of Max put a smile on my face. It was like the sun breaking through cloudy skies. As I marched into *Glenwood High*, I held my head up high with my eyes wide opened. And for the first time in a long time, I felt radiant and confident.

•••

I scribbled my final response on mitosis and meiosis, got up from my desk, and submitted my test paper. I was never one to suffer from exam anxiety, but it felt so relieving to exit *Glenwood High* today. There was an overwhelming feeling of sickness in the pit of my stomach as I nervously started calculating what grade I needed to get to pass the class. In all these years of high school, I'd never been this doubtful of my exam performance. I secretly cried to myself, hopeful that I guessed my answers correctly.

There were still two hours before my next study session with Max. I took out my phone and contemplated whether I should message Clara and Rachel for some much-needed girl time. It has been months since we got together, got drunk on coffee, and chatted excessively about life's most complex problem—*boys*. Though, I resisted the urge as I reminded myself about Clara's blabbermouth syndrome. She couldn't keep a secret even if her life depended on it.

Quietly, I sat on a bench right outside *Glenwood High* and strummed Jimi, bringing life to a new song in my black Moleskine.

♪♫♪♫♪♫♪

Always running, training for life's race

Always climbing, over hurdles I face

And when the sun goes down, I'm left in the dark

But it doesn't mean, it doesn't mean that I've lost my mark

♪♫♪♫♪♫♪

Fifteen minutes to four. I ordered our usual double-shot espressos and sat in the corner booth, patiently waiting for Max's arrival. My Physics notes were sprawled out across half the table, and my head started to feel very tense. I decided to take a small break before Max arrived, so I set aside my notes and transferred my newly written song onto a sheet of neon green paper. At exactly four o'clock, Max entered *Amore*. I discreetly tucked my musical paper airplane under my Moleskine and pulled back my Physics notes in front of me.

"What do you call a girl who drank too much coffee?" Max said as he causally slid into his seat in the booth.

"Umm, a caffeine addict?" I answered.

"Nope," Max shook his head.

"The Energizer bunny?" I guessed.

"Nope," Max said as he paused to add suspense. "Emily McGregor," he laughed. "Wait a second. I always thought that pink, mechanical drummer was a male mascot."

"Ah, poor Max, are you blinded by the cultural stereotype that all mascots are males? No, wait, even worse. You are from one of the world's most chauvinist countries and totally disapproves of girl power," I sighed.

"Woah! Are you insane, Emily? Where on earth did you get that idea from? At least I don't stereotype in believing that pink is only a feminine colour. Pink isn't really my thing, but Jason Momoa has a penchant for wearing the colour pink," Max said defensively with his hands up.

I let out a heavy sigh. "You're right about that. Jason looks stunning in the colour pink any day. Pink sweaters. Pink suits. Even his iconic pink scrunchie on his wrist. That guy is a true style icon," I chuckled as my mind wandered off to my typical daydream.

Then, Max grabbed my hand, almost like he was desperately trying to explain himself. "Emily, trust me when I say this. I just thought that the Energizer bunny was a dude simply because he's buck naked with only a pair of blue and black striped flip-flops. Consider Bugs Bunny versus Lola Bunny," Max explained, raising his right eyebrow.

"Oh, I never thought of it logically like that," I said, slightly embarrassed with my outburst while wiggling my hand out of his grasp. I bit the bottom of my lip and blushed.

"No sweat. Your reaction just legitimizes my point. You usually aren't this sensitive when I joke. Are you normally like this during exam week? Though, I could get used to it. It's pretty cute," Max smirked. He pointed to my nearly empty espresso cup and whispered, "This must be your fifth cup, or you started substituting energy drinks at home just to keep up with me."

"Well, if a caffeine high is anything like a sugar rush, then this roller coaster is only going up," I said, winking.

•••

After five hours of studying and many more cups of coffee, we decided to call it a night. I started to feel very tired, and to make matters worse, my headache was not getting any better. Fortunately, I had a couple more days to cram before my Physics exam.

I stuffed my notes into my bag and carelessly dropped my neon paper airplane on the floor as I got up from my seat. Max noticed it immediately.

"What's this? I had no idea you had a hidden talent for origami. Where's this one soaring off to?" Max asked as he swooped up my paper airplane and began unfolding it.

I quickly snatched it out of his hands and replied, "Some mysteries should remain untold, Max Miller."

"But Emily, you can trust me with your secrets," Max pleaded.

"Sorry, Max. Not today," I said bluntly, stuffing the paper airplane blindly into my bag before Max could sneak a peek.

I turned my head towards André and waved, hoping that Max would forget about the whole paper airplane mystery. I wasn't ready to expose all my secrets to Max, even if he was my best friend. Max followed suit and waved to André as I finished clearing our booth.

We walked out of *Amore*. It was past nine, and the stars were glistening brightly in the clear sky. My migraine lingered, but the fresh air was gladly welcomed. I clutched Jimi tightly as we silently stared into the night sky.

"See you tomorrow?" I asked, breaking the silence.

"Umm, ya, of course," Max said, fidgeting.

Max seemed flustered about something, but I couldn't seem to figure it out. I noticed that he consumed double the amount of coffee this evening, but I assumed that he was just tired. Though, I was certain that Max was hiding something from me. I spent enough time with him to figure out his quirks, like how his fidgeting was a telltale sign that something was wrong. Despite my intuition, my migraine had become more and more unpleasant, so I decided not to press on. I shrugged off my hunch and turned to Max to wave goodbye.

Chapter Seven

It was morning. T-minus three days before my most dreaded Physics and Calculus finals. But I wasn't in the mood to study today. My migraine was still bothering me, and I barely slept last night. And I refused to blame my sleep deprivation on the possibility of a coffee hangover. How could anyone ever drink too much coffee?

I laid in my bed, arms and legs stretched out like a star, and just stared out the window. I started counting. One. Two. Three. Three butterflies fluttered across my view. One landed on my windowsill. I got up and walked towards the window. The vibrant orange glow on its wings was magnificent. And for a brief moment, I imagined what it would be like to be beautiful and free like a monarch butterfly. I let out a loud sigh and closed my eyes.

I imagined myself flying like a butterfly and felt the beginnings of a new song. Quickly, I grabbed my Moleskine from my bag and started to write.

♪♫♪♫♪♫♪

When the rain clears in the sky, I soar like a butterfly

Stars all around me, that's when I feel free

♪♫♪♫♪♫♪

My songwriting was interrupted by an ambrosial aroma that warmed my heart and made my stomach grumble. Aunt Brenna was home today, and according to my nose, she was already awake, making my ultimate favourite breakfast food. Pancakes. I tossed my phone onto my bed, ignoring the missed calls and voicemail notifications, and rushed down to the kitchen.

"Good morning, Emily dear! It's a beautiful sunny day to enjoy some delicious and super fluffy pancakes on our patio. And do you know what would make these pancakes even better?" Aunt Brenna asked in a cheerful voice, smiling.

"Strawberries?" I said grumpily.

Aunt Brenna nodded and replied, "Well, yes. That and—"

"Blueberries?" I interrupted.

She responded, looking a bit frustrated now, "That too. But also—"

"Bananas?" I continued with zero enthusiasm.

"Emily, for Pete's sake, can you stop naming all the fruits in the fruit basket and just let me finish my sentence?" Aunt Brenna yelled in frustration, tugging on her apron.

"Sorry, Aunt Brenna. I guess I got carried away. Umm, I thought you were asking me a question, though," I said defensively.

"It was rhetorical, Em. Rhetorical," Aunt Brenna huffed with her arms positioned firmly on her waist.

"Oh, well, then. Go on," I whispered, nodding for her to continue.

Aunt Brenna smiled and continued, "I wasn't thinking of toppings. I was thinking of pairings."

"Oh! I see where this is going," I said. Then, I covered my mouth quickly, afraid that she would yell at me for interrupting her train of thought again.

Aunt Brenna winked, and we both chanted in unison, "Double-shot espressos with a healthy sprinkle of cocoa and cinnamon spice!" We both laughed.

She waved her hands in the air like she was performing some sort of magic trick at a kid's birthday party. Then, with the snap of her fingers, she moved aside to reveal a brand new Breville espresso machine hiding behind her. I shrieked with excitement. Finally, I could practice the fine skills of a barista in the comfort of my very own home. This was totally awesome!

"No way! You got an espresso machine! I thought you said that instant coffee was good enough at home. Didn't you say that espresso machines were not *essential* kitchen gadgets and that we weren't classy enough for such a sophisticated device? Hmm? You got some explaining to do, Aunt Brenna," I exclaimed, hinting for her to spill the beans.

I waited for Aunt Brenna to respond. Suddenly, I was hit by an epiphany.

I shrieked, "No way! Yes! You hooked up with André!"

Aunt Brenna's cheeks flushed redder than a Red Delicious apple. She sheepishly grinned. Was I so absorbed in my own little world that I foolishly missed all the telltale signs that Aunt Brenna was finally dating again? That totally explains why she never fussed about me meeting up with Max on her days-off and why André, who used to be glued to his shop, was sometimes mysteriously missing from the front counter. I put on a huge smile and giggled. Once I started to connect the dots, I'd realized that Aunt Brenna and André were probably dating for a month or so already.

I leaned in closer to her, eager to hear more juicy details about their relationship. My Aunt could only blush while giving me the knowing nod that had 'yes' written all over her face.

I couldn't contain my excitement much longer. I screamed like a little schoolgirl, grabbed my Aunt's hands, and started jumping up and down like a total psycho. My Aunt probably thought I was high on some sort of strong stimulant. But she did not put a damper on the mood and joined in on the celebration.

Aunt Brenna was on cloud nine. And I was so excited to finally have the chance to bombard her with personal questions about her love life. Yes! This was going to be awesome! There was no way I was going to spare her any grief.

For years I'd dealt with her teasing me about any and every Y-chromosome I met, even if they could have passed as my Grandpa. Aunt Brenna was one of those people who believed that guys and girls could never be *best friends*. She insisted that the laws of physics justified her silly proclamation that *opposites attract*. I was positive that Aunt Brenna's secret profession was matchmaker in our family. So knowing that she finally worked on herself for a change put a huge smile on my face. I twiddled my fingers and widened my smile. It was funny how the tables have now turned.

"I'm so, so, so happy for you! When? How? Does anyone else know? Why didn't you tell me sooner? Why didn't André say anything? Does he speak French to you? This is so romantic! I'm so jealous! You two are totally meant for each other!" I blabbered on and on.

I stopped to gasp for air, but Aunt Brenna held out her hand to stop me from continuing. Perhaps today was *actually* going to be a good day.

"I'll answer all your questions soon. But I think our breakfast is calling us. Wouldn't want our pancakes and espressos to get all cold, would we?" Aunt Brenna said, winking as she ushered me to set the table.

Aunt Brenna shared *all* the juicy details of their newly bloomed relationship while we indulged in fluffy pancakes and espressos. Falling in love was a beautiful thing, and those two lovebirds had *love* written all over their faces. After hearing their stories, I could affirm that André, not to my surprise, was definitely a romantic partner. I thought it was super sweet for him to gift Aunt Brenna with her very own espresso machine just so she could think of him every morning. Absolutely adorable!

According to the countless dating blogs online that I'd read, actions really do speak louder than words when it comes to men. The saying went something like this, 'if he always gave you the better half, then he believed that you *were* his better half.' Aunt Brenna was truly a lucky gal. Note to self. I should look into finding a French boyfriend.

•••

No matter what type of relationship we're talking about, it was always the *little things* that counted the most. They can be relationships between friends, family members, or lovers. And it was these pivotal moments when *little things* are said or done that would make or break that connection. *Little things* added up very quickly. And all those *little things* eventually evolved into *big things* that emitted beautiful energy. Energy we called *love.*

In all relationships, we experienced love. And although I'd never been in a romantic relationship before, I loved my parents, my Aunt, and my friends. But what exactly was *love*? This was one of life's enigmas? A puzzle without a solution. We tried so hard to make sense of it. To hold it. To label it. But love was truly undefinable.

Like life, love wasn't just *one* thing. It was decisions and actions. Thoughts and emotions. Moments and challenges. It was about continually learning (and accepting) how those we loved could fit into the chaos of our lives. It was perhaps all of this, plus the messiness, the confusion, and the flaws. Love was saying that despite the impermanence of human existence, we should not just *give* but also *forgive.*

I was not a narcissist. I knew the world did not revolve around me. And I deeply valued the practice of feeling happy for others. I called it a *practice* because, frankly, it took *a lot* of practice to be good at it. But, feeling happy for others seemed like second nature to me. Probably because I'd never liked being in the spotlight. It was a true wonder whenever my compassionate voice guided me. The more I'd felt happier for others, the happier I'd become.

Aunt Brenna went inside the kitchen to grab another round of espressos. I was extremely happy for Aunt Brenna and André. Plus, my giddiness sparked a sudden urge to cover everything with heart emojis.

We spent the rest of the morning chatting about André, laughing about celebrity mishaps on social media, and re-watching *Aquaman* for the one-hundredth-and-one time. It was a nice break from studying. By afternoon, I felt much more energized to study, so I headed to *Amore* to congratulate André and meet Max for our study session.

When I entered *Amore,* I was welcomed by a huge smile and hug by André.

"She said, yes! Oui, oui! I'm so happy mon amour said oui!" André exclaimed, beaming a proud smile on his face.

"I'm really happy too, André! Aunt Brenna shared the news with me this morning, and I came in to congratulate you. The two of you are perfect for each other," I chimed as I high-fived him.

I was thrilled that André finally had the courage to call Aunt Brenna and profess his love for her. He had a crush on her for so many years, and I knew the feeling was mutual for my Aunt, but she was too oblivious to notice. Today was going to be an awesome day!

I ordered my usual and took the corner booth to start studying. As I waited for Max, I started to doodle heart emojis on random pages in my Moleskine. It was almost 6 o'clock, and it was unusual for Max to have not shown up yet. Perhaps he was delayed from practicum and was now caught in rush hour traffic. By 7 o'clock, I began to lose tolerance for Max's unorthodox silence. He always would text if he would be late, and he had impeccable memory, so there was no way he could have forgotten.

I didn't want to sound needy, so I resisted the urge to text him. Though, by 7:30 p.m., my patience was growing thin. I finally sent him a text to ask about his whereabouts. The past few hours were a real struggle. I felt like some invisible force just sucked the life right out of me. I felt lonelier than I had ever felt before. Why on earth did Max have such a huge impact on me? We were *just* friends.

Today was supposed to be awesome, but Max's unexplained absence made my happy mood turn sour, and my espresso tasted bitter on my tongue. Max never did reply to my text messages. I eventually left *Amore* at a quarter past nine but was still upset about him being MIA.

Max was no Superman. And I was no Wonder Woman. Fictional comic book characters, yes, but the character traits they exhibited were impressive. How could someone be so strong in all facets of their life—physically, emotionally, mentally—and still have the strength to save the world 24/7?

We could not deny the existence of our emotions. If Netflix had the power to leave us in a glass case of emotions when watching those tragic, tear-jerking, cry-off-your-mascara romances, then crying was surely a natural catharsis. I was certain that superheroes cry too, even if it was behind closed doors. Sometimes, all we needed was a good cry to feel better at the end of the day.

As I rode the bus home, I thought to myself, why only humans routinely cried to communicate what they were feeling. Sadness. Happiness. Anger. Crying was one of our most natural forms of communication to convey our emotions in a way that language could not. Often, our emotions went beyond just 'happy' or 'sad.' Crying was a form of nonverbal social communication aimed to cleanse our minds and elicit comfort from others. Humans are highly social beings. We liked to share our personal experiences. Perhaps the ability to cry was what truly distinguished us from other species. It was what made us human. I began to tear up as I approached my stop, but at least no one was watching.

•••

When I approached my street, I saw the lights on in the living room. Aunt Brenna must have returned from her evening shift. She noticed the disappointment on my face and waved me to the kitchen for a chat.

"Do I need to call André, or are you going to spill the beans?" Aunt Brenna asked, crossing her arms firmly across her chest.

"No, André isn't responsible for this. His coffee is always amazing," I said with a sigh.

"I'm not asking about André's coffee. I'm wondering if something happened at his shop," Aunt Brenna continued, trying to pry out more details.

"But this espresso machine," I pointed to Aunt Brenna's new

kitchen gadget, "it may put André's most favourite customers on hiatus." I winked and forced a smile before continuing. "Actually, I probably spend more money on coffee than on transportation these days. I think my bank account is thankful for this new appliance. I could probably go back to studying at home nowadays," I joked, letting out an uneasy chuckle.

"Don't be silly. You don't go to *Amore* for André's coffee, silly bean. You go there because of Maximus," Aunt Brenna retorted.

It was like Aunt Brenna could read my mind. I was just thinking about him. Why did he not show up today? A sour taste filled in my mouth. My head tensed. I did not want to tell Aunt Brenna, and I refused to let Max ruin what was supposed to be an awesome day.

"Aunt Brenna!" I yelled.

"I'm serious, Emily. He's totally your type, and he's quite the looker," she insisted.

"No, he's not. And I don't want to talk about him now, okay?" I snarled, turning to face the wall instead.

"Is something wrong, Emily? You usually don't shut me down so quickly when I tease you about Maximus. Something's up. Talk to me," Aunt Brenna pressed.

"I said that I don't want to talk about it. Can we just talk about you this once? Please!" I pleaded, hoping Aunt Brenna would continue sharing gossip about her relationship instead of prying into mine.

Aunt Brenna nodded. She knew that I wasn't going to budge. Sometimes we cannot win all our battles. And Aunt Brenna knew that at least for tonight, it wasn't worth meddling with my private affairs.

We had grown a lot since our last argument. We'd learned how to compromise with each other's needs and to recognize better when it was appropriate to press each other's buttons.

Aunt Brenna started telling me about the plans for their next date night, but my mind was elsewhere this evening. I kept zoning in and out of the conversation. I couldn't stop thinking about Max. I started to mentally list a hundred different possible reasons to explain Max's disappearance. But none of them made sense. The only plausible explanation was Max losing his phone so that he couldn't contact me. Maybe it was just that simple. No, it couldn't be right. He had practicum, so he had access to plenty of *phones* in the hospital. But why? Why would he not tell me if he wasn't planning on coming? It was just rude and irresponsible to leave me hanging like that!

Stupid Max. Even when he wasn't around, he still had the power to preoccupy my mind. Man. Max always had such impeccably good timing to be a bother. Why was life so complicated?

"Aunt Brenna," I said softly.

"Yes, Emily dear," Aunt Brenna replied, putting a hand on my shoulder.

"Thank you," I whispered.

"Thank you for what, Emily?" Aunt Brenna asked, slightly confused.

"For sharing your happy news. I really like André. And I finally have something to look forward to," I said with a small smile.

"Oh Emily, I'm glad you like André too. But you know, dear, there's plenty to look forward to. You just need to open your eyes to look more carefully," Aunt Brenna said with a smile. "An evening round of double-shot espresso drinks?" she asked cheerfully.

"Most definitely," I said as my lips revealed a tiny smile.

•••

By midnight, I completely forgot about Max, and I was in a much better mood for bedtime. It was never good to go to sleep angry. Being angry at someone was emotionally exhausting. Surely enough, it was easier to be happy with someone than to be angry.

I tossed my bag onto my desk roughly, knocking the empty to-go coffee cup onto the floor. Max. For some strange reason, I kept that coffee cup from our second *Amore* encounter. I bent down to pick up the coffee cup and rubbed my fingers over Max's scribbles. The thought of Max made me angry again. Who wouldn't be peeved if their best friend just ditched them? I let out a huge sigh. I was still unsure of what to do.

My bed was screaming my name and my head felt really tense. I was sitting at my desk, looking out the window at the few stars that shone through the clouds. Stargazing was the best to clear the mind. My migraine returned, but I blamed it on the six rounds of espressos over a short time span. I was a coffee addict but rarely drank *that* much coffee all at once. Eventually, I gave in to temptation, knowing that however long I slept, the rest was much needed.

I jolted awake at 3 o'clock in the morning and looked out the window. It stopped raining. Cloudy skies. Even the moon was hiding tonight. My head felt better, but I was still a mess. I grabbed my phone on my bed to see if there were any missed messages. None. What was going on? Something just didn't add up here.

We'd never ignored each other's text messages for this long before once our friendship matured. Did I do something wrong? Why? What did I do to deserve this type of silent treatment? Friends are supposed to have each other's backs and never leave the other hanging. What gives Max! Where are you?

I put down my phone again and wished that there was a book that I could refer to for guidance to life's medley of problems. That would have made things a lot easier. I grabbed my Moleskine to scribble down my thoughts. Sometimes, the best escape was through song.

♪♫♪♫♪♫♪

This race, I'll keep running

This life, I'll keep fighting

And if I had enough, I would just stop and say

Be bold, be strong, be brave

Just hold on for one more day

'Cause nothing else matters

'Cause nothing else matters

♪♫♪♫♪♫♪

I wrote in my Moleskine religiously. It held my deepest emotions muddled in musical notation. My thoughts. My stories. My problems. I always felt better whenever pen hit paper. It was the perfect stress reliever, and today was a *very* stressful day. Rarely would I possess the imaginative energy required to whip up a musical composition this early in the morning.

And as fate would have it, my phone finally rang. I refused to look at my phone, assuming it was Max. He must have been drunk to have the nerve to call me at 4 a.m. I didn't want to answer it. I was still peeved with being blown off. Plus, the more I thought about it, I was more upset about the fact that he *broke* his promise. I hated broken promises. Didn't he promise me that we'll meet at *Amore* every day this week to cram? It was a matter of principle for Max to keep his word. And it was downright disrespectful not to inform me if he was going to skip out.

I thought he knew that I had a low tolerance for broken promises. We are the promises that we keep. When we made commitments, it was all about honouring our word and refusing to tolerate anything less from others. I used to believe Max was a man of honour. But maybe there were no guys nowadays who *actually* had honour.

My phone stopped ringing. One missed call. Caller ID: Max Miller. After a couple of seconds, my phone rang again. And again. By the third time, I did not have to think twice and accepted his call.

I knew I couldn't avoid him forever, and frankly, I wanted to know why he didn't show up. An awkward silence hung in the air, but I continued to wait for him to speak first.

"Emily! Oh good, you're finally answering my calls. I'm sorry about today. Don't be mad at me. Emily? Are you there? Say something!" Max exclaimed.

I tensed up once I heard Max's voice. I bit the bottom of my lip as my emotions swirled inside. I was fuming.

Max decided to continue talking, "Emily, I want to make it up to you. But I need you to talk to me first. I hate the silent treatment. It hurts, you know. I love hearing your beautiful voice. Emily?"

I bit my lip again and whispered with an irritated voice, "You're sure you still want to hear my voice if I'm angry?"

"You don't sound very angry. Okay, maybe a little. Well, sorry?" Max teased. "If it makes you feel better, go ahead and yell at me. You could be yelling and screaming right now, and that's absolutely okay. It's all music to my ears. At least you'd be talking to me. I like silence when I'm thinking. But not silence between friends," Max reasoned.

"Ditto with the silent treatment. Friends?" I huffed.

"Of course, we're friends. Wouldn't have it any other way," Max said sympathetically.

"So, if *you* hate the silent treatment, don't you think *I* would feel the same way?" I replied, beginning to raise my voice.

"Oh, about that. I forgot. I was busy," Max responded nervously. I heard the scratching sounds of clothing rub against a surface; he was fidgeting again.

"Oh, really? How did you suddenly get so forgetful? Or is there something else you're hiding from me? Spill it, or I'm hanging up," I raged, unable to contain my anger any longer.

"Okay, okay, you're right. I lied and lost track of time. I left early from practicum and went to my friend's farewell party. I planned to stay for a couple of hours and then arrive fashionably late at *Amore* to study with you, but you know how it is when you talk with old friends. Three hours only feels like thirty minutes, so I forgot. I called you right away when I got home," Max blurted out as he admitted defeat.

"You never planned to come, did you? You could have just told me the truth and saved us from all this grief. But you lied, Max. You're responsible for telling me. Frankly, if you decide to cancel with anyone, you're supposed to tell before the event, not several hours after. I respect your priorities, but you need to respect mine as well. I waited for you, Max. I even messaged you. Honestly, it sounds like you don't think it was a big deal," I screamed as tears began to trickle down my cheek.

"One of my buddies is leaving town, so a group of us set up one of those farewell surprise parties. He's moving to a beautiful city called Queenstown to start a new chapter in his life. It's in New Zealand. That's like on the other side of the world, so it'll be a long time before we can save up to visit him in-person," Max said quietly. "You should have been there to meet my buddies. I mean, the guys have been asking about you. Well, I mean, like they weren't asking directly about you. But they were curious why I'd been ditching class more frequently, that's all. When I mentioned a girl's name, it got their attention."

I knew what Max was doing. He was trying to stir up a conversation without going too off-topic to give me some time to 'calm down,' but it wasn't helping. Max just didn't understand how lies could jeopardize trust in our friendship and that the damage was sometimes irreparable. I let out a very loud sigh in frustration.

Our promises were posited on the premise of positive validation of self-identity to others. We made promises, not just to form a foundation of trust. We made them to validate some important aspects of our own identity and how we would like to think of ourselves. And, as it turned out, that was exactly the problem. Max wanted me to think that he was my saviour because he was egotistic. And surely, I fed into the problem. If I had called him out three months ago, then perhaps I could have avoided all of this.

Max was the kind of person who saw himself as an exceptional, better-than-most friend. So, understandably, if I told him what I *really* was thinking, then Max would undoubtedly call me out for sprouting pretentious nonsense. My intuition was telling me that it was not a good idea to speak my mind. I muttered some profanity under my breath and bit the corner of my lip before collecting my words. I contemplated if I should end this conversation. I knew that there was no way either one of us was going to change our minds. Max thought he was right, and I thought he was wrong. Stubbornness was another common character trait that we shared.

"Well, you kinda can't go to a party if you never knew about,

Max. If you and your buddies were planning this, then you knew about this all along. If it makes you feel better, I wouldn't have attended anyway, so thanks for the late invite," I said sarcastically. "You see, I really do want to get to know you better and meet your friends. But you don't need to pretend to be the good guy here. If you wanted to go to this party yourself, you could have just been honest and told me earlier. We aren't joined at the hip, Max. Best friends *do* hang out separately with their other friends from time-to-time. You haven't even met my girlfriends Clara and Rachel yet, but I hang out with them sometimes before we meet at *Amore*," I explained, slightly agitated.

"But Emily! I didn't mean to lie to you. I really did want to spend the whole week studying with you. I just didn't want you to think that I didn't care about your exams. Let's just forget the whole thing happened, okay?" Max pleaded.

"We are the promises that we keep, Max. And for better or worse, we must try our best to keep all of them. You can't go off and make promises that you have no intention of keeping. It's just wrong to play with someone's emotions like that! We—I mean, I—put a lot of faith into promises. Whether big or small, promises are commitments; you must stick to them. I guess you just don't understand because you don't make any *real* promises. Why didn't you just tell me yesterday that you were busy and none of this would have ever happened?" I said firmly.

"What do you mean 'real' promises? So, what's the big deal if I break a couple of them anyway?" Max asked. "Can't we bend them? You know, make exceptions? Sorry, but I guess I don't see how forgetting and changing plans equate to breaking promises," he questioned.

"No, Max! That defeats the purpose of promises. Promises are meant to be kept. Not broken. I'd dealt with enough broken promises in my life. If you value our friendship, you can't be dishonest. At least not intentionally. You knew about the party, but you were too chicken to tell me when you had the chance. And now, you're just digging yourself into a deeper hole with your excuses and lies," I yelled.

"Emily!" Max interrupted, but I cleared my throat to let him know that I wanted to finish.

I took a deep breath and continued in a calmer tone, "I know you had every intention to fulfill your commitment to helping me study for my exams. And, you also had a legitimate excuse to not show up at *Amore* this time too. But, if it's too much of a hassle to balance your own personal life with my studying, then just be honest with me. I would have never stopped you from saying goodbye to your friend. Trust me. You don't want to regret not saying goodbye. Max, all I'm asking for is honesty. If there's one thing our friendship needs to grow is honesty."

Farewells were just as crucial as greetings. Life ebbed and flowed. There were natural beginnings and endings, and farewells were a part of coping with changes in our lives. If I neglected Max from saying goodbye to his friends, it would only weaken his ties with those he loved. Or, even worse, fill him with regret. I, for one, understood how guilt could eat away at us.

Although I wasn't sure how I would have reacted if Max told

me earlier, I would have supported him when life called for him to say goodbye. I did, after all, cared about Max's well-being. Yes, we had FaceTime and WhatsApp, but the distance does affect friendships no matter how small. I'd lost all my friends once I moved to Glenwood, and we still lived in the same time zone.

"Emily, so, we're cool?" Max asked.

"Not so fast, mister. I'm not going to let you off so easily, and I think you still don't get the point of my frustration," I said seriously, lowering my voice.

"You see, Max. You really hurt me when you broke your promise. I know you didn't mean to hurt me, but you did. And it will continue to hurt every time that happens again. You can't just say you'll do something just to make you look like the good guy," I confessed.

I paused to see if Max was going to refute. Expectantly, he did.

"But Emily, my intentions were good. Honest. It was just one lie. I made a mistake. How could you just assume that it'll happen again? Come on, have some faith in our friendship! You got to cut me some slack here!" Max said defensively.

"Okay, I'll give you that. I can't just let this situation create a negative connotation on your future behaviour. I may have gone out of line there, but you still hurt me. It will take some time to heal," I explained.

"Forgive and forget, Emily. That is what makes the world go-'round," Max recited.

"Just give me some time. Okay? At the end of the day, you got to take your word seriously. You can't just babble your promises carelessly to get what you want at that moment or just to please me. The action of making that promise must be genuine, or it's just noise. If you have no obligation to honour your promises, then don't make them because you're bound to cause more harm than good. No matter how you slice it, the blame falls to the one who made the promise. And that's you," I reiterated.

There was a long moment of silence on the other end. This was painful. I was ready to pull out my hair and start again with a clean slate. That was how much I wanted him just to understand. I had only one goal in mind: to communicate and to do it clearly.

Max's friendship meant a lot to me, but I didn't want to risk getting hurt again. Actually, I never had the courage to speak up for *anything*. I was always one to just accept and let things be, even if I completely disagreed. I would navigate *around* the obstacles rather than *over* them.

However, if the passing of my parents taught me anything, silence actually hurts more than words. I'd come to realize that as long as I withheld my opinion, I would be colluding with the wrongdoers and thus mistreating myself for not speaking up. If I'd failed to speak up and hold Max accountable for his lies, then I would, albeit inadvertently, be part of the problem. And I would only expect more of it. More broken promises. More excuses. More stress. I would much rather avoid following the path I took when I dealt with my parents.

This was a life-changing moment for me, maybe because I cared too much. I was actually doing *something* about my problem; I was vocal and not afraid to share my opinion.

I kept feeding him subtle hints about the truth of the matter, waiting for a light bulb to go off in his head. And suddenly, it did. Max then spoke. "I'm sorry that I didn't take my promise to you seriously. I never thought much about promises, which is why I usually don't make them. But perhaps it's my greatest flaw. I was trying to please you, and in doing so, I just said 'yes' to everything without thinking."

"We are the promises that we keep," I replied.

"I know," Max said. There was a long pause before he continued, "I can't promise that I won't hurt you again. I may do something stupid. You never know. But I can promise that I'm going to try my hardest not to let that happen again. You have my word. Scout's honour."

I was relieved. A smile crossed my face, and I spoke softly, "Thank you, Max. I'm glad you understand how I feel."

I just had my first argument with Max if I excluded our first encounter. There was nothing wrong with some disagreement in a relationship. I'd argued with Clara and Rachel all the time, and we were still friends. All things aside, I wasn't going to let a little fight come between our friendship. We were better than that. At least I hoped to be. Anyway, wouldn't things be awfully boring if we just agreed with each other *all* the time? I was relieved that we could finally move on from this. Plus, I desperately needed a glass of water after all that lecturing.

"Thanks for being honest with me, Emily. I should learn a thing or two from you," Max said. "Friends?"

"Friends," I replied.

I remembered playing out in my head all the possible outcomes to our conversation, just to determine if all outcomes were equally likely. Like the grand experiment that is life, which is both random and unfair, the outcomes for my conundrum were not equally likely. So, I was truly satisfied with the turn of events.

I was willing to give Max another chance because I valued our friendship. I only hoped that time would prove that we could be open and honest with each other. Dependability was a pillar in any type of friendship. The foundation being honesty.

"Emily, can I ask you something?" Max asked.

"Okay," I replied.

"So, are we still on for later today?" he asked.

"Only if you want to be there. You can say 'no' if you have other plans, okay?" I replied.

"No, I want to finish what I started. Half-past five?" Max replied.

"Sure. But I'm only getting the first round. You've lost the privilege of unlimited refills for tomorrow," I responded, knowing that only I had the authority to barter coffee for his time.

"Punishment accepted Emily McGregor," Max chuckled.

"Goodnight, Max. Umm, maybe good morning," I yawned.

"I'll be there! Goodnight-Good morning to you too!" Max said excitedly.

I smiled. It was nice being on the *same* page again.

Doris Siu

Chapter Eight

Morning. T-minus less than two days before my Physics and Calculus finals. Missed call. Max Miller.

For a moment, I feared for the worse. He wasn't going to bail on me again, was he? I decided to call him back to find out the deets.

"You called," I said bluntly without having the courtesy to say 'good morning.'

"Not even a good morning? Someone must have woken up on the wrong side of the bed today," Max chuckled to lighten the mood.

"Don't toy with me, Max Miller. You normally don't call me this early in the morning. Spill the beans, or you'll be covering the next three espresso rounds," I huffed.

"Huh? I must have butt-dialed you. Sorry. If I didn't know better, you just wanted to hear my voice. You know, med students are notoriously poor. We survive on ramen noodles and freebies because we spent all our savings on the overpriced education program," Max explained.

"Don't tell me you only hang out with me because of the free coffee!" I exclaimed, worried about his reply.

"What can I say. It's hot and steamy. It's the first thing I think about in the morning, and it's what keeps me up all night," he paused, as though he was putting emphasis on what was just said. "You know, I'm just kidding, Emily. I'm sure you know by now how addicted I am to this fine caffeinated beverage. But trust me when I say this. I really just butt-dialed you. I guess every part of me wants a piece of Emily McGregor."

Although I could not see his expression, I was certain he was wearing his mischievous grin. "Umm, I'm going to pretend I didn't hear that last part," I said awkwardly.

Even Max was acting weirder than normal. Or maybe my mind was just hyperactive from our intimate conversation last night. Either way, I had to end this conversation pronto before it got any weirder.

"Ditto," Max said, embarrassed.

"I'll see you later tonight. Have fun in class," I exclaimed.

"I'll probably be sleeping. But thanks," Max said before he hung up.

•••

It was like any other day at *Amore*. I waited for Max at our usual spot—the corner booth at the back—with two cups of double-shot espressos. My phone lit up from an incoming text message that read, "Emily, I'll be a couple of minutes late. Got Mom's Highlander today. Need to pick up something. Will be there just before six."

I wondered what Max was up to. He wasn't avoiding me, was he? I assured myself that he was probably just running errands for his Mom. I had to stop thinking of the worse. I already forgave the guy. Though, I hoped Max wouldn't arrive much later. It would be a shame to waste such a deliciously warm cup of coffee. Cold coffee that wasn't intentionally prepared cold, like a Frappuccino, was just *sad* news.

I replied to his text, "No problem." Then, I sent a smiley face emoji before placing my phone aside on the table. I sipped my cup of coffee and waited for Max to arrive. The silent hum of the espresso machines sparked my inspiration for a new song. I busied myself with my Moleskine while I waited for Max, careful not to smudge the ink with the drops of coffee that dripped from the rim each time I stirred my espresso.

Max rushed in a couple of minutes before six. He held a mysterious brown paper bag on his right. Max placed it beside Jimi, sat down across from me, and then began opening the bag. He looked at me and breathed in the scent of the mysterious contents deeply before he spoke. "Ah, I love the smell of this!" Max playfully smiled and then quickly rolled the bag shut without letting me take a sniff.

"You're either holding an empty paper bag, or you're trying to build suspense by not showing me what's inside," I said as I crossed my arms to appear upset.

"Patience, Emily. The night is young," Max said, raising his right eyebrow. "Oh, and sorry for being late. I had to drop my Mom off at work. My car is in the shop, so I asked to use hers today," Max explained.

"It's okay. At least you texted and didn't leave me hanging. But the suspense here is killing me. What's in the bag?" I questioned.

Max straightened himself in his seat and spoke. "You see, Emily. Differential equations have the remarkable ability to predict the life cycle of food. Mold, you see, is a normal part of food as it ages. It basically grows on food once it is exposed to excessive amounts of oxygen. Certain foods, like Exhibit A here, are notorious for getting moldy very quickly."

Max opened the bag, removed a half-eaten French baguette, and placed it on the table. He then continued, "Let's say I left this baguette here for several days, which I know is not possible because I would have eaten the other half by then, but let's just keep going with this story. You would start to see mold growing, called *P*, that changes with time, *t*. So, if mold splits by binary fission, then through observation, we would translate this mathematically as—"

"*dP* over *dt* equals *kP(t)*," I interrupted. Max's face lit up, and he nodded for me to continue, "This means that the rate of change in a population is a function of the current population at time *t*, multiplied by a constant factor *k*. So, in Layman's terms, the rate of bacterial growth is proportional to the size of the bacterial population."

"Exactly!" Max exclaimed, completely satisfied with my response. "Don't you love it when math is *this* delicious!"

"I can't believe all this gibberish is starting to make sense," I said confidently. I patted Max on the shoulder and held up my cup of coffee, triumphantly. "You're a great teacher Max!"

Max blushed and reacted instinctively by raising his cup too. He fondly spoke, "Well, I'm not so sure if you can call me *great*, but I am *hungry.*" Max started nibbling on the baguette, "I would have had more of Exhibit A to showcase, but I just couldn't resist that fresh bread smell after leaving the bakery."

I laughed and grabbed the baguette out of his hands. I ripped a small piece off and tossed it back over to Max. I nibbled it and quietly shouted, "Delicious! Victory has never tasted so sweet."

Max chuckled and stuffed the rest of the baguette in his mouth. After several hours of studying, André's carrot cake, and three more rounds of espresso refills, we finished reviewing Calculus well before midnight.

•••

It was a productive night, but I was exhausted. I looked down at the mess of empty coffee cups in front of me before flashing a smile. "Well, I'm glad we did this today. Thanks, Max!" I exclaimed.

"No need to thank me, Emily. It was all you," Max said, tipping his baseball cap to commend my excellent performance today with the material.

"You know, Max. I'm glad to have you as a friend even though I suffer severely from black cat syndrome. I mean, I've been pretty unlucky all my life. The way I see it, I'm like some sort of bad luck magnet. I hope I haven't infected you," I said with a sigh.

"Bad luck isn't contagious, Emily. I feel pretty lucky to have met you. Oh, Emily. What goes on in that head of yours? The only thing contagious here is that smile. You should wear it more often. It looks good on you," Max chuckled.

I knew Max was right, but my whole life had been a living roller coaster. So, I had a gut feeling that something else was going to go wrong. Whenever things seemed to be running smoothly in my life, I was destined to hit some sort of hurdle and go tumbling down. Fortunately, I'd survived *all* my falls so far.

Suddenly, I felt a bit nauseous as I got up from my seat to pack my belongings. I sat back down to rest for a moment. My right hand began to tingle as I reached over to grab Jimi. It was like pins and needles. The feeling was strange and very uncomfortable. I tried moving my fingers like how I did when I played scales on the piano to increase blood flow to my extremities. Max looked at me, confused but didn't say anything.

I grabbed Jimi with my left hand instead, but my guitar felt strangely heavier than normal. I didn't think much about it at the time, but all those late nights studying must have finally caught up with me. I just wanted to go home and sleep. I had one more night before the big Physics and Mathematics showdown. Just one more night before I could go to bed at a *normal* hour again. I tried to reassure myself that everything was going to be okay. After all, I had two months of summer coming up to catch up on sleep, so I just had to hold on a bit longer. I closed my eyes and repeated to myself quietly, "Just one more night. Just one more night."

I started to sit up but grimaced with pain as I sank back in my seat. I rubbed my temples and felt weak. Very weak. Max then got up from our booth and walked over to my side of the table.

He placed his hand on my shoulder and softly spoke. "Emily, is everything okay?"

"I'm fine. Just a little tired," I said weakly.

"Let me give you a ride home. I got the car," Max insisted.

Although I knew well enough that we lived in opposite directions of town, I decided not to refuse his offer today. I really did feel awful. And I just wanted to get home as fast as I could. So, I nodded, and immediately Max held out his hand, invitingly, "Shall we?"

I nervously reached out to touch his hand. He smiled and grabbed my hand as he held it tight. His chivalry seemed suspicious, but I was too braindead to fuss over it. Max's smile got even wider as he helped me to my feet.

"Emily McGregor. I must be dreaming because I'm finally holding hands with the girl I *tripped* over. Oh, how I wished you could have given me a fair warning. I would have taken a shower today and put on a fresh shirt too," Max teased.

I giggled and tried imagining Max in a shirt nicer than what he already had on. Max was one for fashion, so he always had impeccable taste, freshly ironed clothes, and his signature baseball cap to complete his look. It was unique. Uniquely Max Miller.

"Is this what you say to all the girls you meet?" I joked quietly.

"No, just the pretty ones," Max chuckled.

"Just because I need a little help today doesn't mean you have to rub it in my face Mr. Prince Charming," I exclaimed sarcastically.

"Well, at least I'm a *prince* in your eyes," Max beamed proudly. "Let's stop nipping at each other's words and get you home."

We walked towards the red Highlander parked down the street. It was 9 p.m., pitch black, with only the glow of the moon lighting up the sidewalk. Although I'd never been scared about walking home alone late at night, his gentle touch made me feel safe. The way his fingers intertwined with mine was both innocent and special. It was human nature for us to gravitate towards people who made us feel happy and secure. Whether it was a kind word, a smile, or a hug, these actions helped us temporarily relieve stress and pain. The simple act of Max's touch relieved the tension in my head. Surprisingly, I actually felt safe with him.

I smiled and looked up to study his face, "Thank you, Max," I whispered.

Max smiled and replied, "It's no biggie. Didn't want you taking the bus alone when you're already not feeling too well. What are friends for?"

We were just steps from the Highlander when I felt lightheaded and nauseous again. I tightened my grip, and he squeezed back reassuringly. "You know, you don't have to rush it. Baby steps, Emily. We're almost there," Max said quietly and patted my shoulder.

At the car, Max opened the passenger door and gave me another squeeze before he let go of my hand. I curled up in the passenger seat as Max drove to Aunt Brenna's. I made a mental note to cut back on caffeine once examinations were over.

Max kept his eye on the road as he sang and hummed to songs from Ed Sheeran's second studio album, *x (Multiply)*. "Photograph" began to play softly in the background, and Max quietly sang along.

I started thinking about my parents and all the photos we'd taken together. All my childhood memories were captured as single moments in time. Each moment was photographed and stored in an album. It was the only album in the universe that had the power to bend time. I wiped a tear from the side of my face and closed my eyes.

Max turned to face me at the next red traffic light, "Emily, are you sure you're alright?" he asked.

Obviously, I was not okay. But I wanted to save him from the glory details. More tears trickled down my cheek. I was having trouble keeping my emotions in check, and it wasn't because it was *that* time of the month. So, I decided to ask him a question instead.

"Max, have you ever missed someone so much that you feel incomplete without them?" I asked.

"I know the feeling, actually. I haven't seen my Dad for like over ten years. And even though he's completely unreliable at times, I do miss him. All I have left are photographs and some memories," Max said softly.

I sighed, "Sorry, I had no idea. The song just got to me."

"I know," Max nodded with an understanding smile. "But remember, all stories have two sides. Some may have ended, but many continue. Life goes on. You may feel miserable, but we can't just stop in the middle of the road and expect not to get hit. We can either keep driving to see what lies ahead or park and be stuck in our memories. I prefer to be in the driver's seat. You should try it sometime, Emily."

Apart from the music playing in the background, it was silent the rest of the way back. Max switched his playlist to more upbeat tunes, and we both sang along to Pharrell Williams' "Happy." Just before ten, Max pulled up onto the driveway and parked behind Aunt Brenna's Mazda. He grabbed Jimi and my backpack from the backseat and then helped me to the door.

"We better get you inside. You look paler than white bread," Max noted.

"So, it's bread talk again. Do you always think of food?" I asked as I fumbled with my keys to unlock the front door.

"Only when my stomach is dominating. And I can definitely hear the 24-hour drive-thru calling my name right now," Max chuckled. He continued, "But, first, let me help you with the door. You know you don't have to be so nervous about inviting such a hot guy, like me, to stay the night. It must be your *first*, right?" Max playfully joked as he grabbed the keys out of my hands and unlocked the door.

I quickly entered and rushed to find a seat on the leather sofa in the living room. Max snuck past the front door and placed Jimi on the cluttered coffee table before plopping down beside me. "Comfy. But I think we should take it upstairs?" Max continued, raising his eyebrows.

Max was flirting well above his normal quota for charm. It

was probably because I couldn't think of anything witty to say for retaliation. Normally, my witty remarks would kill the mood and make him *behave*. But I didn't have anything at my disposal tonight. I was finally home, my head was pounding intensely, and I just wanted to collapse in my own bed to sleep.

He was inches from my face. I struggled to shift my gaze as our eyes locked. I could feel his heavy breathing as he removed his baseball cap to run his hands through his hair repeatedly. Suddenly, in one fluid motion, Max lifted me up and swooped me into his arms. I knew I had to say something to kill the mood. I firmly pulled his baseball cap down low over his eyes to distract him.

"Woah, easy tiger. If Aunt Brenna wakes up, then I'll be dead meat. She doesn't know you're here," I shrieked, intuitively calming him down. He flashed a devilish grin and set me back on my feet.

I took a couple of steps by myself towards the stairwell before I spoke, "See, I can take it from here. I'm walking perfectly fine, Mr. Miller. I'm high on caffeine, not ecstasy." I pointed to the door, "Now, why don't you uninvite yourself out so I can get some rest, and you can get some takeout."

"Call me in the morning?" he asked as the intensity toned down in his eyes.

"Definitely," I nodded with a smile.

Before Max exited, he took off his baseball cap and tossed it into my hands. "For good luck!" he said and closed the door behind him.

Chapter Nine

It was exam day, and like any other morning, I pressed snooze three times before dragging myself out of bed. I made two double-shot espressos and took it quickly like a shot of tequila. My head spun, and I felt dizzy. I honestly thought double caffeine intake this morning would solve all my woes. Rather, it just caused double the trouble. It was the first time in a long time that coffee could not fix *all* my problems.

I sunk to my knees and held myself in a fetal position on the kitchen floor. The pain in my head was unbearable. But I knew I had to fight the pain. I had to get to my exams. I couldn't let my parents down. I couldn't let myself down. I just had to push on.

I decided to forgo my usual bowl of *Lucky Charms* and headed straight out the door. Luckily the bus was empty, so I got a seat in the back to stretch out. I guess luck was still on my side. I was wearing Max's lucky baseball cap, and its magic seemed to be working. It was nice knowing that I could still be lucky without consuming large amounts of colourful marshmallows. Though, I wasn't a fan of hat hair. But, if it meant that I would ace my finals, then I frankly didn't mind if my hair stayed messy for awhile.

As I entered *Glenwood High*, I walked like a zombie down the hallway until I reached Room 105. The time had come to take my most dreaded examination. Physics. Ugh. I closed my eyes when I settled in the room and tried to recite all the things Max taught me. My head constantly swirled, throbbing on both sides. I wanted to go home.

Surprisingly, the exam was easier than I expected. Or perhaps Max was really a good teacher. I handed in my exam and walked confidently out the door.

I grabbed a quick coffee from the cafeteria before heading to my Calculus exam. The coffee at the cafeteria was absolutely disgusting. It was so watered down that even the black coffee didn't taste bitter. But I needed the caffeine rush, so I gulped the whole cup down in less than thirty seconds flat.

After my final hour of torture, I was freed from the responsibility of studying. At least for two months. And it felt so awesome. I was relieved. And to my surprise, my headache disappeared once I exited *Glenwood High*. So I concluded that my headaches were definitely stress-induced.

I met up with Clara and Rachel, who were sitting outside at a nearby bench. It was like the scheduling staff followed a secret rule at *Glenwood High* for all upper-year students. We actually conducted a thorough research study on this a few years back. We concluded that every eleventh and twelfth grader was guaranteed to have at least one examination on the last day of exam week. It was like the staff here enjoyed seeing the older kids suffer. It was an evil and cruel form of punishment in my opinion.

"I haven't seen you around for a while. What have you been up to?" Clara asked with hands folded across her chest like I owed her an explanation.

"Studying," I said.

"We ought to go out and celebrate. Party at my house tonight. Bring sparklers, and just maybe I'll spike our coffee with some of my Dad's finest collection," Clara exclaimed, clapping her hands with excitement.

"I like my coffee just the way it is, thank you very much," I said bluntly.

"Emily, you take the fun out of everything," Clara scoffed, looking towards Rachel.

"Ya, Emily, loosen up, won't you? It's okay to party sometimes. We're young. We're bold. And we're beautiful," Rachel exclaimed.

"You tell her, girl!" Clara screamed.

"No, thanks, guys. I'm busy," I insisted.

"Busy with what? School? Ah, Emily, last time I checked, you're done exams," Clara exclaimed. "What's with the hat?"

"Nothing. I'm just busy," I repeated. I wasn't ready to tell Clara and Rachel about Max. Especially since I wasn't really sure what he meant to me. So, I refused to admit that I had a date with him tonight at *Amore*. Well, not *really* a date per se. It was more like a meetup.

•••

I took the next bus to go home. Max had a meeting with his supervisor, so we weren't going to meet up until a lot later in the evening. Like right on cue, my phone buzzed. It was Max.

"So, how was it? You aced them, didn't you?" Max asked excitedly.

"I'm not sure. But they were both a lot easier than I thought. I guess you did a good job preparing me," I said.

"It wasn't me. It was all you. I could teach you a million things, but if you had no idea how to apply them, then it'll be useless. I could have just drilled you like an army sergeant, and you could have still passed. But, to ace exams, you got to look beyond the basic questions in the textbook," Max insisted.

"Don't you have a meeting to get to?" I asked.

"I still got five minutes. I got time," Max replied. "Umm, Emily, do you have a dress?"

I wasn't sure where this conversation was going, but it was apparent that Max changed the subject for a reason. I had a strange feeling that I wasn't going to like it. Hesitantly, I responded, "Umm, yes."

Max quickly responded, "Perfect! I'll pick you up at five. Don't forget my hat. See you then." Max hung up immediately afterward.

What on earth did Max have up his sleeves? I hated wearing things that were *too* feminine. Okay, maybe *hate* was too strong of a word for a piece of clothing that was specifically made for females. But I believed that *real* women didn't have to wear dresses to look beautiful. There was absolutely nothing wrong with wearing loose-fitting clothing or stylish alternatives. After all, Mom did teach me never to sacrifice comfort for fashion.

I'd extremely disliked frilly garments all my life. Even as a little girl, I wore skorts because it gave me maximum playtime mobility without the worry of flashing anyone unintentionally.

As I entered adolescence, I owned a few dresses but rarely wore them. And when I did wear them, I'd never liked how I had to act like a *lady*. It wasn't because I was a tomboy or that I was so subconscious about my tiny legs. I just didn't like how I couldn't sit the way I wanted without flashing my underwear or something.

And don't even get me started about my extreme distaste for three-inch heels. By the end of the day, I'd be limping like I worked out at the gym for six-hours. My ankles would be near bleeding, and my toes would be all blistered. Just being in a dress made me feel a bit naked around my most private body parts. I wondered if other girls had the same problem. Fortunately, being friends with Clara had taught me about the joys of leggings, sandals, and jumpsuits. I totally felt hot in leggings. Like I rocked them. And my foot was no longer crushed when I wore sandals. I may have had tiny legs, but I had humongous feet.

I stared at my closet. Most of the dresses I owned were either too childish or too revealing. I couldn't say yes to either type. I didn't want to give Max mixed signals. And because he was older than me, I didn't want him to feel superior. I felt hopelessly lost with the whole situation. And I only had three more hours before he arrived at my door.

"Aunt Brenna!" I screamed.

Aunt Brenna rushed into my room. She was panting heavily. I rarely would scream out unless it were from a nightmare. But right now, it kind of felt like a *nightmare*. She noticed the piles of clothes sprawled out across the floor and instantly knew why

I was panicking.

"Boy trouble, Emily dear?" she asked.

"Max trouble," I said.

"Yes! Yes! Yes!" Aunt Brenna smiled before correcting her tone. "I mean, No! No! No!" she said sarcastically, smiling.

"Can you help?" I asked.

"Hit me!" she shouted.

"Max just called and asked me to pick out a dress for tonight. I have no idea what type of shenanigans he's up to, but you know how much I hate wearing dresses. Do I have to?" I cried.

"Emily dear, do not disappoint your sweet Maximus. Friend or mate?" Aunt Brenna said sympathetically.

"Friend, Aunt Brenna. Friend," I said, annoyed.

"Okay, so no for the outfits with a plunging neckline then. But yes, for the cutesy ones. And I think I have just the thing. You're lucky we're about the same size. It'll be a bit longer on you, though, but it'll look presentable," Aunt Brenna explained.

"The longer, the better. I extremely dislike dresses," I pleaded. "Can't I just wear a cute top with flowy pants or something?"

"How would you feel if you asked Max to do something and he didn't do it. He's your best friend. It's not like he's asking you out to a nude beach," Aunt Brenna exclaimed.

"Aunt Brenna!" I shouted.

"I'm just saying! Okay, but forget the last thing I just said if it makes you uncomfortable," Aunt Brenna winked.

"It's not a date. I never promised," I huffed.

"It's a date, Emily. It's definitely a date. Now, I know you didn't promise anything, but you also never said no either," Aunt Brenna insisted.

I sighed loudly. Why are we always so oblivious when it comes to love in our own relationships? Aunt Brenna was absolutely right. If whatever Max had planned required appropriate attire, then I would have just ruined the whole night before it even began. I would probably have fewer eyes on me if I just followed suit with his request. I despised being the center of attention, so I wasn't going to risk it.

"Okay, fine. I'll try it, but it's not a date," I agreed reluctantly.

"Call it whatever you like. I'll be right back. Oh, my little Emily is growing up! Can I do your hair?" Aunt Brenna exclaimed excitedly.

"Aunt Brenna! And don't give me that look. I'm not putting on any makeup," I barked, annoyed.

"Come on? I need the practice. I spend two hours in front of the mirror on days that I would be seeing André. I had no idea mascara, foundation, and the flat iron could be so difficult. YouTube makes everything look so easy!" Aunt Brenna confessed.

"Only lip gloss," I compromised.

"Fine by me," Aunt Brenna winked as she bolted out the room to grab the dress she had in mind for my evening out with Max.

I spent the next hour getting ready. It was my ultimate life struggle of wanting to look good but being too lazy to try. Makeup, like dresses and heels, was my enemy. Why did I despise so many feminine products?

Many of us girls relied on makeup to cover up our *imperfections*. At least what we considered to be imperfect. Nonexistent eyebrows. Acne. Uneven skin tone. Our imperfections were endless. And to make things even more complicated, there were probably a thousand-and-one different variations of one product. Lipstick. Foundation. Eye shadow. And I was definitely not one of those people because I hated the hassle of doing something that wasted a ton of time and money. I was certain celebrities still looked beautiful without their makeup. I knew I didn't *need* this gunk on my face.

I dreamt of perfecting the most flawless, natural look one day. But, emphasis on the word 'dream.' I would be lying to myself if I never thought about it. But it was too stressful to make sure both sides of my face were relatively symmetrical in shape and tone. Ugh. It was a nightmare. And to add to my further displeasure, makeup was such a pain to remove. I had to wash my face twice just to remove everything. And because of my acne-prone skin, I had to make sure to remove everything, or I'd clog all my pores with those nasty chemicals. Why did girls have so many *problems*?

•••

At exactly five o'clock, Max knocked on the door. He held a beautiful bouquet of flowers. A mix of lavender and daisies. He nervously held them as Aunt Brenna invited him into the house.

She greeted Max warmly with a hug. He handed the flowers over to her and smiled, "For you," he said uncomfortably, unsure if Aunt Brenna was going to accept them.

"How could I say no to such a beautiful bouquet of flowers? But I am taken already. Though Emily over there is still on the market," Aunt Brenna winked, pointing to the corner of the room.

I nervously stepped forward, clutching Max's baseball cap tightly, afraid that he might explode with laughter over my *costume.* I called it a 'costume' because I felt like a clown. Or at the very least, pretending to be someone else. I was thankful that I refused to paint my face with concealer, or it would have totally sealed the deal. I looked at my reflection in the mirror and sighed. This was so *not* me.

I wore a flowy baby blue strapless chiffon dress that was supposed to be just above my knees. Obviously, being Aunt Brenna's dress, I wore it slightly longer. I still felt like I was showing off a bit *too* much skin, but with the 40 ^{0}C heatwave, it didn't seem like *too* much. Though, I was beginning to regret asking for Aunt Brenna's help. She was all giddy like a schoolgirl, and that made me even more nervous. What was her deal?

"Wow!" Max exclaimed in awe. "You look beautiful!"

"Thanks, I guess. You don't look too shabby yourself," I said quietly.

Max actually looked ravishing for a dude. I mean, he was wearing a suit that was much fancier than his normal suits for clinic duty. And he had his hair all gelled back. I desperately wanted to scream. I'd never seen him style his hair before! It was always hidden under his baseball cap and messy looking. Max's dirty blonde hairdo was far from 'dirty' today; it was so slick and surprisingly very attractive. Man, I just used *very attractive* and *Max* in the same sentence!

I wished I had the guts to take his picture to capture this rare moment. But, as if intentionally, Max quickly grabbed his baseball cap out of my hands and positioned it back on his noggin. The action was so sudden that it befogged me.

He wore a flawlessly tailored light grey velvet suit, paired with a sleek pale pink shirt that had the first three buttons unbuttoned. I was not a stickler for fashion, but I could tell that Max was a very fashion-forward man. This Max, minus the baseball cap, was a Max that I'd never seen before. And admittedly, I *liked* it.

Now, although Max exhibited maturity through his attire, he was far from it. The Max Miller I knew was just a rebel in disguise. Controversially, I was an adult in a child's body. My attire was a far cry from being sophisticated, but I was more in tune with my emotional maturity than most seventeen-year-old girls.

I'd noticed a paradox among students. We were advanced intellectually but behind emotionally. The speed and quantity of information available for us to consume were unimaginable. We consumed information faster than we could process. Frankly, our brains required more time to actually '*grow up*,' so we weren't ready to apply all that learned material. We were emotionally unprepared for adulthood because we were still stuck in between a child and an adult. Truth be told, we all had a selfish rascal that lived inside us that was constantly running away from responsibilities, unwilling to *grow up*.

From what I gathered, Max disregarded authority and

regulations often. He skipped school as much as he skipped breakfast. He was arrogant, had no real long-term commitments, was terrible at keeping promises (though better lately), and lived life on a whim. Max exemplified these typical behaviours and characteristics for immature people, but it didn't mean that he didn't care about important things in his life. He just seemed to be carrying a lot of *baggage*, and being rebellious was his way of coping.

Max was no open book. He rarely talked openly about his past. We both still had our secrets. Granted, I never told him about my parents or my life in Calgary. But Max probably knew more about me than I did about him. The problem with arrogant guys was that they hated being vulnerable. In my presence, Max's aura always radiated invincibility and power.

The only thing I gathered about Max's childhood was that his Dad left his family when he was young. Although I didn't know much about Max's past, *big* life-changing moments like that normally caused kids to mature at a faster-than-normal pace. But maybe Max was one who defied convention.

•••

I'd often wondered what the source of my stage phobia was. It was probably when I was three. The other girls at my daycare ostracized me because of the way I dressed. They laughed at my braided pigtails because they weren't just braids or just pigtails. They laughed at my skort because it wasn't a skirt or a pair of shorts. They laughed at me just because they *could* laugh at me.

It was so uncomfortable being the centre of unwanted attention, being ridiculed. And from that moment, I grew up to be very shy and solitary. I liked being alone and hated the limelight, but on the flip side, I was always very ambitious. Mom used to tell me that we had to do things out of our comfort zone. Because to be successful, we had to stand out and speak up. I guess today, I'd flipped to a new page in my book of life. I nervously bit the bottom of my lip and forced a smile.

Max held out his hand and dragged me out of the corner. He smiled and spoke invitingly. "Shall we?"

And just like that, Max whisked me off my feet and into the passenger seat of his yellow Civic. Well, not literally. But it felt exhilarating to do something different today. Something out of my comfort zone. I thought for a moment. Perhaps the only reason we felt uncomfortable outside our comfort zone was that we were too self-conscious about what others thought of us. The more I thought about it, I'd realized that no one actually had the time to pay that much attention to me. So, maybe I should have stopped thinking that there were millions of eyes watching my every move. Maybe. Though it would take some time to convince myself to feel comfortable.

I kind of wished Max could just forgo his beloved baseball cap. It always hid the top portion of his face. I would never have known he had a row of freckles across his forehead if he had never taken his cap off. It was quite cute.

Max turned on the radio as he backed out of the driveway. Queen's "We Are the Champions" started playing, and we sang along together.

Singing with Max together in the car reminded me of the times when Dad and I organized karaoke nights. Mom was our audience, and the winner would score the last chocolate chip cookie on the plate.

As we drove downtown towards *Amore*, I wondered what was to come this evening. We stopped at *Amore* to grab our usual double-shot espressos with a dash of cocoa and cinnamon spice. Today, though, Max requested our order to-go.

Earlier in the car, Max actually asked me if I wanted to be more adventurous today with mocha lattes, but I told him that some things were better unchanged. André complimented our outfits and winked at Max as he closed the register. I was positive that I heard André whisper, "Finally!"

Back in the car, Max switched the radio station to classical music. He turned down the volume and began to speak, "Emily, I know I told your Aunt that we were going to hang out at *Amore*, but I actually wanted to take you somewhere else. It's to celebrate your successes this term."

"I don't know what to say. I had a feeling we weren't just going to hang out at *Amore* if we were dressed this fashionably. Where to?" I asked.

"That's for you to find out. Patience, Emily. Patience," he insisted.

So, I patiently looked out the window, trying to figure out where Max was going. As we inched closer to the restaurant, I held my breath as familiarity seeped into my mind. I'd recognized the tiny colourful houses and the miniature statutes at each intersection. I knew exactly where we were heading. I turned towards him and looked at Max with excitement.

"How does dinner at *Rue 143,* followed by a night at the carnival sound to you?" he asked with a smile.

"Amazing!" I exclaimed.

Rue 143 did not disappoint. It was the most luxurious restaurant in Glenwood. *Rue 143* was featured on *The Food Network* several years ago as one of the country's finest fine dining restaurants. It was home to Canada's best chefs that graduated from world-class schools from across the globe. This very same restaurant brought thousands of tourists and celebrities annually to Glenwood. It was probably the only thing that put Glenwood on the map.

It was almost impossible to get a last-minute reservation. I'd always been a foodie, but never in my wildest dreams would I have ever imagined dining here. Ever! Even Dad never brought me *here*. I knew of the place since we would always pass by it on our way to the fair every summer. But this was *surreal.*

"How did you get reservations, Max?" I asked, intrigued to learn how he scored the table.

"I got my ways. If you can have secrets, then so can I. There's nothing wrong with a little mystery, right?" Max replied. I knew where he was coming from. He was still bitter that I didn't share with him what was written inside my paper airplanes.

"Right," I agreed. I didn't want to start any sort of argument. Not today.

Max smiled and turned his attention back on the road.

"Maximus Miller, how many surprises do you have planned for me tonight?" I squealed. Then, I quickly covered my mouth as my face turned as pink as a flamingo's bottom. I just called Max 'Maximus!' How could I be so careless? This was absolutely embarrassing. I mean, it just rolled off my tongue. Aunt Brenna! Why did she always call him Maximus when we talked about him at home? Oh my, I sounded utterly ridiculous!

I sunk into my seat and covered my face completely. I desperately wished Max had a lapse of momentary deafness in the last thirty seconds of my life.

Suddenly, Max started to laugh, "Maximus? Where did you come up with that nickname?" He continued to chuckle as I continued to shrink in my seat. "I had no idea my name could sound that cool! Like Optimus Prime sort of cool," he chuckled again loudly.

"Sorry, Aunt Brenna likes to call you that," I said apologetically.

"Emily, for the record, I like it. But, just don't go off calling me that in public, okay?" Max said.

"Okay," I replied.

As we pulled into a parking spot, Max tossed his baseball cap to the back seat. "Can't wear this in there. Lucky or not, it's against the dress code policy. Wouldn't want to get kicked out when I got a beautiful girl with me," Max winked.

"Ha, ha, ha. Very funny, Max," I said sarcastically, sticking out my tongue.

"I thought Max Miller doesn't follow the rules?" I refuted.

"Still the same old Max. Rules are made to be broken. And I probably will continue not following most of them. But I just need to be selective with which ones I don't follow. After all, you'd taught me that I had to do a better job on my commitments. Didn't I promise you a wonderful evening?" Max laughed.

"You did?" I asked, confused.

"I did. Just now," Max smiled mischievously as he ran his hand through his hair before we walked together to the main entrance.

•••

The charming and modern décor was the perfect haven to indulge my senses. It was the most scrumptious, Instagram-worthy, meal I had ever tasted. Everything was delicious. Everything was perfect. The music. The ambience. The company. Even the napkins were folded to a tee.

Fine dining at a Michelin-starred restaurant truly could satisfy all your taste buds and senses. I mean, every sense but my *common* sense that protected my wallet. How could Max afford such an expensive meal? He was a med student.

Throughout the meal, I laughed at his jokes and enlightened Max with stories from *Glenwood High*. I told him about the school bully. The lunch lady who used her own hair for spaghetti once when she ran out. I even told him about Clara and Rachel. We'd come a long way since our first study session. I still remembered the day when my hands profusely sweated as I held my phone, contemplating whether I should or should not give Max a call.

•••

It was hard to top our dinner at *Rue 143*. But the carnival was just as amazing. I haven't been back here since I was ten. Oh, how I missed indulging in classic childhood treats like cotton candy and funnel cake. Unfortunately, I was stuffed from our three-course meal and didn't have much room for carnival treats.

Many assumed that fancy restaurants served food in tiny proportions. But, not *Rue 143*. Their dishes were huge, which was ironic because they were famous for their dessert menu. Why fill up on appetizers and entrees when the dessert table was calling for my attention? *Rue 143* was kind of like an upscaled version of *The Cheesecake Factory*. I was well over my normal quota for sweets, but if there were a day to succeed that quota, today would be the day.

"What are you thinking about? You seem troubled," Max asked.

"It's nothing. I was just thinking about roller coasters. If I want to keep my entire meal in my stomach, I don't think I can ride them tonight. It'll be a pity for such a delicious meal to end up on my dress," I answered shyly.

Max chuckled at the thought of me screaming on the roller coasters. Well, promise me that we can do this again another time. I want to see you ride that one," he bargained, pointing to the wildest roller coaster at the fair. It had almost a complete 90^{0} drop, three gigantic loops, and one fast-spinning tunnel at the end. Just thinking about it made me want to puke.

"Are you having a fever, Max Miller? You never made so many promises in one day before," I asked, looking at him carefully.

"What can I say? It must be the coffee," Max joked.

"Coffee? But we only had one cup. That's well below our normal intake," I said.

"I actually had seven cups before I got here. Tough meeting with my supervisor," Max explained.

"Is that even legal? I mean, that's a lot of coffee!" I exclaimed, looking into his eyes to make sure he really was okay.

"My supervisor told me that I had to stop ditching, or it'll cost me my graduation. He called me a 'pathetic loser who didn't know better.' Which isn't *entirely* untrue. Then he tried threatening me to make changes to my behaviour, or he would tell my Mom," Max said, frustrated.

"Pathetic loser?" I asked.

"Ya. Those were his exact words. Didn't you see me air quote the statement?" Max confirmed.

"Harsh," I replied.

"Totally," Max agreed.

We sat on the bench, picking at our cotton candy until Max finally decided to call it a night and go home. I didn't want the evening to end. I hadn't had this much fun in a long, long time.

•••

It was almost eleven when we got back to Aunt Brenna's. My head started to throb a bit in the car, but I was too concerned about Max even to notice. I wondered why Max enrolled in med school if he hated it so much. It was excruciatingly painful to be forced to do something that you *hated.* I was doubtful that his mother was that much of the monster that Max made her out to be. She was the head of medicine at *Glenwood Medical Clinic,* but I had a strange feeling that she wasn't *that* overbearing.

It was normal for parents to have disagreements with their children. My views on politics, education, and relationships rarely matched up perfectly with my parents. So, if Max was anything like me, he probably was in a similar boat. But it was possible to have a healthy relationship with parents who did not share the same morals. We often assumed that as we matured, we would be more *like* our parents. After all, weren't we mini-mes? Truth be told, having similarities in our DNA sequencing did not equate to having similarities in our mentality.

Max walked me to the door, and I unlocked it. It was late, and although I had the entire summer to sleep now, I knew that Max had practicum the next morning, so I didn't want to keep him much longer.

Aunt Brenna was already asleep. I wasn't sure if she did that intentionally to give us some private time or if she really did have an early morning shift at the hospital.

Max smiled and turned towards me. Our eyes locked, and I felt like I was soaring through the sky effortlessly. The evening was perfect. And this moment felt so magical. Just the two of us staring into each other's eyes.

Then suddenly, my head started throbbing again. I

instinctively placed my hand on my forehead and closed my eyes. The throbbing continued violently. My head felt like an orange, and someone was trying to make orange juice with it.

I desperately wanted to lie down. I shifted towards the entryway, but my right leg went numb. My body burned in pain as I started falling forward. Max's sweet eyes were now laced with fear as he moved forward to try to catch my fall. I stumbled hard onto the ground. I screamed loudly and cried.

He rushed over to me and pulled me up towards his chest. I could hear his heartbeat quicken. I felt safe. I gave him a faint smile as my eyes became very heavy. I fought to keep them open.

My lips trembled in fear. I stared at Max's face to seek comfort. But his brows were furrowed; his eyes darted about in concern as though they were searching for a place to hide. He looked like he'd just seen a ghost. I just scared the life out of him, didn't I? He placed his arm around my bare shoulders and looked torn between his duty and his heart.

Max may have been a med student, but he only had the most superficial knowledge of medicine. It was like being in a creek without a paddle. He was temporarily incapacitated. Max lifted me from the ground and cradled me in his embrace. He refused to leave me stranded alone.

He barged through the entryway, carrying me inside, and screamed up the stairwell, "Help! Help!" I knew he wanted to get Aunt Brenna's attention. Max screamed even louder, "Ms. McGregor! Ms. McGregor!"

With the last of my strength, I lifted my left hand and placed a finger on his lip to hush him. I wanted to tell him that I was fine and just needed rest. But I could not speak. I put on a faint smile; my head throbbed intensely again. I was drowning. My eyes began to close. And the last thing I remembered was the sheer panic in his eyes and his worried voice calling my name.

My body began seizing uncontrollably. Pain set in immediately, and Max continued screaming my name over and over at the top of his lungs. And just like that, I was gone. My vision blurred, and everything went black.

Chapter Ten

I woke up lying in a hospital bed with dozens of tubes coming out of every part of my body. There was beeping and bopping noises around me. I could hear the sounds of chaos beyond the hum of machines in my room. The bed was covered with sterile white sheets, and it was somewhat lumpy. My body sunk into the mattress as I tried to wiggle out of the tight clasp of the pale blue blanket wrapped around me. I felt like a newborn baby swaddled tightly under the covers. Trapped. Helpless. Alone.

I heard a sweet, yet unfamiliar voice mixed into the rhythmic hissing sound of a machine. It was hard to make out what this mysterious voice was saying, but it sounded like a song. Like a familiar nursery rhyme.

The voice sang softly, "Rain, rain, go away. Come again another day."

It was a little girl's voice, and she sounded near. But it was hard to make out what she was singing. I thought to myself, was this voice my conscience? I slowly turned my head to see if anyone was in the room. But all I saw were the plain white walls, my bed that dominated, and a chair for potential visitors. I *was* alone. But, where did that voice come from?

The voice continued, "Anna Minor wants to play. Rain, rain, go away."

Suddenly, I noticed the light green coloured curtain to my right. Ah, the infamous curtain partition that gave each patient in shared hospital rooms a little bit more *privacy*. So, I wasn't *alone*. I was relieved to know that I wasn't going insane and that there was a real little girl, Anna Minor, to be exact, behind that curtained wall. Clearly, these curtains only physically separated patients but did absolutely nothing to block out sound.

My head felt like it was swimming. Instinctively, I wiggled harder to break free of the swaddle. My arms felt weak. No matter how hard I tried, I just couldn't get my right arm to move. It was like my brain got angry at my arm and gave Mr. Right the cold shoulder. I started to panic. What was wrong with me? My blood pressure and heart rate spiked, setting off an alarmingly loud beeping sound. I wanted to rip out the IV attached to my hand so badly. I felt stupid being connected to a bag of saline solution hanging from a pole that beeped every time I tried to move. I was extremely frustrated. I did not want to be here. Not today. Not tomorrow. Not ever.

As the monitors continued to beep, I looked out my window to seek comfort. There I saw a lonely, old Laurel Leaf willow tree positioned directly in my line of sight. I wasn't sure exactly where I was, if I was dreaming, or if I was even alive. I stared at the willow tree's slender, graceful branches, and hummed a peaceful tune to put my mind at ease. That was when I'd realized that my voice box was still functional. At least I wasn't all broken. So I screamed as loud as I could, "Aunt Brenna? Max? Someone? Anyone?"

The once silent room with just the methodic beat of my heart rate monitor suddenly turned loud and chaotic. A nurse rushed in and frantically pressed buttons before writing something down on her clipboard. She was a young lady, likely in her early twenties, with her dark brown hair tied back in a tiny neat ponytail. I squinted to read her name tag. It read, 'Mabel Brown, registered nurse.' I looked at her burgundy scrubs as she meticulously worked away at the machines. It had an oddly familiar logo and pattern. Then it dawned on me. I was at *G&C*, the very same children's hospital that Aunt Brenna worked at. I muttered some swear words under my breath. I'd finally become a patient at her hospital, and I was horrified.

Mabel finally got the monitors to stop beeping before she spoke with a friendly smile, "Tell me your full name, date of birth, and something about yourself."

"Umm," I whispered as she adjusted my pillow to help me sit up in bed. "Emily Anne McGregor. Born exactly 23 days after the 2002 winter equinox. Love music."

Mabel nodded her head and wrote something down on her clipboard, "Wonderful. And how are you feeling?"

"I know it's obvious because I'm here, but not *normal.* My head is pounding like I'm listening to some sort of imaginary heavy metal rock band. I can't really describe it. Tired, of course. But I'm always tired. And I'm having trouble moving the right side of my body."

Mabel scribbled more onto the clipboard and replied, "Dr. Waters will be in here shortly. Let me page him." Mabel turned towards the window and fiddled with her pager.

"Where am I?" I asked.

She turned back towards me and spoke. "You're in room 55, ICU, at *G&C*." Mabel paused to look at her pager, then asked, "Do you remember how you got here?"

"No, I don't," I said, ashamed.

Mabel just smiled and, in a warm voice, said, "I'll let your Aunt know that you're awake. She's in the waiting room—"

I interrupted, "Max? What about Max?"

"Oh, you mean that nice boy with the baseball cap? He's with her too. The two of them haven't left your side since you were admitted to the hospital," Mabel said as I turned my head to check the room again. "Well, your Aunt kept touching all these buttons here, so I eventually ushered them both out and made them wait in the waiting room."

"That's classic, Aunt Brenna," I sighed, shaking my head. "My Aunt's a registered nurse here for the pediatric dialysis unit. She's a bit overprotective, I guess. She's even worse than a mother bird protecting her hatchlings. Sorry about that."

"Not to worry. I'm new here, so we never met before. But I figured that she worked here once she started yelling medical terms and policies at me, and then threatening to report me to my supervisor, Dr. Roscoe Hank. Between you and me, Roscoe is not a common name. So, I put two and two together and realized that I was treating her niece this whole time. All is forgiven. Though, I better make sure I take good care of you if I value my life," Mabel chuckled. "Your Aunt is quite the character."

"How long was I out for?" I asked.

"Almost half a day," Mabel replied while reviewing my charts.

"So, just tell me straight. What's in my charts? I'm dying, right? I mean, I'm in the ICU. Only patients in dire need of attention get admitted here," I questioned.

Mabel just smiled warmly and said, "We are all dying, Emily. Just some faster than others. ICU stands for intensive care unit, not automatic death sentence. You were admitted here because you were unresponsive and required more attention. Trust me. You rather be here than in the ER. It's crowded, overpacked, and loud down there. Things that someone suffering from a migraine would frown upon, am I right? Anyway, being here isn't so bad. You got to meet me," Mabel said as she winked.

I liked Mabel. She was straightforward and witty, absolutely loveable, and so easy to talk to. All of which were extremely important character traits for a nurse, apart from empathy and attentiveness. I thought to myself, Aunt Brenna and Mabel could have been great friends if Aunt Brenna washed her potty mouth and sanitized her frustration.

Mabel opened the curtain to let herself out as she waved goodbye. I heard the click of the door, and I slumped back into a resting position on my lumpy bed. I wasn't an idiot. Being transferred to the ICU from the ER was already a telltale sign of something serious.

•••

Aunt Brenna busted into the room anxiously as Max trailed just steps behind her. Max clutched his baseball cap nervously in his hands and quietly sat in the visitor chair. Aunt Brenna grabbed my hand and kissed the top of my forehead.

"Emily dear, don't scare me like that," Aunt Brenna exclaimed through her tears.

I looked at Aunt Brenna, then Max. I noticed Aunt Brenna's eyes were bloodshot and puffy, and Max's suit jacket was soaked right through on his entire left shoulder. It was a bit sad to see a perfectly good outfit ruined. Max held a small packet of tissues and endlessly passed them to my Aunt until he ran out. They both looked like a terrible train wreck. And I was the cause of it all. That made me feel even worse.

"Sorry, Aunt Brenna," I cried.

Max stood up from behind her and spoke. "Your Aunt has been wailing like a lost coyote the past few hours. And if you don't hurry up and get out of here, then I think I'll have to look in the lost and found for another shirt," Max said as he pointed to his left shoulder.

That was classic Max. The same guy whose sarcasm could annoy me and please me all at the same time. Gosh, I felt better just seeing him. I chuckled. It was good to laugh again. The seriousness of being strapped to machines in the ICU was rather depressing. I would totally swap positions with a homeless dude if it meant that I could get out of here. I wished so badly that I was at home, strumming Jimi and studying for exams.

Aunt Brenna and Max continued babbling, asking questions about how I was feeling and all that jazz. But I zoned out for most of it. I just kept nodding my head like a natural reflex. I thought of George Orwell's *1984* novel. It was a novel that shown how in human nature, there were more grounds for despair than hope. Basically, we were all pessimistic robots and slaves to fear. Only those who deciphered the secret code had found the gift of optimism, freeing their mind from the negativity virus.

It was natural to let our fears consume us. Simply the concept of buying insurance was based on our greatest fears, like fires, floods, and death. But negative thoughts feed off each other just as much as positive ones. When my parents died, I fell victim to thoughts like 'my life sucked,' 'the world hated my music,' and 'I would be miserably single for the rest of my life.'

But three years after moving to Glenwood, things changed. Almost like something unlocked the gateway to curing my negativity. I started to think: life was great, I was so lucky to have Aunt Brenna and Max, and although I was still single, I loved that I was alive with good enough health to make music. Well, today, I wasn't completely sure about the last point, but I enjoyed my transformation into an *optimistic realist*. Even if I was doubtful now if it still applied.

Despite sleeping for over twelve hours, I still felt very tired. I intentionally tried ignoring the conversation Aunt Brenna and Max were having to put my mind at ease. That was until they raised their voices and started to argue.

"I was not! You're overexaggerating!" Aunt Brenna shouted defensively.

"Really? Exhibit A here tells otherwise. Right, Emily?" Max

said playfully as he waved his hand around the soaked spot of his fancy suit jacket.

Then, a tall, balding man entered the room, who I assumed was Dr. Waters. Everyone turned their attention to him, and Aunt Brenna stepped forward protectively.

Immediately, Aunt Brenna took charge. She bombarded Dr. Waters with questions before giving him a chance to answer. "Alan! So good to see you! I mean, Dr. Waters! I know we got to keep this professional here, but I'm so glad you're here taking care of my niece. What's wrong with her? Is she pregnant? Why would a perfectly healthy person just faint like that? She's pregnant, isn't she?" Aunt Brenna demanded.

She glared at me then at Max and screamed disappointingly, "Emily! Max! Why didn't you guys use protection!" Aunt Brenna paused and shook her head before switching to a softer tone. "I made a huge mistake letting you hang out with a college guy, Emily. I should have gone through the whole 'birds and the bees' talk when you turned sixteen. What have you two gotten yourself into? You're both way too young to be parents." Aunt Brenna stopped again, but this time to compose herself. Then, she looked upwards and whispered, "I'm so sorry, Tom. I failed you, my brother."

"Brenna! Please. Calm down," Dr. Waters said as he placed a reassuring hand on my Aunt's shoulder. "You need to breathe. I didn't even say anything yet."

Clearly, the two of them knew each other very well. After all, Aunt Brenna did work at *G&C*, so I was positive she was acquainted with most of the staff at the children's hospital. I peered over at Max, who looked rather embarrassed and uneasy about the accusation. Aunt Brenna was clearly losing her mind. As a full-time registered nurse, she should've known better for jumping to conclusions before checking the paperwork. Aunt Brenna was always one for numbers, but probably acted out because *I* was the one in the patient chair.

"Brenna, Emily is not pregnant," Dr. Waters said with a chuckle.

"Oh, what a relief!" Aunt Brenna exclaimed. She exhaled loudly before she gave Max one of those 'I got my eyes on you' stares. Max was sweating profusely now. Though, I couldn't blame him since we did raise all the red flags. I would be completely satisfied if my Aunt's shenanigans wouldn't make our friendship awkward once I could finally leave the hospital. I really hoped Max would forgive me for Aunt Brenna's *very* active imagination. At that moment, I thought my life was ruined. But the worse had yet to come.

Dr. Waters turned to Max and spoke. "Young man, would you mind stepping out so I could talk with Brenna and Emily privately?"

Privately. Ugh. I hated those words. They sounded so *adult*. So important. So serious. Oh boy, I was in hot water and had no personal flotation device in my possession. I'm dead. Max looked at me and nodded. He knew that he couldn't argue. All medical information was typically only given to immediate family members. Being my caregiver, Aunt Brenna was the only other person allowed in the room for the next part of the conversation.

“It’s Max. Max Miller,” he said as he shook the doctor’s hand. “And yes, I respect Emily’s privacy. I will leave you all now. Thank you, Dr. Waters. Please take care of her,” Max said politely.

Max walked up to me and squeezed my right hand. “I’ll wait for you in the waiting room, okay?” he said softly.

I tried to squeeze back, but I couldn’t. So, I flashed a small smile and whispered, “Thank you.” I longed for him to stay, but I knew he couldn’t. Max stepped past the curtained wall and exited.

•••

Dr. Waters cleared his throat and started explaining everything written in my charts. “Emily actually had a seizure. But I’m more concerned with why Emily is having temporary paralysis of her right extremities, particularly her fingers. I reviewed her bloodwork from the ER, and there were no indications of B-12 deficiencies or diabetes. That young gentleman, Max, mentioned in the ER that Emily experienced a seizure before being admitted and has been experiencing migraines recently. Emily, is this all true?”

Dr. Waters looked at me. I wasn’t sure about the seizure. I couldn’t remember how I ended up at the hospital, but the migraines were true, so I responded with a nod. Aunt Brenna looked hurt. I could tell that she was upset that I’d never mentioned anything about my reoccurring migraines.

I tried to downplay the situation; lying through my teeth, I said, “Yes, Dr. Waters, over the past few months, but it never bothered me. I just joked about it with Max whenever he said something annoying.”

Aunt Brenna looked more disappointed than angry. But I could tell she was fuming inside; her eyes were like a fiery flame. Clearly, she was annoyed about how I kept secrets from her, especially ones that revolved around my health. I never meant to hurt her. I really thought it was nothing. But I guess I was wrong.

I started to desperately plead to Dr. Waters. “The headaches weren’t really anything. I never had trouble studying or sleeping,” I lied.

I refused to tell Dr. Waters the *full* truth. At least not in front of Aunt Brenna. Oh how I just hated being the center of attention. Honestly, my migraines were pretty bad. Each was more intense than the last, and they occurred almost daily. But, I’d already dug myself into such a deep hole that I had no choice but to continue with this lie.

“I actually feel much better, Dr. Waters, so can I please go home now?” I pleaded as I attempted to stand. I shifted in the bed and stood momentarily before my right leg buckled, and I stumbled hard onto the floor. My body was sprawled out awkwardly in a very straggling fashion. I was so embarrassed by the whole ordeal and had a lovely bruise on my knee to serve as a reminder of my stupidity.

Aunt Brenna and Dr. Waters eventually helped me back up onto the bed. The room was silent momentarily before Dr. Waters continued. “Well, temporary one-sided numbness could be a symptom of many things. Most are not too serious and completely treatable. But I would like to rule out some *other* possibilities, especially if you'd been having episodes of migraines over the past few months."

Dr. Waters sympathetically stared at me with one of those 'just cooperate and let me do my job' looks. I sighed and nodded. There was no point fighting with inevitability. I was tired anyway.

He looked at my chart and asked, "Emily, did your parents ever have a history of multiple sclerosis or stroke?"

I looked at Aunt Brenna. She did not look back but responded, "Tom's side of the family had a history of dementia. I'm not sure about Liz's family."

"Well, I would like to run some tests to rule out some possibilities. I suspect we may be dealing with encephalitis," Dr. Waters said bluntly.

"Acute inflammation of the brain, causing partial paralysis in the arms and legs," Aunt Brenna interrupted. "But how is that possible?"

"Yes, Emily's CBC indicates a dangerously high white blood cell count, which I suspect is due to a viral infection. Given the symptoms, I believe this infection explains what she is currently experiencing, but we require additional testing to be certain. Elevated WBC count could be something minor, like stress, to something more serious, like cancer," Dr. Waters explained.

Aunt Brenna began to cry. Dr. Waters placed a hand on her shoulder and spoke reassuringly. "But, the diagnosis of leukemia is very doubtful, Brenna. It is likely encephalitis, which is rarely life-threatening, and there's a handful of antiviral medications that are extremely effective in treating it. We will take good care of Emily. I promise," Dr. Waters said.

I muttered under my breath, "Promise? I thought doctors don't make promises."

Chapter Eleven

Dr. Waters scheduled an MRI for tomorrow morning and kept me in the ICU under observation overnight. Aunt Brenna had an early shift, so she entrusted Max to keep watch at the hospital. He went home to grab a shower and change of clothes, so when I saw him again, Max was back in his more casual outfits. I felt bad that Max was thrown into this whole ordeal. It wasn't fair for Aunt Brenna to task him with such responsibility. He was *only* my friend. Ok, *best* friend. But, *still.* It didn't feel right. Though, he kept his word to Aunt Brenna. Maybe I was starting to rub off on him. Maybe.

The more I thought about the situation, the more my mind filled with all sorts of conflicting thoughts. Was *I* his bestie? Was he genuinely worried about me? Or was it pity? I started to innocently treat all those thoughts as if they each deserved consideration. But why did it all matter so much to me? Confused, I let out a loud sigh.

I stared at Max curled up, uncomfortably asleep in the visitor chair by the window. The moonlight lit up his face, and I felt like some psychopathic weirdo as I studied him. Watching Max sleep was like tweeting about my belly button. It conflated both our vanity and vulnerability because we were the most *exposed* when we sleep. Often, we feel embarrassed when we doze off in public. We put down all our guards, have our most unpolished faces, and sometimes even make the most awkward sounds. Yet, Max was right here in front of me. Exposed. No walls, lots of drool, and a cacophonous snore. This *was* Max Miller.

Suddenly, Max twitched and turned his face towards the window. He probably felt my eyes burn into his skull. Granted, if I had laser beam eyes, I would have already burned a hole right through his face with the intensity I was staring at him with.

I looked around the room to find something else to entertain my troubled mind. It was definitely going to be a long night. I disconnected myself from the heart rate monitor and used the rest of the strength in my arms to lift myself up from my lumpy bed. Using the IV pole for support, I slowly tip-toed to Jimi. Then, I heard something. That sweet voice again, singing the same nursery rhyme.

"Rain, rain, go away. Come again another day. Anna Minor wants to play. Rain, rain go away," the voice whispered.

I knew instantly that I wasn't the only one struggling to find sleep tonight. Likewise, my roommate, Anna, was still awake too. I thought of her. I wondered why Anna always sang that same nursery rhyme. Perhaps it brought her comfort. A memory of good times? I wasn't sure. But music's ubiquitous influence was felt by everyone in the world. Music had the uncanny ability to lift my mood whenever I was down, so I wasn't surprised to hear her sing during these lonely hours.

When we connect with music, we connect with not only ourselves and the individual notes, but also with others who hear the same tune. I knew that Anna wanted someone to hear her song. I was certain. I just wasn't exactly sure who.

I turned to face the curtain partition that separated me from my mysterious roommate. I hadn't left my side of the room since I arrived, but tonight I was eager to venture past those green curtains. I slowly inched towards the curtains, but as I approached, the singing suddenly stopped. Anna's sweet voice was replaced by a loud muffling sound that resembled a high-speed hairdryer. I didn't hear Mabel enter, so I was intrigued about what surprises stood behind that curtained door.

I cautiously pulled open the curtain and saw a little girl, about seven years old, who laid very still in her bed. She was wide awake and held an adorable fluffy white teddy bear. There was a bright pink ribbon that held together a tiny braid twisted in her long brown hair. She looked up at me and waved.

Anna wore a strange mask attached to some sort of ventilating machine that made the same strange whistling noises I heard earlier. The mask hid most of her face, but I could tell that she was smiling. Her side of the room looked identical to mine, except for the array of breathing apparatus and colourful drawings taped to the walls.

My IV pole got caught in the madness of cords twisted together across the floor. I wiggled free and continued towards her bed. Anna's face lit up with excitement. Quickly, Anna removed her Iron Man mask and pulled up her nasal cannula that rested around her neck. She took two deep breaths, smiled, and waved again.

"Hello, neighbour! I'm so glad you finally came over to say

hello. Did you meet my friend George?" Anna said, pointing to her stuffed teddy bear. She picked up George and dangled him in the air like it was saying hello to me.

I waved back and smiled, "Hello, George. Nice to meet you. And you must be Anna Minor."

"You know who I am?" Anna asked, surprised.

"You're famous, Anna," I joked.

"I'm not on YouTube!" Anna replied.

"Not yet, but I did hear you singing. You have a beautiful voice," I exclaimed softly.

"My Mommy told me that too!" Anna said fondly. She then held up George towards the window and whispered, "Is it still raining, George?" Anna then playfully made George nod his head as she pulled him in for a tight hug.

"Anna, do you like the rain?" I asked, confused.

"No!" Anna said firmly. "It's always raining. I'm tired of the rain. I want the sun to come out again," Anna whined. "Can you ask Mother Nature to stop crying? I want to go out and play. Mommy said I must stay in this room until it stops raining. I can't see out the window. So, George has been helping me check. Right, George?" Anna said as she lifted George above her head as though he was peering out the window again. "Why does spring rain so much?" Anna said, frustrated.

I considered telling her the truth. That it wasn't raining outside. And how her Mom had employed the rain as a ploy to buy time at the hospital. But it would only make Anna even more miserable. So, I played along.

"Sorry, Anna. I'm not friends with Mother Nature either. It's raining for me too," I said with a sigh.

My adrenaline rush began to fade. I started to feel very tired and desperately wanted to sit down. My bed seemed so far away from where I was standing. Anna smiled as I wheeled myself towards the visitor chair by her bedside.

"You don't mind if I hang out on your side for a bit," I asked.

"What is your name?" Anna asked.

I straightened myself in her chair, then said, "I guess I never gave you a proper introduction." I held out my hand and greeted her, "Hello, my name is Emily McGregor."

Anna shook my hand and responded, "And my name is Anna Minor. I like my new roommate. Can we be friends?"

I smiled. Who would have known that during these dark hours, I would be adding a plus one to my social circle. Four. We may have been a decade apart in age, but we lived a lifetime together on the same wavelength. It was nice having someone to talk to who understood how much it sucked to be stuck at the hospital.

Anna was like a breath of fresh air. I mean, kids used to scare the bejesus out of me. And as an only child, I never had much practice. As a rule, I was wary of anything that was smaller and probably smarter than me. I'd seen the way kids look at adults with those puppy dog eyes. Wow, those kids were pure geniuses to make even the toughest punks turn into softies. I was just glad that Anna, too, was desperate for some company.

I started to think about her nursery rhyme. Slowly, I began to piece together a new version of the nursery rhyme in my head. I sang it out loud to Anna.

♪♫♪♫♪♫♪

Rain, rain, go away
Children here want to play
Skies are gloomy, it's all grey
Just go on a holiday

Stop the rain, make it shine
Skies are dark, please be kind
Rain, rain, go away
Children here want to play

♪♫♪♫♪♫♪

After we shared our own stories about how we ended up in room 55, I drew a picture of a silly-looking monkey with a curly moustache and taped it onto her wall. Later, we had a staring contest that sparked an eruption of giggles, especially when George was crowned the title of undefeated champion. Mabel rushed in after she heard all the commotion.

"Anna! Emily! Why are you both still awake?" Mabel asked with her arms crossed and a stern look on her face.

It was way past midnight. Almost 3 a.m. So, I could imagine

why Mabel would be upset about our slumber party. I bit the bottom of my lip and said, "Umm, there are monsters under my bed," I innocently claimed.

"Your side of the room seems better than mine! I want to see your monsters! Can we switch, Emily? Please. I'm not afraid of any monsters! Mike Wazowski and Sulley are my friends," Anna exclaimed excitingly.

Anna was such a sweet little girl. It was heartbreaking to see someone so young suffering from severe asthma. And although I was unaware of the extent of her condition, I knew Anna's weather forecast was going to be rainy for, at least, a little while longer. Anna may have been small, but when it came to bravery, she was big.

Mabel interrupted our little shenanigans and ushered me back to my side of the room. I whispered, "Goodnight, Anna," before she pulled the curtain partition shut.

Mabel helped me back into my bed and reconnected me to the cardiac monitor. Mabel whispered, "Seems like Max here is getting more sleep than you. But you really need the energy in the morning. Oh, honey, I know it's hard, but try to get some sleep. Okay?"

"Okay, Mabel. I'll try," I replied.

Before Mabel left the room to check on Anna, I asked, "Mabel, what is that strange machine in Anna's room?"

"That's a BIPAP breathing machine. It pushes air into the lungs by keeping the lungs open to allow enough oxygen to enter. Anna has trouble breathing on her own when sleeping, so at night, we hook her up to the machine. But Anna has been here for quite some time. She's a smart girl. She figured out how to detach herself from the BIPAP machine as she prefers using the nasal cannula."

I let out a loud sigh, and solemnly spoke, "Illnesses really don't discriminate. Anyone and everyone can get sick. Anna's not even double digits in age."

"We are not immortal, which is why we all need our rest," Mabel said with a wink.

Max suddenly jolted awake and panicked when he saw Mabel in the room.

"Mabel, is everything ok? How's Emily?" Max asked.

"Well, good morning, sleepyhead. Emily is fine. I was just helping her back into bed," Mabel replied.

"Back in bed? Emily, where did you go? You should have woken me up if you needed something. That's why I'm here," Max said, concerned.

"I couldn't sleep. I'm so nervous about my MRI. I went next door to visit my roommate, Anna," I said defensively.

Mabel placed a hand on Max's shoulder and nodded. She opened the curtains and disappeared behind them, leaving me alone with Max once again.

"Max, I'm sorry. I didn't want to scare you or anything. I just couldn't sleep. Then I heard Anna singing, and you were sleeping like a baby, so I just felt obliged to investigate on my own. It was just a peek," I said.

"Emily, I'm not mad. It's just you know better. You need

your energy. Your body is still recovering, and sleep is the best medicine," Max exclaimed.

A concerned look crossed my face as I spoke. "It's just. What if sleep doesn't fix it. What if it's not encephalitis! What if it's something more serious? Ugh, that six-letter word. You know—"

"Nothing," Max interrupted.

"No, cancer, Max! What if it's cancer!" I blurted out as tears trickled down my cheek. Max just looked at me, and then I realized. "Ah, just so you know, *nothing* has seven letters," I said with a smirk. We both smiled at each other and chuckled.

"Well, your brain seems to be working just fine. You can count better than me," Max laughed. "Didn't I tell you before that there are always two sides to every story? Well, the same applies here. You can worry yourself sick, or you can get some rest and find out what you really have first before you start all this worrying. I think I prefer the last option more. It means *I* get to sleep," Max said with a smile.

"Sorry, Max," I whispered.

"Stop apologizing. There's nothing to be sorry about," Max insisted.

"I truly am sorry for getting you involved in all of this. You know you don't have to be here. I got this. I have Aunt Brenna. There's Anna now too. I'll be fine. You should go home," I said, looking away towards the window so he couldn't see me shed another tear.

"And be stuck with my Mom all day. No thanks! This totally beats having to do chores. Emily McGregor, you just saved me from doing my week's worth of laundry. I could kiss you right now," Max said sarcastically.

My brows furrowed. Did Max just joke about kissing me? Was Max subconsciously flirting with me? Or was I so sleep deprived that I was already dreaming while awake?

"Oh?" I exclaimed, surprised.

Max replied, "Emily, I want to be here. No one can make Max Miller do anything unless he wants it." He walked over to my bedside and caressed my hand tightly in his grasp. "Whatever you have, Emily McGregor, there's absolutely no way I'm going to let you face it alone. Do you hear me? You are not on your own. Let me be here so we can face it together," Max said confidently, straightening his baseball cap.

Max looked at me and flashed one of his infamous devilish grins. I couldn't help but smile and stare into his emerald green eyes. I just nodded.

"Do you need me to sing you to sleep?" Max asked. "I won't take no for an answer, so I hope your roomie doesn't mind."

I knew instantly that Max was totally serious. He flipped his baseball cap backward and picked up Jimi. He spoke softly, "May I?"

I grinned and nodded. Max continued, "Let me serenade you with Bobby McFerrin's "Don't Worry, Be Happy." This one's perfect for the occasion."

As Max sang and methodically strummed Jimi, I closed my eyes to indulge in this beautiful moment. My mind swirled with a plethora of emotions, and I didn't want this moment ever to end. My eyes felt too heavy to open, and soon enough, I fell fast asleep.

Chapter Twelve

It was morning, 8 a.m. MRI in T-minus two hours. Mabel was in the room already when I woke, and Max had disappeared from the visitor chair. I looked a bit disappointed. I knew Max wouldn't have stayed the whole night in that uncomfortable thing for a bed.

"Oh, honey, you got it all wrong. That sweet boy of yours was here all night. He flagged me just moments before you woke up so he could grab a coffee. He didn't want you to be in the room alone. He's a keeper!" Mabel said as though she was reading my mind. She winked and chuckled, "Oh, the beauty of adolescence."

I breathed out a sigh of relief. I wasn't sure why I cared so much about Max being here with me. Maybe Mabel was right. Maybe I didn't want to deal with *this* on my own. Maybe I *needed* Max.

The passing of my parents forced me to grow up way too quickly. I'd felt the weight of adulthood before I was ready to shoulder it. But life as we know it never promised to be easy. When our plans go awry, sometimes we are forced to persevere through non-ideal circumstances where the only limiting factor was time. That was exactly what killed me. Even if time were endless, we would still never have enough. So, while all my friends focused on hot celebrity crushes, hormones, and the latest fashion trends, I was robbed of *this* normality.

Although I was wary of classifying any teenager's life as *normal,* I became the 99th percentile in my social circle. I dealt with my new realities, which consequentially made me always on the outside looking in. It was almost unreal how the cost of one moment could be that astronomical. But this was my story. My ravaged life. Like the Great Plague that wiped out almost a quarter of London's population in a span of 18 months, I was soiled with despair because of one moment in my life.

But today, I'd realized that Max was right. I'd failed to see something that was there all along. Being the 99th percentile also meant that I had a second chance. A clean slate in life. There were *always* two sides to every story. Although my past was immutably fixed, my future was partially undefined. I could be the *one* percent. And this singularity contained such a wealth of possibilities. In this perspective, time was no longer a limiting factor because the only limit was in our minds.

•••

Max returned, holding two cups of coffee in hand. He approached my bed and smiled at the sight of me awake.

"Good morning, Emily! It's a beautiful sunny day. You got Jimi, and of course the star of the show, *me,* all here with you on your big day. And, what better way to start off your day than with a piping hot cup of coffee in your hands," Max beamed as he handed over one of his coffees that was simultaneously intercepted by Hurricane Mabel.

"Hey, what's the big idea? That's *my* liqueur of courage! No sharing!" I pouted, unamused.

"No way you're drinking that this morning, Emily! Haven't you read the patient handbook?" Mabel exclaimed.

I shook my head, confused before Mabel recited, "No food or drink two hours before an MRI exam." Mabel glared at me while pointing to the corresponding page. "I would like to minimize your risk of nausea simply because if *you* puke your guts out, then *I* have to clean it. It's a very simple equation. And I'm sure if you were smart, you'd choose wisely. You got that, Miss McGregor?" Mabel said as she wagged her finger and shook her head sternly.

"You're serious?" I asked.

"Oh ya, I'm *dead* serious. Not even a sip," Mabel said bluntly.

"Mabel, please? I can't live without my caffeinated beverage. I'd been wasting away ever since I got admitted to the ICU. Don't you see how pale my complexion has become? And it would be almost cruel to let a perfectly good cup of coffee go to waste," I pleaded.

Honestly, I was just making stuff up, but I didn't mind sounding stupid. If someone was going to take my coffee away, I wasn't going to go down without a fight. I haven't tasted even a sip of coffee since entering room 55. Living off saline water was a far cry from caffeine. But I knew instantly that I'd already lost the battle. Clearly, today was going to be a bad day.

"Well, Max could always graciously forfeit a cup of coffee to someone else," Mabel said as she winked at Max.

"Over my dead body!" I huffed and crossed my hands across my chest like a toddler having a temper tantrum. If there was one thing I hated in life, apart from inevitability, it was when others rubbed inevitability in my face.

"Emily! This is a serious matter. You cannot afford to have your MRI rescheduled," Mabel shouted.

"Afford?" Max asked, concerned.

"Oh, it's nothing. Just that I'm new here, so I would prefer if everything ran smoothly under my watch," Mabel pleaded, ignoring Max's concern.

I was still upset. But I was too tired to continue. I raised my hands up in defeat and shouted, "Fine! But I want you to know that I'm listening only because I want to get out of here ASAP."

"You and me both, Miss McGregor. You and me both," Mabel said reassuringly.

Max turned to face Mabel and held out *my* cup of coffee towards her. "Mabel? I have an extra coffee, would you like–" Max said as Mabel interrupted with a sarcastic voice.

"Oh, why thank you, Max. What a kind young gentleman!" Mabel said, flattered. She snatched the cup out of Max's hands and scurried out the room.

I was still fuming over the fact that someone laid their dirty paws on *my* coffee. And Max could tell that I was *still* pretty upset. Whenever anything bad happened in my life, I could always turn to coffee as my escape. But today, coffee was like forbidden fruit, and it could not fulfill all that it promised. Max cautiously sat on the corner of my bed. He'd never seen me this angry before, so I felt embarrassed about the whole ordeal.

Max placed his hand on my shoulder and looked me in the eye

before he spoke. "Sorry I wasn't here when you woke up. Didn't I tell you before that you're quite attractive when you're angry? Your nose wrinkles up in the cutest way. And–"

"Max, save your flattery for your future girlfriend. Nothing you're going to say is going to make me forget about the whole coffee fiasco. You know, I'd trade in my soul for a cup of coffee if the grim reaper came for a visit right now. So, don't even try," I said bluntly.

"Emily, how do you wake up Lady Gaga from her sleep?" Max asked.

"Huh? What kind of question is that? I dunno. You just wake her up. Do celebrities use alarm clocks? Maybe a rich butler, like Alfred?" I replied, confused.

"None of those things. Just poke her face," Max joked.

A smile crept onto my face, and suddenly we both burst out in laughter. It was hard to contain the giggles. Max put on a goofy smile and continued throwing out jokes and riddles to cheer me up.

His comedy showdown was absolutely hilarious, and soon enough, he gained a small crowd in room 55. Even Anna joined us to laugh at Max's puns. Although I normally would have enjoyed the silence, it felt comforting being in such an uplifting environment with patients alike. Laughter was truly life's best medicine. I guess this was how support groups felt like.

"What's the difference between a piano and a fish?" Everyone looked at each other and shrugged. "You can't tuna fish," Max laughed.

"And here's a special one just for Emily's roommate, Anna Minor," Max said while he looked in Anna's direction. She smiled and clapped her hands excitedly. "Middle C, E flat, and G walk into a bar. The barman stopped E flat and said, 'sorry, we don't serve minors here,'" Max joked.

The crowd roared for an encore, Anna cheered, and I smiled. Max was amazing. He really did know just what to do to keep my mind from worrying.

•••

MRI in T-minus thirty minutes. Mabel cleared the crowd in my room and started to prep the examination room. I couldn't help but watch the hands on the clock inch closer to ten. Max sat back down in the visitor's chair and grabbed Jimi, who was sunbathing by the window.

"I'd been working on a song. It doesn't have any words yet. But the melody goes something like this," Max said as he strummed a beautiful melody that was both soothing and gentle. I closed my eyes and took a deep breath.

"Max, it's beautiful. I thought you said you haven't created your own music in years," I said.

"That's absolutely right. But that day when I accidentally discovered your Moleskine, I was inspired. El couldn't have been happier. Thanks, Emily," Max said with a smile.

I blushed. Max was usually the one inspiring me, not the other way around. He was a very talented young musician, so it was unfortunate that Max chose medicine over music. I had a long way to go before I could even be half as good as Max. He definitely gave Jimi Hendrix some tough competition.

"I think curiosity got the best of you when you laid your hands on my Moleskine, Mr. Miller. I think *intentionally* is a better adverb," I teased.

"Ok, let's say I *did* intentionally open your Moleskine. Then did you *intentionally* leave your Moleskine at *Amore* for me to discover?" Max teased back.

I could only smile. Sometimes the best things that happen in our lives are those decided by fate. Some people called it a coincidence. But I called it fate.

In life, our fortunes and misfortunes were closely intertwined, and although many things came unexpectedly, I believed that everything happened for a reason. And once destiny guided us to where we wanted to be, it was our choice to decide whether we stayed on course or maneuvered elsewhere. Perhaps Max was my *fortunate misfortune*. He did have the uncanny ability to find the good in the bad. To me, Max served as a reminder that whenever misfortune striked, fortune was just around the corner. I just had to be strong and get through this life hurdle.

•••

The clock struck ten, and Mabel showed up right on time to wheel me to the basement of *G&C*. I left my phone on my bedside table and slowly got up from my bed. Max helped me into my wheelchair and gave my hand a tight squeeze. I looked up and flashed a weak smile. Mabel went through the safety questionnaire as she began to wheel me towards the curtained partition. I fidgeted in my chair and held up my hand to stop her. Mabel paused, and Max jogged up to see what was wrong.

I wasn't ready. My mind was plagued with doubt. What was the radiologist going to find? The thought of someone looking through my head felt like an invasion of privacy. The brain was probably the most complex organ in our bodies, and perhaps the most remarkable. It produced our every thought, action, memory, feeling, and experience of the world. The complexity of the one hundred billion neurons inside my head was mind-boggling. It was *my* personal space that made me who I am. My heart pounded so loudly that I could barely hear Max whisper into my ear.

Max placed his iPod on my lap and winked. "Listen to this when you're in there, okay? Escape in these melodies, and it'll be over before you know it. Trust me," he insisted.

I nodded and placed my hand over his iPod. I whispered, "Are you going to be here when I get back?" I felt needy, saying that. But I really didn't want to do *this* alone.

Max smiled, "Promise."

"Promise?" I said, surprised to hear the word slip from Max's tongue.

"Promise," Max whispered, placing a hand on my shoulder. He nodded again and flashed me one of his devilish grins.

As Max disappeared down the hallway to wait in the waiting room, Mabel wheeled me down the opposite direction towards the elevator.

Chapter Thirteen

As I entered the examination room, I felt queasy. Mabel greeted the radiologist, Dr. Lancaster, and together, they explained the procedure at hand. I tried to put on my bravest smile, but I was absorbed in thought. Then, that was when I saw it. A massive white machine that looked like some sort of opening to a parallel universe. There was a long movable table in front of this strange circular tunnel, and the shock hit me hard. My face turned pale. My palms were all sweaty. And my whole body shook uncontrollably. I kept repeating, "No, no, no!"

It was utterly insane how the sight of a narrow cylinder portal, which housed the MRI scanning magnet, could cause such a powerful reaction. I closed my eyes and clutched Max's iPod tightly in my grasp. Immediately, Dr. Lancaster took over and put her hand on my shoulder.

"Emily, do you like barbeques?" Dr. Lancaster asked.

I shook my head, not sure where this conversation was going.

"Well, this machine here is like a ginormous barbeque, and these computers behind that glass window allow us to see exactly what's inside the barbeque," Dr. Lancaster said while she pointed to the MRI scanner and then to the glass window where her computer was stationed.

"I don't get it," I whispered with a loud sigh.

"Have you ever wondered what's inside a hot dog? Well, rather than just looking at the ingredients on the package, we can use a machine like this to see all the tiny details inside that frankfurter. So, today you are going to be the hot dog, and this is your bun," Dr. Lancaster said as she pointed to the long table. "The only thing you have to do is stay perfectly still and let me do the barbequing. Okay?"

I was still uncomfortable about the whole ordeal, but the thought of transforming myself into a hot dog was amusing, so I played along. "Hmm, is it hot inside?" I asked, pointing to the machine.

"Nope. But you may feel a little sweaty, so I guess someone could say it really is like a real barbeque," Dr. Lancaster laughed. "But don't worry. We have a fan inside there to cool things off if it gets too hot inside."

I was still wary about being inside such a confined space, but I started to warm up to the idea. At least they weren't going to probe my brain physically.

"Any more questions before we begin?" Dr. Lancaster asked as she nodded to Mabel to start prepping the table.

"Just one more. Can I listen to this?" I asked, pointing to Max's iPod.

"Of course. We can plug it into our sound system while we work. But you'll have to use our pneumatic headphones," Dr. Lancaster explained. "You're also welcome to sleep there if you like. Some of my patients found the scanning sounds to be rather therapeutic. Others have said that they felt like pigs in a blanket.

So, whatever makes you comfortable. Okay?" Dr. Lancaster said as she took the iPod from my lap and handed it to Mabel.

I got up from my wheelchair and slowly lifted myself up onto the examination table. This was it. I was now Emily the Sausage.

I laid down as Mabel positioned my head on a pillow. She then lowered a headpiece onto the table that coiled around my head snuggly. After, she strapped the rest of my body with Velcro and reminded me to stay perfectly still during the whole procedure.

"Emily, if at any time you feel pain or discomfort, then let me know by raising up your hand. I will stop the scan immediately and move you out of the cylinder. Okay?" Dr. Lancaster said softly.

I gave Dr. Lancaster a thumbs up. Mabel positioned the headphones over my ears and gave my shoulder a small squeeze. The lights above me were bright, almost blinding. I closed my eyes as the table moved into the strange portal. Suddenly, I heard a series of loud, repetitive pulsing noises, like a flurry of rain that rattled against the windowsill.

Although I was wearing a hospital gown, I felt so naked inside. The MRI machine exposed everything that was seemingly invisible to the naked eye. It was like a million eyes were staring into my soul and crawling beneath my skin. I had only been inside for less than a minute, but those seconds felt like an eternity.

"Emily?" a voice erupted from my headphones. "This is Dr. Lancaster. Can you hear me?"

I intuitively wanted to nod my head but remembered that I was strapped down to the table in a headpiece. I responded with a thumbs up. The machine hummed again, and a gentle breeze whooshed into the tunnel and tickled my toes.

"Emily, you are going to hear a lot of weird swirling noises. That's okay. It just means the machine is working," Dr. Lancaster explained. She paused to speak to someone, probably Mabel, and then continued. "In a moment, I will put on your music, but it's super important that you remain perfectly still when I'm taking pictures. I will be taking many pictures, and it can take up to ten minutes for each set. You should be in and out in about half an hour. Okay? Let's rock 'n roll."

Dr. Lancaster's voice was soon replaced by a musical playlist featuring a mix of artists from various genres. The playlist started off with Elvis Presley's "Jailhouse Rock," followed by Billy Joel's "Piano Man," Eminem's "Lose Yourself," and Sara Bareilles's "Brave."

As Dr. Lancaster scanned my brain, I drowned my thoughts with these wondrous melodies. Instantly, I felt at ease. It was almost like Max was speaking to me in this parallel universe. Perhaps music was just an abstract form of language. Like he left some sort of cryptic message for me to decipher behind the modulations of pitch, intensity, and tempo.

Dad lived by Hans Christian Andersen's words almost as much as the lessons I learned in Andersen's fairy tales. Whenever Mom was enraged by Dad's supercilious attitude, Dad would always turn to songs to make things better. Dad was the epitome of Andersen's words, "where words fail, music speaks." And it was at this very moment that I finally experienced the true meaning of those powerful words too.

Since music was a unity of emotions, we sometimes turn to music to articulate what we couldn't quite say with words alone. Happiness and sadness. Love and envy. Hope and fear. Max was using his music to comfort me when I felt lost and alone. With my mind now at ease, I rested my eyes and drifted off to a sweet slumber.

•••

I woke to the sweet aroma of freshly ground coffee beans. I must have been dead. How could my imagination conjure up something so delicious? I opened my eyes. I was back in room 55, and there in front of me was Aunt Brenna and Max. I turned towards the delicious smell and saw a cup of *Amore*'s double espresso on my bedside table.

"I must be in heaven to smell coffee that sweet," I said, pinching myself just to make sure I wasn't dreaming.

"Max picked that up for you after Mabel wheeled you back to your room. You fell asleep in the MRI machine, sweetie. You must have been extremely exhausted if you could fall asleep inside that loud machine," Aunt Brenna chuckled.

"Ya, I had to run some errands for my Mom. I thought you would like your favourite and I was in the area. It's nothing really. Oh, and André wishes his most favourite customer a speedy recovery," Max said as he removed his baseball cap to run his fingers through his hair.

"Nothing! Are you insane? This is everything. I mean, Max,

thank you!" I exclaimed, blushing.

I grabbed the warm cup of coffee from the table and held it tightly in my hands. Slowly, I sipped my espresso to take in its full, rich flavour. I felt alive again. Everything was *almost* perfect.

•••

Dr. Waters invited Aunt Brenna and me to his office to discuss my MRI results. Max wheeled me down the hallway as Aunt Brenna and Dr. Waters spoke quietly behind us. I overheard Dr. Waters mention complicated names of tests that I'd never heard of, let alone knew how to pronounce. I zoned out for a bit. And reached out to grab Max's hand for comfort.

I was terrified. My heart pounded violently, and I started to hyperventilate. Max squeezed my hand in response to my nervousness, and I tried to compose myself before the onset of a mental breakdown.

When we reached Dr. Waters's office, Max flashed a thumbs up and escorted himself to the waiting room. Max knew the protocol. Once the door clicked shut, Dr. Waters began to talk, and Aunt Brenna exploded in tears.

"Now, I'm not going to jump to any conclusions until we run more tests," Dr. Waters said as he flipped through my charts. "Brenna, once I conduct more tests, then I can better explain to you the realities of your niece's situation."

"Alan! Don't patronize me. Just tell me straight. I've drunk a quadruple shot espresso before with no milk or sugar, so I can take it," Aunt Brenna exclaimed.

Aunt Brenna reached out to hold Dr. Waters's hands. "Alan. Please. Just tell me exactly what's wrong. You know I understand all the medical terminology. And I am fully aware of the protocol to sugar coat everything for patients and their families until we are definite about our diagnosis. So, just save me from that grief and just tell me what's going on. What are we talking about? How many weeks before Emily is back on her toes?" Aunt Brenna questioned, concerned.

Dr. Waters shook his head. "I'm afraid Emily's case is much more complicated than that, Brenna. I'm not trying to annoy you, but—" Dr. Waters paused and turned on his computer. He turned his screen towards us and continued, "You see, Emily's MRI shows a large mass on the left side of her brain. We thought that we'd find lesions, but there's this abnormal outgrowth of tissues here."

"What! There's a massive tumour inside Emily's brain! This can't be happening! Alan, why didn't you just call me when you looked at her scans? It's serious, isn't it? It's malignant. All those additional tests you mentioned aren't just for precaution, is it?" Aunt Brenna screamed before huddling over in her seat. Aunt Brenna muttered to herself, "I'm so sorry, Tom. I'm so, so sorry. I'd failed you."

The shock finally registered as I stared closely at the strange blob on the MRI. It had to be a mistake. How was it possible for something like *that* to be inside my head? It was like a bug entered through my ear, crawled into my brain, and made itself a home on my left hemisphere. Gross! I shuttered with the thought of a bug squirming inside my body. "But how?" I blurted out in horror.

I looked at Dr. Waters, and he spoke warmly. "I don't know how exactly it got there. I only know that this is likely a tumour. It could be benign or cancerous. I am not certain just from these results. We need to schedule a biopsy to get to the bottom of this."

"You mean you have to cut open my head and look inside of it!" I said in disgust. "That's not just gross, that's inhumane. What if my whole brain is full of cancer? Do you just cut open my head and remove the whole thing? You can't just remove pieces of my brain. Those are my memories!" I exclaimed in fear. I was scared of what the permanent side effects would be from brain surgery.

"Emily, please calm down. It is just a biopsy. And the tumour is only on one portion of your brain. The frontal lobe in the left hemisphere," Dr. Waters explained.

"Frontal what?" I screamed in horror.

"Emily, you'll be under anesthetics. Don't worry about anything. You won't feel a thing. If you like, we can conduct some more tests before deciding on the surgery," Dr. Waters assured.

I turned to face the back wall of his office. The results of my MRI were completely unexpected. I thought, at most, I would be stuck taking antibiotics for two months because of a viral infection. But this was far worse than a viral infection.

I breathed heavily and let out a loud sigh. My worst fears were coming true. What if I had *cancer*? What if I was *dying*? All I could think about now was Mom and Dad. I was already *dead*.

Chapter Fourteen

Dr. Waters suspected that I might have glioma. We ended up deciding on more tests to confirm his diagnosis before opting for any surgical procedures. Although my medical knowledge on the topic was minimal, I knew of only one type of glioma. It was called glioblastoma. Honestly, I had no idea how to pronounce that terrible word, but I referred to it as GBM for short.

GBM was one of the most malignant brain tumours out there that took the life of Tragically Hip's lead singer, Gord Downie, back in 2017. Even Canadians who normally didn't follow the band tuned in to watch his farewell tour.

Admittedly, I refrained from learning more about GBM at the time because Downie's story was almost unimaginable to the music world. But looking back, I'd wished I watched the Hip's documentary *A Longtime Running* so I could be better prepared for *this* moment. My moment.

The Tragically Hip's "Ahead by a Century" began playing in my head. I visualized Downie on the stage in Toronto, singing this song as his final farewell. The more I thought about it, Downie's final chapter was intertwined with mine. The thought stuck with me. I had no idea what type of glioma I had in my head, or whether I really had *that* inside. After all, the doctors were wrong about my preliminary diagnosis. Technically, I could have been worrying over nothing.

But since I honestly had no idea what glioma really entailed, I did what any other teenager would do whenever they had a burning question on their mind. Turn to their all-knowing friend, Google. All of life's answers were right at my fingertips. And Google never complained whenever I asked stupid or personal questions. All I knew was that I was terrified to discover *my* truth. So any means to alleviate the drama was welcomed.

I spent the next hour reading up articles on the Internet about glioma. I discovered that it was a fancy medical term for a brain tumour, and that headaches were a common symptom. But Google was a dangerous place to seek medical advice.

The thing with the Internet was that the quality and reliability of websites varied greatly. Often, it was hard to tell what was right and what was wrong. Aunt Brenna always told me that there was a higher chance of Dr. Google telling us that we had some rare and incurable disease and that Google only worsened the phobia. She insisted that online symptom checkers were simply glorified personality quizzes that were not sourced from a trained professional. Granted, Aunt Brenna worked in the business, so she had every right to doubt my faith in Google. And not until today, I couldn't agree more.

I was now traumatized over the whole matter. I couldn't stop thinking about how my brain, the most personal space in my body, was being attacked by some sort of invasive species that enjoyed nibbling on my brain for lunch. I cringed with the thought of something creepy and crawly moving around inside my head. Ugh! I kept hoping that the doctors were wrong again.

I tried distracting myself by thinking of a clever tune. As I closed my eyes, I thought of words that expressed my current emotions. Unfortunately, my mind was clouded with dark thoughts today.

♪♫♪♫♪♫♪

Hold back your tears, push away your fears
Feeling like you're all alone, power taken from your throne

♪♫♪♫♪♫♪

I went through a series of medical tests over the next few days. Each one was scarier than the last. I started to wonder if I would ever leave the hospital. Max came to visit every day after his classes. I insisted that Max stop skipping if he wanted a chance to be on good terms with his supervisor. I enjoyed his company on good days. But, for the most part, my days were bad. Most times, I wasn't even awake when he arrived. I only knew he came because Mabel told me the next morning.

Dr. Waters eventually transferred me to the neurology department and assigned me to Dr. Babinski, my neurologist. I said goodbye to Anna on my moving day and promised her that if I ever made it out of *G&C*, I would negotiate with Mother Nature to bring her some sunshine. That made Anna smile.

I shared a new room with three other patients, but we were all too sick to initiate pleasantries. It was even grimmer in this ward than in the ICU. I referred to my roommates as simply A, B, and C, with A being the closest in proximity.

Later that day, I underwent a thorough neurological exam that included checking my vision, hearing, balance, coordination, and reflexes. Nurse Zita, who was keeping watch on me in neurology, was a tall Persian lady with gorgeous hazel eyes. The day I met her, I whispered, "khoshgel," which was pretty in Farsi (probably the only word I knew in her home language). She smiled and called me 'Pretty Emily' ever since.

Zita conducted my neurological exam, and I knew immediately that I failed my coordination test. She initiated the most popular test of coordination: the finger-nose-finger test. I was asked to alternately touch my nose and then Zita's finger as quickly as possible. I missed my nose and her finger countlessly. Maybe, just maybe, I came close once. But no matter how hard I tried, it seemed impossible. It was probably the first time I failed anything. Well, I guess I couldn't spell *life* without an *F,* or I would be living a *lie*.

Late afternoon, Dr. Babinski ordered another MRI. But this time around, Dr. Lancaster injected something strange into my IV. I asked about it, but Dr. Lancaster only responded with, "it's a contrast called Gadolinium." I felt even more scared because I was left in the dark.

Fortunately, Dr. Lancaster noticed my eyes twitching with fear and decided to explain Gadolinium further. Apparently, it was a special yellow highlighter for my head. Tumours absorbed this kind of dye, which meant that any abnormalities in my brain would glow like a lightbulb on my scan.

Although I wasn't as nervous with the MRI this time around, I still wasn't convinced how another MRI would provide better insight into my tumour. I doubted that they really needed another look just to be sure. There was a gigantic blob on my first MRI scan. And it was pretty huge.

I was in the MRI machine for almost two hours, and unfortunately, I slept so much prior to my scan that I just couldn't fall asleep this time. So, I just stared at the walls of my barbeque, feeling just a tad bit claustrophobic, and patiently waited for it to all be over. Although I knew I had to stay perfectly still like a statue inside, I couldn't help myself from wiggling my toes because not being able to move for two hours was painfully excruciating.

Day after day, they stuck random needles into me. Everywhere. They hooked me up to machines that made strange whirly and whiny noises. And my blood. Well, let's just say that it was a hot commodity at *G&C*. It was either the doctors here were secretly bloodthirsty vampires, or they really thought I had an unlimited supply in my body. There was only one thing I wanted more in this world right now other than sleep. Home. I just wanted to go home.

•••

Dr. Babinski popped into my room at exactly four o'clock. Aunt Brenna left for her shift about an hour ago, and I was alone wall staring to pass the time. Dr. Babinski was sporting a very slick, heavily greased combover that covered his receding hairline. He probably had more hair on his chin than his head, but nevertheless, he was at least a friendly doctor.

"Good afternoon Emily! How are you enjoying your new room and this gorgeous view out your window?" Dr. Babinski said joyfully.

I frowned. Although the view from my window was still of my willow tree from the ICU, the atmosphere in the ICU was much more ambient. Moving to neurology did not seem like an upgrade. Seriously.

"I would like to go over your test results. Is that okay, or would you prefer to wait for your Aunt?" Dr. Babinski asked.

I put on my bravest smile and said, while I bit the bottom of my lip, "I'm ready."

The test results confirmed the worse of all the scenarios I googled. The MRI confirmed the presence of my tumour. It was located in the left hemisphere of my brain, and it wasn't small. That stupid contrast highlighted almost the entire top of my head. I wanted to cry. This blob was aggressively taking over my brain and if I did nothing, my entire brain would become a highlighter.

"Malignant?" I asked with my eyes closed, although I already knew the answer.

"Unfortunately, yes, Emily. I'm sorry," Dr. Babinski said softly.

Words from the articles I searched up on the web flashed

before my eyes. Deep down, I knew that my poor neurological test results hinted at the extent of the damage.

Dr. Babinski carefully explained that my on-again, off-again headaches, were the initial symptom that something was wrong. And because the glioma was on my frontal lobe, it likely interfered with my muscle coordination that caused my temporary one-sided paralysis. I was overwhelmed with all the medical details and wished Aunt Brenna was here beside me now. It was hard to digest everything, and I began blurring what I read on the Internet with what Dr. Babinski was explaining.

"Emily, you see this tissue box here," Dr. Babinski said, pointing to the tissue box on my bedside table. "Well, our brain is actually like a tissue box, holding hundreds of delicate tissues that protect our skull. So, whenever we get headaches, it would feel like I'm crushing the tissue box. And when a tumour decides to get cozy in there too, then there just isn't going to be much wiggle room. It is virtually impossible to stuff more tissues into a full box without damaging it. Sometimes the box may just explode open if we attempt such a task."

I looked at Dr. Babinski and asked, "Are you saying that my head is about to explode?"

Dr. Babinski shook his head and replied, "Not literally, but if you don't let us open your tissue box, then we might not know if or when that explosion may occur."

I nodded and took a deep breath, knowing exactly what Dr. Babinski was alluding to.

"The next logical step is to opt for surgery. At that time, we can take a biopsy to find out exactly what type of brain tumour you have. Also, we can attempt to remove as much of the tumour as humanly possible. Once we confirm our diagnosis, we would have a better guide for treatment options that would best work for you," Dr. Babinski explained.

I nodded but had nothing more to say. I refrained from looking at Dr. Babinski. Unable to function from shock, I decided to look out the window at my willow tree instead.

"Remember, medicine has advanced so much in the past decade. If there's any positive to all of this, the location of your tumour is quite favourable for removal via surgery," Dr. Babinski reassured.

I knew Dr. Babinski was right and that I shouldn't believe all the nonsense I read online. Still, I wanted some 'me' time to digest the whole situation. Was it possible to use the words 'favourable' and 'tumour' in the same sentence?

Dr. Babinski left me with a leaflet to review. There were large words on the cover that read, "Brain Surgery." I knew it was best to review its contents before my surgery and familiarize myself with the procedure, but I lacked the courage to open it.

My surgery was scheduled in T-minus three days. I thought to myself how much my life had changed since I rolled into the ER unconscious. I was shocked at how harsh reality could be. But the unknowns seemed worse than reality, and I had no idea what to expect on my journey ahead. It was blatantly obvious, though, that my days outside *G&C* were merely a distant memory.

•••

I was awake when Max arrived that evening. I wasn't expecting any visitors. He took one look at me and instantly knew that something was wrong. Max cautiously approached me and sat on the edge of my bed. Unsure how to respond, he just stared at me. The concerned look in his eyes said it all. He wanted answers. Now.

I struggled to put my thoughts into words. My mind was momentarily paralyzed. I hesitated. Internally, I sighed. If only my brain would cooperate. I didn't know why it was so hard to tell Max. It wasn't like I meant anything to him. We were *just* friends. And I was *just* another fish in the sea. Well, maybe not just *any* fish. I was a very sick one who had trouble swimming.

And probably after the longest, most intense staring contest that we'd ever shared, my chin trembled, and my body wracked with an onslaught of sobs and tears. I tried to look brave, but a flood of uncontrollable tears escaped me and gushed down my ashen cheeks. My tears continued to flow, robbing my ability to speak, barely allowing a breath to be drawn. And as my sobs tore through the curtained walls, it threatened the fall of a thousand stars in the night sky. I leaned my head back and looked at Max, helpless and defeated. My bottom lip quivered, and my shoulders dropped in resignation.

And just like that, another promise was broken. We are the promises that we keep. And I felt emotionally taxed for failing to keep my emotions in check. I promised myself to never, in a million years, cry like *that* again. But I just did. And it wouldn't stop.

How could the fourteen-year-old Emily McGregor pledge to be mentally strong for the rest of her life? What on earth was I thinking? I was human. Had no superhuman strength or invincibility cloak. I was just an immature teenager who had no sense of my limitations. I hated breaking my promises. Though, it seemed inconsequential now to be caught up in my own disappointments. I had bigger things to worry about. And I was scared out of my mind.

"Oh, Emily, I—" Max said before pausing mid-sentence.

His arms spread wide, welcoming me in, and I immediately entered them. He pulled me into a gentle embrace. It was a moment of exceptional bonding that somehow took away my pain and made me feel safe. I became oblivious to the world around us. I leaned in closer, closed my eyes, and all the noise in the room stopped. Then, more tears welled from deep inside. Deep emotions stirred with no other outlet but through my long-lasting sobs. Max's eyes bled with pain. Tears stained my face.

Then, Max spotted the brain surgery leaflet that I stuffed behind my pillow. Max grabbed it. His eyes widened as he spoke. "It's this, isn't it? This is what's making you so upset," Max asked, waving the leaflet in front of my face.

He knew my condition was not something to be taken lightly. But he knew that I needed his strength more than anything now. His body looked calm compared to how tangled his mind was. Max was at a loss for words. And so was I. So, we just sat there in silence as he held me in his arms. I melted from his warmth. I felt his heart beating steadily with mine. The silence. His touch. None of it seemed to end, but I didn't mind. I wanted this moment to last as long as it allowed us.

After what seemed like hours, Max held my hand and let out a loud sigh. "Emily, I'm sorry. I'm so sorry. I know brain surgery is not going to be easy, but you can talk to me. Okay? I'm not going to let you do this alone," Max said softly as he looked deeply into my eyes.

"I can't. I just can't. I'm scared, Max! I'm not as strong as you think I am. I'm just Emily McGregor," I blurted out in frustration.

Max's eyes held mine a moment longer before he confidently spoke. "Not *just* Emily McGregor. *The* Emily McGregor. The girl with a mind full of songs and a heart of gold. The same girl that makes guys trip over her. Someone who is both strong-willed and strong-minded. I don't think I ever met a girl stronger than the strongest coffee in the world, until I met you. And you of all people know, I like my coffee black. Jet black."

I was awestruck by his sweet comment. Was Max? No. Couldn't be. I blushed and pulled back from his embrace.

One of our deepest desires to be in a relationship with others was closeness. It was what gave us a sense of belonging and what we needed most when we were struggling. Yet, when we struggled, we often were drawn to isolate ourselves. Not because we were depressed, but because we were convinced that reaching out to someone would be a great burden on them. A sign of weakness. Vulnerability.

I was afraid of getting close to Max because I was afraid to lose him. And once we discovered what was truly going on inside my brain, I was certain that he wouldn't be patient enough to work through it with me. I know. It was probably best for me to push back now before I got too attached.

I wiped the tears from my cheek and decided to move forward with my decision. "You must not know a lot of girls then. Do you need me to introduce you to some hot chicks from *Glenwood High*? Or are you more of an older gal sort of guy?" I joked.

Max looked confused, but I continued. "You totally need to get out more. Go to bars, pool parties, maybe the beach. You don't need to rely on a fake ID like me, so what's stopping you from living your life, mister," I pestered.

"Are you calling me *old* Emily McGregor?" Max asked coyly, raising his right eyebrow and smirked.

"What?!? No! Are you insane? You look like you worked out eight days a week if that *was* possible," I said, slightly embarrassed.

"Are you blushing, Emily McGregor? Are you checking me out? Like what you see, huh?" Max boasted as he flashed that insanely attractive devilish grin that any girl would swoon over.

I turned away and blushed again. Why was I helping him boost his ego? Clearly, my approach was not working.

I bit the bottom of my lip and sniffled as I turned to face the window. I loved looking at my willow tree. Each time I focused on the gentle swaying of the leaves blowing in the wind brought a sense of calmness to my mind.

Max sat closer and gently turned the side of my face so I would look him in the eyes. "Emily, I'm not going anywhere, okay? I see what you're doing and don't think for a second it'll work. I'm just going to stay right here by your side no matter how many times you try pushing me away," Max said with a sweet smile.

Even in the darkest of times, Max always knew how to put a smile on my face. There was a discernible change in the air. And that was when it began. From this moment, my life would change forever. Despite all the uncertainties that lingered in my near future, *I*, Emily McGregor, was most definitely falling for Max.

Chapter Fifteen

Life was full of surprises and unexpected turns, and no matter how thoroughly we planned things, life always had its way of taking us by surprise. Some of these surprises were good. Like super good. We were talking about those truly remarkable, mountain top moments that made even the impossible seem possible. It was like living in a dream. And I would gladly welcome more of those mountain top moments because frankly, who doesn't like a good view.

Where there was good, there was bad. The bad encompassed those 'oops' moments. Like 'I made a mistake' sort of bad that turned out to be okay after profusely apologizing. But there was also the 'ugly bad.' The moments that were so terrible that even the word *terrible* wouldn't be sufficient enough to articulate how incredibly bad it was. I wouldn't even wish it upon my greatest enemy.

Two separate moments at opposite ends of the spectrum. Good and bad. And together, these moments made up our lives. And whether we had more of one than the other, it didn't matter. Because that was the beauty of life. There was no predictable pattern. No guaranteed 50-50 split. Just a lot of random surprises (and maybe a little bit of fate).

My life had too many of the 'ugly bad' moments. And being stuck in the hospital with a brain tumour was one of them. I knew I dug myself too deep of a hole to climb out of this time. But I did not want to be the victim of my own crime. So, either someone had to come and rescue me, or I could continue digging even deeper until I reached a manhole.

I wasn't sure what fate had in store for me. Frankly, I wasn't sure if Max was my knight in shining armour. Or if there was a level lower than rock bottom. But I wasn't going to sit there and just wait for an answer that may seemingly never come. Whatever illness I had, I couldn't let it consume me.

I remembered feeling overwhelmed the first two years after my parents passed. I used to think that every day was a nightmare. But I mostly got over that hump. I guess you could say that I became slightly fire-resistant. However, it seemed as though I entered another nightmare. And it was discouraging that this one seemed a lot worse. How was that even possible? I wished to see the light in this dark path ahead, but at least I was still *living*. Maybe everything was actually grey. I cried enough yesterday. Today I was ready to face the music.

•••

As I inched closer to surgery day, I felt weaker by the minute. I wasn't sure if it was my nerves or a side effect from my glioma. The most frustrating moment was when I was too weak even to hold Jimi in my arms. I felt Jimi calling for me, so I got up from my bed one night to reach him. I tried to lift Jimi up, but I couldn't. My knees then buckled, and I plunged towards the floor, and everything swirled into darkness. It may seem counterintuitive, but we do heal when we're sleeping. The only downside was that rest did not fix *everything*. It only temporarily made us *feel* better.

After that night when I blacked out and started convulsing beside Jimi, Max stationed himself in my room to be my personal watchdog. I appreciated his kind gesture for taking care of me, but I felt terrible knowing that Max was slacking from med school even more than usual. He'd always been a slacker for lectures and practicum, but missing assignments and evaluations were a bit uncalled for. Even though I secretly enjoyed his company, I hated being his scapegoat.

Everyone, at some point in their lifetime, had been blamed for something that they didn't do, especially if they grew up with siblings. I was one of the fortunate souls that had no siblings. Only child. But I heard stories from Clara about how she always got blamed every time her little brother did something naughty. Like the time when he drew on the walls, stole snacks from Clara's lunchbox, or broke an expensive vase in the living room. More than half of the time, when her brother did something naughty, she wasn't even present. So, it seemed absurd to be blamed for something that wasn't even her fault.

But being an only child did not spare me from this callous blame game. I, too, was a victim of it. The problem with scapegoating was that it wasn't fair to the person being blamed. It was bad enough to get in trouble for doing something wrong, but when you haven't done anything wrong in the first place, it was even more difficult to accept the consequences. This totally would ruin anyone's self-esteem. Seriously. The other problem was that it encouraged the innocent victim to start acting out because they knew that they would be punished whether or not they misbehaved.

At school, I was always the 'butt of the joke.' I mean, every classroom had a class clown, Brainiac, and jock. But every classroom also had a class scapegoat. I always got picked on in class. For my clothes. My music. Even for getting perfect on a test. Sometimes when I looked back on my earlier years, I wondered how I survived so much verbal abuse. It came to a point where I was so afraid to do anything in the classroom because I feared that anything I did would get blamed. Being a scapegoat was not, by any means, a *fun* thing. I truly believed that my scapegoat experience totally messed with my self-esteem, making me afraid of ever being the centre of attention.

But just this once, I wasn't worried. Why? Because from what I gathered, Max was not the type of guy who would blame me if his position in med school was ever jeopardized. Though, I did feel *slightly* guilty for influencing his poor attendance habits.

•••

There were many times when I'd contemplated why Max enrolled in med school. Everyone dreamed. Some dreamed bigger than others. But becoming a doctor was a pretty big dream. It was a career. And I couldn't help but wonder why, even before we met, Max didn't take his schooling seriously.

Although I knew little about his past, I still believed that dreams were like promises, and that we had to be committed to them for a positive outcome. I remembered Max telling me about how his supervisor called him out for his tardiness. And it seemed ludicrous for Max to risk his entire career by spending time with someone who wasn't even of great significance. I mean, I could die today, and Max would be totally unaffected. He may miss his free coffee at *Amore*, but I was positive he would get over me very quickly. I was *just* a friend. *I* may have been falling for him, but he had plenty of fish in the sea that wasn't disease-ridden.

The thought of dying made me cringe. I wondered, do patients die on the operating table for brain surgery? Did anyone ever come out of an operation braindead? I was scaring myself for no apparent reason, and it absolutely sucked to be stuck in this mindset. I mumbled to myself and stared at my willow tree for serenity.

In two more sleeps, I would be under the knife. Although I would have appreciated Aunt Brenna's company just as much, Max's presence was better than having 'mother bird' hovering over me like a newborn baby. I'd wondered if Max just pitied me, felt responsible, or was just being a good friend. There was no clear sign of which feeling was stronger. Or maybe Max came to support me for *all* those reasons. Frankly, Max *was* my pillar of emotional and mental support. Seeing him kept me sane. And talking with him made me feel better. Though, I felt so selfish to want him here with me.

Although all the doctors and nurses were focused on me. My condition. My vitals. Me. I'd realized that I wasn't the only one fighting. We all were. Sometimes I wondered if it was more stressful on the outside, looking in. I worried about Max. I really did.

•••

Brain surgery posed several risks because my brain sort of controlled how the rest of my body worked. Doctors don't just open up your head simply because they can. I mean, I had a ginormous tumour that was likely cancerous. There was only one direction to move now, and that was forward.

According to the pamphlet Dr. Babinski left me, the dangers of brain surgery, apart from allergic reactions to anesthesia, were coma, impaired speech, and vision or coordination loss. But those weren't the worse of them all. The risk I feared the most was memory loss. I couldn't bear the thought of forgetting my parents, Aunt Brenna, or even Max. It pained me to know that I could wake up post-surgery and be a complete dud living inside my body. It meant that I would be *alive*, but not actually *living*. The thought was insanely disturbing. And all my life I'd thought death and clowns were the most disturbing things I could *ever* encounter. Boy, was I wrong.

Whenever I was stressed or felt that my life was a little out of control, I get very organized. I do my laundry. I clean my house. I would sometimes even arrange my homework into neat little piles on my bedroom floor, which was an utterly pointless exercise because I immediately would vacuum the floor right away after.

When life got crazy, I tried to impose order in whatever way I could. I just felt better knowing that there was something in my life that I could control. But, being stuck at *G&C* meant that I didn't have many organizational options. So, instinctively, I felt even more stressed about the whole procedure.

"Emily, what's wrong?" Max asked.

"Nothing. Just go back to bed. I'm just thinking," I exclaimed.

"Can't fool me, Miss McGregor. Spill the beans, or I'm going to tickle it out of you," Max chanted.

"You dare!" I taunted.

"Try me," Max smirked.

I gave in and admitted to Max what was on my mind. "I'm stressed."

"Tell me something I don't know. It's more than just that. There's something else bothering you," Max said softly.

"Caught me red-handed. Gosh, you got to stop reading me like a book, Max," I confessed.

"Well, it's one of my many talents. And I like the book that I'm reading," Max winked.

"I'm worried about forgetting the things that mean the most to me. This glioma has already taken my music away from me. I'm not even strong enough to hold Jimi anymore. What if I lose all my childhood memories? What if I can't even remember you!" I blurted out before I covered my mouth, realizing what I just said out loud.

"Emily McGregor. How could you forget a face like this?" Max said, posing with a cocky grin. "I bet you can never forget this mug. I'm sorry to disappoint you," Max joked. "You know, even if you do forget everything, that's ok. We don't keep our fondest memories in our minds. We keep them in our hearts. You're never going to forget how to read music notes or your family. It's brain surgery, not heart surgery. And trust me, if you ever do forget any of those things, then I'll just have to work extra hard to help you remember. Promise?"

I smiled and spoke. "Promise."

After a long awkward silence, I asked, "Umm, Max? Can you do me a favour?"

"Sure, shoot," Max said with a thumbs up.

"Can you get me a box of double chocolate chip cookies and a Tupperware container?" I asked.

"Umm, sure? Got a sweet tooth, don't you? Or maybe the hospital food just doesn't cut it?" Max laughed.

We turned to face each other and chimed in unison, "Absolutely bland, but we got to eat it whether we like it or not!" A loud chuckle escaped both of our mouths.

"So, a box of cookies, eh?" Max asked with another chuckle.

"It's not what you think. I just need to organize," I insisted.

"Organize?" Max asked, confused.

"Yes, organize. When I get really super stressed about something, I like to organize," I explained.

"Ok, I don't see how organizing can be stress-relieving, but to everyone their own. I'll get you your cookies if you can promise me that you'll come over to my house and organize my room the next time you're feeling stressed. Okay? It'll save me from doing it myself. My Mom's always on my case about keeping my room clean," Max chuckled.

"Mr. Miller, making promises again, are we? Don't start making more than you can keep," I grinned.

"Well, you need something to look forward to when you get discharged from here. So, do we have ourselves a deal?"

I shook Max's hand, and he gave me a tight squeeze. He then grabbed his jacket and raced out the door.

We spent the afternoon stacking double chocolate chip cookies to see who could stack the tallest tower. After, I counted the number of chocolate chips on each cookie and sorted them by size and chips in the Tupperware container. Max snagged a couple while I was organizing, so each time I reorganized the stash, it got progressively smaller. By the end of the day, 99% of them ended up in Max's stomach. But I managed to eat the last one. Delicious.

•••

After being stuffed in the room all day, I desperately wanted some fresh air. So, I asked Zita if it would be alright for Max to take me outside for a short stroll around the perimeter.

"Not for too long," Zita said. "And you better be back before it's dark."

"Yes, madam!" Max exclaimed, saluting Zita like he was some sort of military soldier in training receiving orders from the commander.

Max helped me to my wheelchair, and he grabbed Jimi before we headed out the door. We wheeled past the fountain and towards the statues nestled in the cluster of willow trees. It was so peaceful here. The gentle whistling of the willow leaves rustling in the wind put my mind at ease.

I breathed in a deep breath of fresh air and closed my eyes. I imagined myself back at home, jamming with Max. I had Jimi, and he had El. I had no wheelchair. No bandages. And I looked strong, holding Jimi on my own. I sighed loudly. Oh, how I wished for those days.

"Max, do you mind if we sit under my willow tree?" I asked.

"Your willow tree?" Max questioned.

"Ya, the one that I can see right out from my window. The lonely one that's away from this cluster," I explained.

"Of course," Max said as he started to wheel towards the willow tree I was seeking.

We stopped under the lonely willow tree and sat in the shade as we watched the children running around in the field. I smiled at the sight of laughing children and wiped a tear from my eyes. Suddenly, the chorus of the Backstreet Boys' "Show Me the Meaning of Being Lonely" repeated in the back of my mind. My eyes felt moist and a tear trickled down my cheek.

"Max, can you do me a favour? Can you grab my Moleskine in the pouch underneath my wheelchair," I asked.

"Ya, sure thing," Max said as he peered into the pouch and pulled out my black Moleskine notebook. He passed it to me, and

I flipped it opened, searching for a song. I flipped page after page until I found what I was looking for. A lot of my songs were dark. I mean, I mostly wrote about loss and adolescent troubles, but I did have a couple of motivational tunes.

I looked up to Max and pointed to the page I was on. He smiled, knowing that I was permitting him to look into my private notebook.

"I've been working on this recently but don't know how it sounds. Do you mind playing Jimi so I could sing it?" I asked.

I lifted my Moleskine from my lap and handed it to Max. He nodded and smiled.

"This is like gold Emily. Wow, you never cease to amaze me. Even when you're ill, you still find the energy to make music. It would be an honour to play this with you," Max exclaimed.

Max picked up Jimi and started to play the melody as I sang along. I closed my eyes to indulge in this moment. It was really special to give my music life.

♪♫♪♫♪♫♪

Always running, training for life's race

Always climbing, over hurdles I face

And when the sun goes down, I'm left in the dark

But it doesn't mean, it doesn't mean that I've lost my mark

Got one life, blessed with all this love

Feel no pain, if I keep looking up

My fighting spirit is what keeps me alive

Like a bullet train, I'm flying in this ride

This race, I'll keep running

This life, I'll keep fighting

And if I had enough, I would just stop and say

Be bold, be strong, be brave

Just hold on for one more day

'Cause nothing else matters

'Cause nothing else matters

♪♫♪♫♪♫♪

After we finished my song, I opened my eyes and realized that a small crowd formed around us underneath the willow tree. I started to get really nervous. There was like a gremlin inside, loudly screaming at me to run away. The eyes of what seemed like thousands of children burned through my skin like kryptonite. I desperately wished to be covered by Harry Potter's invisibility cloak or to be flying in Wonder Woman's invisible jet just to get out of here.

Max! Why didn't he stop me when an audience began to form? Though, I secretly blamed myself for keeping my eyes closed the whole time. I felt like hyperventilating.

I was on the edge of a panic attack. I felt so embarrassed that someone else other than Max or Aunt Brenna got a taste of my music. My words. My thoughts.

At this very moment, I felt so very small. I closed my eyes even tighter. My mind filled with water. I had that panicky feeling of being underwater in a dream and thinking that I was drowning, but I was actually breathing just fine.

A single applaud broke the silence. Soon, more people applauded. And eventually, everyone cheered. I looked up to see what all the fuss was about. Everyone was smiling around us. But how? Why?

Then, a family screamed, "Encore! Encore! Encore!" I was shocked at the positive reception. This was impossible. Max had a huge smile on his face as he looked down at me, patting my shoulder to acknowledge a job well done.

Max turned to the crowd and bowed. "Thank you, everyone. This beautiful song was written by my best friend, Emily. This amazing lady here was the brains behind all of this. Let's give her another round of applause," Max cheered as the crowd followed.

"Max, stop it," I whispered, quickly grabbing my Moleskine out of his hands. I was not ready. Not today. Not ever.

Max was a bit disappointed that I didn't want to relish in the spotlight. After all, he did tell me back at GMC that sometimes 'all we needed was an audience.' But Max also didn't want to make me feel too uncomfortable the day before my surgery. So, he thanked everyone again and ushered them to leave.

"Thank you, Glenwood citizens. Show's over. Thanks for stopping by," Max said, waving to the crowd.

As the crowd began to dissipate, my breathing slowed to a more normal pace. We sat together for a couple more minutes of silence before Max wheeled me back into my room.

•••

That evening, Zita wheeled me to the MRI room, where I met with Dr. Lancaster. She began affixing these small stickers that looked like white doughnuts on my scalp. It didn't hurt or anything. They were painless. I just felt like an idiot having stickers on my head.

"What are these for?" I asked, confused.

"We need to get an MRI scan with these stickers before the surgery," Zita explained.

Dr. Lancaster turned to me and continued the explanation, "These stickers here are called fiducials, and we actually need them on you to create a 3D map of your head."

"Why do you need that?" I asked.

"During surgery, this 3D map would help Dr. Babinski navigate through your brain. Your head isn't labeled like the pictures you see in a school textbook. Doing this will ensure that we can safely find our way around your brain and precisely locate the tumour. It's like a GPS system for your head," Dr. Lancaster clarified.

"Okay, but can I take them off after. I feel like an idiot," I said, biting the corner of my lip.

"We will remove them once your operation is complete. You cannot shower or wash your hair tonight. We need to keep them in place, understand?" Dr. Lancaster insisted and gave me a stern look.

"Understand," I said quietly.

I knew that fashion shouldn't have been high on my priority list at the hospital, but that didn't mean I had to sacrifice my personal hygiene. Boy, why was everything against me?

It was like a lightbulb went off in my head. Now it made sense why Zita reminded me to shampoo thoroughly this morning. I remembered that she gave me a special soap to wash the rest of my body with. It had the acronym CHG on the packaging, but I thought it just meant 'Children's Hospital in Glenwood.' Was I stupid enough to make such an assumption? Clearly, the longer this *monster* of a tumour stayed inside my head, the more brain cells I was going to lose.

Medical names for everything were always so long and complicated. It was like scientific names for plants and animals. Almost like understanding a completely different language. I skimmed through Max's textbook before, and even he said it would take years to memorize every single one. It seemed like medical practitioners had to be both a linguist and an etymologist because trying to pronounce some of these words was more difficult than the English language. I guess that was why so many acronyms were used to avoid errors when providing verbal instructions or written prescriptions.

I wished I carefully reviewed the brain surgery pamphlet Dr. Babinski gave me earlier in the week. If I did, then I wouldn't be so upset right now.

The thing is, I hated dirty hair. I had those lazy days when all I did was lounge around in the house, sleep in, and binge watch Netflix shows without ever leaving my room. My hair held excess sebum, and a day's worth of grime collected on my scalp easily. It was like double-sided tape. Everything just stuck to it. And it was absolutely disgusting. Plus, all that excess debris meant itching and scratching and then dandruff-like flaking. Ugh. Luckily, I didn't get many visitors, and Max already left for the day. I was going to look downright ugly tonight, and I couldn't do anything about it.

I was so distracted with the whole no hair washing or showering fiasco that the MRI scan felt like a breeze this time around. Or maybe the third time was a charm. I wasn't sure. But I was hoping that I never had to test that theory out again because I was tired of being forced to stay still for several minutes, even if my life depended on it.

I now fully appreciated the Queen's guards at Buckingham Palace that were trained to remain unflinched despite everything from extreme weather to screaming abuse a few inches from their faces. Respect. I read about how they technically were permitted to move and, in certain circumstances, even react to hecklers, but still, what they did took discipline.

•••

It was D-day at the *G&C* neurology department. Aunt Brenna took the day off and was with Max in my room. I felt very tired and wished to still be sleeping. Admittedly, I fantasied about just falling into a coma or contracting schizophrenia so I could leave the real world behind. I'd tried to funnel my feelings into music. It would certainly make for some bleak subject matter, but at least it would help me find some peace inside my chaos. Alan Walker's "Faded" was on repeat in my head. I pinched myself and wondered if the *monster* running wild inside of me was just a fantasy.

I kept my eyes closed, but I felt their presence. Max paced in circles around my bed while Aunt Brenna methodically tapped her hand on her lap. Everyone was nervous. If sleeping meant that I could avoid the inevitable, then I would sleep for a thousand more years. I refused to open my eyes today. But I knew that I had to bite the bullet and face the music. This was the moment. My moment. And today, whether I liked it or not, I was the star of the show.

Aunt Brenna saw me flinch, but I turned my back towards her and pretended to still be sleeping. "Rise and shine sugar plum," Aunt Brenna cheered.

I knew instantly that she drank too many cups of instant coffee. That horrible combination of poor sleep and high caffeine intake had the power to make just about anyone hyper and perky. Instant coffee was one of those 'last resort' coffees. It was like poison to coffeeholics. I could tell you with 100% certainty that if you drank any brand of instant coffee, it would taste like a stale, blank, water-downed version of the fresh stuff. In short, it just tasted awful.

Now truth be told, Keurig brewing systems and powdered

coffee stick packs were found in almost every office or home across North America. Honestly, we even had one in our home. But despite its popularity, only second to traditional drip coffee pots, this sort of coffee tasted at best mediocre. The problem with instant coffee was that by the time the coffee was made, the coffee had already begun going stale. Think about it. The coffee had been grounded days, weeks, or possibly years before you actually would drink it. So, it lost a lot of its nutty, irresistible smell and taste.

Don't get me wrong. I'd drank probably hundreds, maybe thousands, of pre-grinded coffee that was packed into little vacuum-sealed pods or sticks. But it didn't seem justified to sacrifice taste for convenience.

The grinding process immediately exposed the beans to oxygen, which zapped the true flavour and fresh aroma of the coffee bean. Any barista would recommend brewing coffee shortly after grinding the beans. Just ask André. He taught me that good things in life should never be rushed, including a tasty cup of coffee. Making the perfect cup of coffee was an art. The perfect water temperature, brew time, grind, and brew method were the things that really made coffee deliciously irresistible. Even I haven't perfected the art yet. If it were *that* easy, I wouldn't still be going to *Amore*.

"Aunt Brenna, can you not be so excited? You drank all the instant in the staff lounge, didn't you?" I fussed.

"Sorry, Em. You know, when I'm nervous, I start acting this way," Aunt Brenna confessed. She turned to Max and continued.

"I may be a nurse, but that's my niece going under the knife in a couple of hours."

Max just stood there in the corner of the room. He stared out the window, silent. So, I reverted my gaze to the window to look at my willow tree with him. There was a small nest cradled on one of the limbs of the willow tree. A mother robin was sitting in its nest of grass, lined with mud, watching over her eggs. The robin family chose an excellent tree for its home. There was decent shade, and whenever the wind blew through its branches, the musical sounds were no finer.

Willows were beautiful trees, known as the tree of immortality because of their ability to regrow from a fallen branch in moist grounds. I felt a bit better knowing that this willow tree was watching over me. Maybe Max felt the same way too.

"Good morning, beautiful," Zita cheered, clapping her hands excitedly.

"Hi, Zita. You look beautiful, as always. But I don't feel very pretty today. My hair is a mess. I smell like trash. And I feel absolutely terrible. I look like some worn-out ragdoll with buttons on my head," I sulked.

"No one is judging. Don't be silly. We are just going to get some bloodwork done before your surgery. If your family here can give us some space," Zita said softly as she ushered Aunt Brenna and Max to the far corner of the room.

Zita worked quickly, drawing blood and checking my pupils. She then gave Aunt Brenna and Max a thumbs up before leaving the room. The nurses at *G&C* were amazing. I guess they only hired the best. I mean, Aunt Brenna was one of them, and she was amazing at her job too. Although Zita was not as talkative as Mabel, she was very attentive to detail. There were many nights when she brought me an extra pillow or a cup of water during her evening rounds. She knew exactly what I needed before I requested it. She was like an angel.

•••

The silence in the room was killing me. I knew everybody enjoyed a little bit of peace and quiet from time to time, but the room was so silent that I could hear A, B, and C snoring next door. The quieter the room, the more things we could hear. I could hear my heart beating rapidly and my stomach gurgling loudly. I felt like an astronaut in an anechoic chamber because *I* became the sound.

"Ahh!!!" I screamed, pulling at my hair and burying myself under my pillows. Immediately, Aunt Brenna and Max turned in my direction.

"Emily dear, it's okay. Everything is going to be okay," she repeated reassuringly.

"This is just torture. There is nothing more that I can do but sit here until doomsday. This is just so horribly depressing," I sulked.

Max turned away from the window and walked up to me. He held out a pinky finger and winked, "Come on, Emily, hold out your pinky finger," Max insisted.

"Why would I do such a childish thing?" I scoffed.

Max looked at me as I kept my arms folded and all my fingers hidden.

"Because I want you to remember that no moment lasts forever. I know you're scared now. Who wouldn't be? I admit that I'm probably just as scared as you are. Maybe more if that is possible. But we can never lose hope that better days will come. Promise yourself that you'll believe it. I know that you're not destined to leave any of us yet," Max said inspirationally.

I slowly unraveled my arms and held out my pinky finger. I put on a weak smile and responded, "Promise."

"Promise," Max said and smiled back.

Aunt Brenna was wiping tears away before she barreled in to give us both a huge bearhug. "That was beautiful, Max. I should refer you to the counseling department in the palliative care unit. You're the right man for the job," Aunt Brenna said, proudly patting Max on the back.

"Ah, thanks, Ms. McGregor," Max said uncomfortably.

"Just Brenna. Just call me Brenna. We're all family now, Max," Aunt Brenna smiled.

"Ah, sure," Max said nervously.

"Well, I'm going to freshen up in the ladies' room. Don't have too much fun without me lovelies," Aunt Brenna cheered as she strutted out the room.

Our pinkies remained interlocked together for a couple more minutes. For this brief moment, everything felt right, so I closed my eyes to saviour it a bit longer.

When Aunt Brenna returned, Max entertained us with some

stand-up comedy, and just before ten, Zita came in to prepare me for my surgery. I got up slowly from my bed as Max helped me into my wheelchair. I instinctively grabbed his hand before he let go of me. Max squeezed back gently and nodded. Aunt Brenna kissed my forehead and told me that she'd pray for a successful surgery.

My Aunt was certainly not classified as the religious type, but for many non-believers, it was an instinctive response to a crisis, and this was their way of feeling *better*. It was kind of like an insurance policy. Was it superstition, or was it something more real? This was all a mystery. But many people were driven to pray at some point in their lives, even if they aren't religious, because it was their way of reaching out. It was inspiring to believe that everything in life could change if we just believed.

•••

Max hummed the tune of Sia's "Unstoppable" as I exited the room; the inspirational tune echoed down the hallway as Zita wheeled me towards the elevator. My palms were so sweaty, and I was shivering in fear. I suddenly felt chills down my spine, and I shuttered when we approached the surgery room.

Zita transferred me to the stretcher. I closed my eyes and kept my fingers crossed for good luck. I muttered to myself, "I believe. I believe," as the neurosurgeons filled the room and surrounded me.

I looked around the room to see if there was anyone I'd recognized. It was hard to distinguish their faces since everyone was wearing surgical caps, face masks, and visors. But I saw Dr. Babinski in scrubs. He gave me a wink.

The anesthesiologist placed a breathing tube into my windpipe, and Dr. Babinski explained that they would be monitoring my heart rate, blood pressure, breathing, and oxygen levels during the surgery. Dr. Babinski introduced the rest of his crew to me before the anesthesia was administered. I couldn't speak with the tube down my trachea, so I gave them all a thumbs up.

"Now, Emily, you are going to count backward from five. Once you reach one, you will be asleep. All you have to do is dream peacefully while I remove that little bugger inside your noggin. Can you do that for me?"

I gave him another thumbs-up despite being extremely nervous.

"Great, I'll see you soon, Emily," Dr. Babinski said.

I closed my eyes and started to count in my head, "Five. Four. Three."

Suddenly, I felt my head spinning, and my breathing slowed down. It was like I was falling asleep fast. I continued to count, "Two. One."

And just like that, there was a sudden pop of darkness that enveloped me. My breath quickened in fear as I plunged deeper into the darkness. The bright lights that shone down on the operating table dimmed. My world turned to night, and there was silence.

Chapter Sixteen

Brain tumours were like fractious children. Even experienced neurosurgeons found them difficult to remove because of the sensitivity of the brain and proximity to critical functioning components. Also, many types of medication could not cross the blood-brain barrier, which added a new layer of complexity to the whole procedure.

Max taught me a very valuable lesson. There was always some *good*—albeit how minuscule or insignificant—in any *bad* situation. Brain surgery was a complicated process, and surgeons, while being as careful and thorough as possible, had to treat each surgery on a case-by-case basis. However, the *good* for me was the location of my tumour. Since it was positioned on my frontal lobe, surgeons could do more than just a biopsy. They were able to remove as much of the tumour as possible during the same procedure.

•••

The surgery lasted just over six hours, but the effects of the general anesthesia made me feel like I haven't slept in years. Technically, general anesthesia was a medically induced coma, not sleep. The drugs rendered me unresponsive and unconscious, but, in theory, I was *awake* through the whole operation but immune to pain. That would explain why it felt like I slept for only one hour despite sleeping well over eight.

I woke just under three hours post-surgery to a sore throat, likely due to the breathing tube. Everything seemed hazy and woozy, my head spun uncontrollably, and I had no idea where I was. For a moment, I felt like I was on a two-minute, eighteen-second rollercoaster ride that soared through five inversions at speeds up to 150 kilometres per hour. I moved up and down, creating a unique combination of vertigo and thrills. The combination that made this rollercoaster ride, not for the faint of heart. And almost instantaneously, I felt an involuntary, forceful push from the inside of me. I expelled the contents of my stomach, or at least whatever was left inside, as I haven't eaten anything solid for hours.

I gasped for air, and my heart, once quickly beating, now slowed in tempo. Tears streamed down my face; my body shivered like I was stuck outside in the Arctic without a winter jacket. I felt very weak and confused, covered in my own vomit. I looked around and saw nobody. My room was empty. I tried to call for help, but my voice was a faint whisper. My throat burned too much to utter even the slightest sound. I tried reaching for the call button, but I could barely move my body. My efforts were rendered useless, and I feared to discover what else was wrong.

I continued my visual exploration until I locked onto the willow tree out the window. I remembered staring at that tree with Max before surgery. I remembered Aunt Brenna tapping methodically by my bedside. I remembered *Glenwood High*, my friends, my room, Jimi. And even the damaged Gibson at the scene of my parents' car crash. I let out a huge sigh of relief. I was thankful that the side effects of my operation were minimal.

When I entered brain surgery, it was not a foregone conclusion that my complete memory bank would be spared. The deep gloom that had overshadowed me had been relieved by one single fact that I still remembered *everything*.

And in the quiet solitude of my room, I thought about how grateful I was for the amazing doctors at *G&C*. One thing was for sure. Wearing a white coat meant more than a symbol of professionalism and authority.

Most medical schools conferred these white coats on new students during a ceremony on day one of the program to mark the momentous start of their careers. To everyone else, it was *just* a uniform. And that was exactly how I felt before my experience at *G&C*. But their white coat was actually a 'coat of honour' that signified their devotion to a lifetime of servitude. To heal and protect the sick and vulnerable, no matter the cost. I had a new appreciation for medical practitioners. Max was lucky to be a part of this *family*.

•••

Fortunately, Zita came in to check on me half an hour later. I was covered in my own vomit and reeked of unpleasant aromas that were worse than stale horse manure. She gave me another gown to change into and swapped my stained sheets for fresh ones. I instantly felt better once the foul stench dissipated from the perimeter of my bed.

After the cleanup, I drifted off to sleep for real this time, and it was probably the best sleep I ever had since, well, *ever*. I felt very drowsy and sleepy post-surgery. I assumed it was normal because of the anesthesia and high dosage of painkillers. My cheeks felt swollen, and my head was sore. It was a bit counterintuitive to still have headaches post-surgery, but maybe it was normal. My head felt like a sumo wrestler was sitting on it.

Zita woke me a couple of hours later to take medicine. Before she handed over the meds, she asked me to take a few sips of water first to make sure I didn't have any swallowing problems. Luckily, I got the green light.

I stared at the many colourful tablets in my hand; I had no idea what each one was for. But knowing that I was already doped up on painkillers, a couple more drugs wouldn't do more harm. I was never the type to drink, smoke weed, or take ecstasy at parties. But drugs were like candy here at the hospital. If they condoned it, then the more, the merrier. Surely, this was just the beginning of my growing list of *candy*.

Zita explained that Dr. Babinski was going to visit tomorrow morning to discuss the details of my operation. Also, she encouraged me to sit upwards with the head of my bed raised to reduce swelling in my brain.

After she adjusted my bed, Zita continued explaining my next steps post-surgery. She said something about a physiotherapist stopping by to move my arms and legs while I laid in bed. I only heard half of what she was saying, but apparently, if I didn't move for a couple of days, then my muscles would stiffen, and I would run the risk of developing blood clots.

Zita continued listing things that I could and could not do. She definitely had everything memorized from repeating it so many times. The only thing I remembered was that she wanted me to stay 'as still as possible' during the first two days post-surgery. I wondered when I could start moving like a normal person again. I tried asking, but Zita couldn't hear my whisper.

Then, the most dreaded 'MRI' word popped up in conversation and I cringed. Just the thought of having to do another MRI made me shutter. I started to think that I always had claustrophobia but was just unaware of it until now. Not again! Although I was intrigued to know if my surgery was successful or not, I was not looking forward to being a sausage again. I made a mental reminder to not ask Aunt Brenna to organize a barbeque for the next two summers.

I wondered if I looked like Frankenstein. Maybe more like a mummy? If these bandages had to stay on 'til Halloween, then I just saved myself the hassle of thinking of a costume for myself this year. I instinctively lifted my hand up to my head but couldn't feel anything under the thick layer of bandages around it. My head started to hurt; I felt overwhelmed with all the information.

Suddenly, I began to panic with the thought that my sutures would burst from the overload of information. My head ached badly and I was scared about how fragile I'd become. I worried that I wasn't paying attention enough to remember everything that was *important*. Gosh, everything was 'important' when it came to anything medical. But it was times like this that I wished

Aunt Brenna was here to be my ears. Everything sounded scary.

Although Zita explained everything slowly and emphasized each word carefully, it was hard absorbing all the information. I pointed to my head and asked quietly, "You don't need to sugar coat it. I'm missing hair around my incision, right? Do I have to come back in and remove the sutures too?"

"Yes, and no, Emily. Yes, we had to remove some hair around the incision, but the sutures will dissolve on their own, so nothing you need to worry about. Just promise me that you won't scratch when you remove the bandages a couple of days later," Zita pleaded.

Honestly, I did not want to know how I looked like in the mirror right now. If I thought white doughnut stickers were idiotic, then I was certain that a random patch of missing hair on my head would look even more absurd. I was so tempted to scratch my wound because it was so itchy. It felt like an army of fire ants crawling into every crevice, crack, and pore. Well, like anything at the hospital, there was a slew of guidelines to follow. The worst part was that I was forbidden to scratch and pick at my wound once the bandages were removed. And, I couldn't wash my hair until the fourth-day post-surgery and could not use a hairdryer. I knew I had to control my obsession to scratch, but it was absolutely unbearable.

I considered ignoring Zita's head care guidelines but then reconsidered only because I wanted a super, speedy recovery. Though, I was bound to break several of them, maybe not intentionally, because my head didn't seem like it was all in the right place. Admittedly, I wasn't completely listening to Zita. It was hard to focus.

Zita wasn't normally this garrulous, but after her fifteen-minute lecture, she finally gave me some peace of mind. Afterward, Zita only returned quietly to record neurological observations on my alertness. I eventually fell asleep but woke to a bright light shined into my eyes.

"Sorry, Emily. I need to check if your pupils are reacting to the brightness. How are you feeling?" Zita asked.

"Sleepy. Alive," I replied tersely.

"How is the pain?" Zita reiterated.

"Bearable," I replied.

"Emily, could you give me a little bit more here," Zita pleaded.

"Sorry, Zita. It hurts when I talk. But, if you need to know, I really want to sleep," I whispered loudly.

Zita nodded with a frown, so I decided to give her a better answer. "I'm feeling a lot better than I expected. I honestly expected to forget the reason why I was even here in the first place, so I'm glad I still remember everything," I replied.

Zita nodded and smiled before she spoke, "I sent your Aunt and Max home after they received word of your successful operation. After brain surgery, you should rest in a quiet environment. I told them to visit in the morning."

"Thank you, Zita," I said with a smile.

Zita puffed my pillows and gave my shoulder a small squeeze before leaving my room. I chuckled at the fact that she said "quiet environment" because Zita was the one causing all the commotion. I closed my eyes again and drifted off to sleep.

•••

Aunt Brenna and Max were by my bedside come morning. I still felt tired, and my head ached, but I knew I just had to be patient. Time healed all wounds. And I was in no hurry to get up today.

"Hey," I said as I opened my eyes. Max's eyes lit up, and Aunt Brenna gave me a huge kiss on my forehead.

"I'm so happy to see you, "Aunt Brenna whispered, holding back her tears of joy.

"Ditto," I replied.

"Emily, why did Carl have a bandage on his ear?" Max asked.

"Who's Carl?" I responded, confused.

"I'm trying to make a joke here. Emily, play along," Max insisted.

"I dunno," I shrugged.

"Because he was ironing his shirts when his phone rang and picked up the iron instead of his phone," Max explained.

I chuckled slightly. Max continued. "But wait, here's the best part. Why did Carl have a bandage on his other ear?" Max paused for emphasis and then said, "Because the phone rang again."

I giggled. Then, I told Max to stop telling jokes, or I would laugh too hard and burst open my sutures.

Dr. Babinski entered the room a couple of minutes later and held a clipboard. He ushered Max to leave the room, as protocol.

Max reluctantly ducked out the door but slipped his baseball cap into my lap as he exited.

"Good morning, Emily. You are looking wonderful this morning. I'm sure Zita already gave you a run-through of this week's itinerary," Dr. Babinski exclaimed.

I frowned. Dr. Babinski responded, "Oh, don't give me that face. You should be happy to hear that I was able to remove about 95% of your tumour during the resection, and if everything goes well this week, then you'll be free to go home."

"Seriously!" I screamed excitedly.

"Yes, Emily. But you'll have to return to the hospital for routine treatment so we can properly manage your tumour. So, you're not scot-free just quite yet," Dr. Babinski explained.

Just the thought of being back in my own room, in my own bed, and in my own home was like heaven. I zoned out until Dr. Babinski mentioned the C-word. *Cancer.*

Cancer was one of those words no one wanted to hear. Even the nonmedical definition of cancer meant undesirable, destructive, and invasive. Those were all bad things. Clearly, cancer was not something for the faint-hearted. I shuttered as these thoughts swirled in my mind. The choice was obvious. I had none. I had to follow Dr. Babinski's plan of attack if I hoped to put a leash on the 5% of the monster that still lived inside my head. Gosh, my life sucked.

"Emily, the biopsy confirmed that you have anaplastic astrocytoma. AA is a grade III malignant brain tumour," Dr. Babinski said solemnly.

"What?" I shrieked.

"Let me explain this to you. There are millions of star-shaped brain cells called astrocytes that form the protecting tissue in your brain. This is exactly why people always ask if you can 'see the stars.' Technically they are not referring to what's above you in the night sky. But rather what is inside of you. Malignant tumours are cancerous, and if left untreated, they could, well, take over all the tissues in your brain. I removed most of it, so it isn't that much of a concern. Now, these cancers do not metastasize to other body parts, but they do grow very quickly," Dr. Babinski explained.

"So, you're basically saying that it's going to come back if I don't do anything about it," I asked to clarify.

"Unfortunately, yes. I would like to start you on treatment to shrink the remaining part of the tumour that I couldn't remove during surgery. Okay?" Dr. Babinski exclaimed with a loud, heavy sigh.

I gave him a stern stare and mirrored his reaction. I sighed, "I guess."

I felt betrayed. Surgery was supposed to fix everything. But my journey to recovery had just scratched the surface. I felt like I was standing at gunpoint, and the doctors held the trigger, only to have them pull when I least expected it.

I just came out of probably the biggest surgery I would ever have in my entire life, and now they were telling me that the surgery didn't fix everything! How? Was I still a ticking time bomb? Seriously! Was this for real? My head really hurt. Really.

And I felt absolutely miserable.

•••

Three days post-surgery, I was discharged from *G&C*. The day was bittersweet. I was happy to finally go home. The road to recovery was still a lengthy one. Maybe I could finally take a breather after the weeks of torment and anxiety. Aunt Brenna was, pretty understandably, kind of overwhelmed between her work and my surgery. She had her first mental breakdown since I was admitted to *G&C*. Fortunately, Aunt Brenna had André, so she was in good hands.

Max agreed to pick me up today at the hospital. I was fortunate to have his support. I still couldn't stay on my feet, so my new mode of transportation was via wheelchair. It sucked being disabled as I had yet to encounter a situation that was easier to accomplish because I used a wheelchair.

Although I was not bed-bound or confined indoors, extensive wheelchair use over the past few weeks caused thick calluses to form on my hands. But I didn't mind. At least it meant I could be mobile without having to wait for Aunt Brenna, Max, or Zita to bring me to the washroom. Being disabled meant that I had to work harder to increase my level of autonomy and independence. I wondered if I would ever get strong enough to overcome my extra limitations. Would Max and I still be friends if he assumed the roles of a caretaker? Although Max insisted that we were going to fight this together, I did not want to impose caretaking on someone I loved.

I was still bitter about the outcome of my surgery. Unfortunately, this was not a goodbye, but more like a 'see you later.' *G&C* was now a revolving door for me, and I was going to get very acquainted with oncology.

After mulling over it the past few days, I'd decided that I had to tell Max about what was going on. He caught a few bits and pieces here and there, but between naps and assessments, I had little opportunity to discuss my post-surgery situation with him. Until now.

I was certain Max was going to pry for details on the drive back to Aunt Brenna's. Though, I couldn't just lie about it. If I truly cared about Max, I had to tell him the truth, no matter how much it would hurt. It would have been selfish to keep it from him, especially if he'd shown his commitment to my battle. Anyway, the whole cancer thing meant radiation and chemotherapy. And it didn't take a genius to know that it meant losing my hair.

The difficulty of sharing a cancer diagnosis with friends and family was that it would have meant that I had accepted the reality. But I wasn't ready to *accept* something that I didn't want or didn't believe I had.

It was very common for people to experience denial of diagnosis shortly after receiving the shocking news. My mind needed time to adjust. But it was time that I didn't have. How could someone request for time to slow down when their days were outnumbered? It seemed almost counterintuitive. I tried to imagine the realities of my situation. I tried to settle into the idea of what it all meant. About how my life would change. And about how these changes would affect those around me.

The denial I felt was unwilful. I mean, it wasn't like I adamantly refused to 'face the facts,' although Aunt Brenna was 100% certain that I was just trying to make things difficult. She called it anosognosia. In Layman's terms, it meant someone who lacked the insight to understand their own condition. I'm sure if I looked up the word in the dictionary, I'd also see my name beside it.

I stared at the mirror in my room for quite some time. I simply didn't see what Dr. Babinski saw. Yes, I looked unwell with the bandages and IV wounds. But I didn't *look* like a cancer patient.

It was a silent killer. Apart from baldness being associated with cancer, there were no other clues that were visible on the outside that would make us believe that there was something wrong inside. Cancer, like death, did not discriminate. It knew no boundaries. It did not spare the young. And it did not forgive.

I wondered what I did in my past life that would make *cancer* hate me so much. I lost a lot of my trust in the medical system following the outcome of my surgery. I always thought doctors could fix everything if patients willingly cooperated. I also felt alone in this long and difficult battle.

But then I thought of Max. I remembered him blindly promising me to stay by my side. Our friendship already braved a couple of small storms, but was it ready for a hurricane? I was worried, though, about Max's reaction once I exposed the truth. Not everyone reacts well to the word 'cancer.'

Max had been my rainbow ever since we met. Mom used

to say, 'the greater the storm, the brighter the rainbow.' I was determined to abide by her words of wisdom. Cancer had already taken so much from me. It was my turn to fight back. I believed that when I could defeat cancer, whenever that was, my rainbow would be so bright that it would never fade.

•••

Max was waiting for me outside. His yellow Civic idled at the main entrance of the hospital. He texted me when he arrived, but there were some things I had to get done before leaving. I knew there was someone I had to visit. I stopped by room 55 in the ICU to hug my friend Anna.

"Knock, knock," I said as I appeared at the doorway of her room.

"Emily! I'm so happy to see you!" Anna exclaimed.

"I'm going home today. But I will be back for treatment," I explained, rolling into the room as I positioned myself by her bedside.

"Are you going to come to visit?" Anna asked as she tugged on the sleeve of my jacket.

"Of course! I got to bring George a friend to play with, so he doesn't feel so lonely when you're sleeping," I said with a smile.

"Yay! A new friend! What's its name?" Anna asked curiously.

"Lucas the Cactus," I said.

"Is he prickly?" Anna questioned.

"Nope. But he's super cute. He has tiny little dimples and a curly moustache. I called him yesterday, and he agreed to keep you both company," I exclaimed cheerfully. I looked at Anna and asked, "Did you ever watch Guardians of the Galaxy? Actually, maybe you are too young for that."

"I know what that is! I saw the trailers on YouTube," Anna said proudly before giggling.

"Well, Lucas is a bit like Groot. But less violent and more musical. Oh, and he doesn't just say variants of his name, like what all those Pokémon do. He should fit right in," I explained.

"Woohoo! I can't wait!" she screamed with excitement. While waving George in the air, she said, "Look, George. You're going to have a new friend soon. Miss Emily is going to bring us a new friend the next time she visits."

I smiled and pasted a drawing of Lucas the Cactus on her wall before leaving the room.

•••

If there was one thing my time at *G&C* taught me was to share our gifts with others. We all have a certain special gift inside of us. Each and every one of us had this special *something*. Some of us used it to make a living, while others locked it away. I was the epitome of the latter. But in any case, this gift was unique to us. No one else in the world had that *exact* same gift. Like a fingerprint.

My time with Anna, and my unexpected live performance under the willow tree, had made me realize that I ought to suck it up and just be brave enough to share my voice to the world.

My fear of sharing my talents with others went beyond my stage fright. My childhood traumas had left me with minimal confidence; I feared that I wasn't good enough. There were millions of songwriters and musicians out there, but what made me unique, different, or better. I knew that if we didn't stand out, then we would just blend into harmony.

Don't get me wrong. I still have those fears. That lack of self-confidence. It may never truly go away. But I'd never realized the *power* of my gifts until I saw the *smiles*. That moment when my presence brought someone happiness and hope. It only takes *one* person to change someone. Maybe that one person for Anna was me. Maybe it wasn't. But I felt super good doing it. Sharing with her my gifts. Being there for her with open arms.

And now, the more I thought about it, I actually felt pretty good under the willow tree too. I saw how happy the children were listening to my uplifting song. I saw the glimmer of hope in their parents' eyes.

Although I was embarrassed at the time, I'd realized that it was my words that brought pure ecstasy. If I just had the courage to face the world, I wouldn't need to look for an audience. Dad used to tell me that if my music had a powerful voice, my audience would naturally gravitate towards it.

Dad had tried endlessly to help me overcome my stage fright. He used to say, "To win over any crowd, you have to want to stand out. You need to suck the crowd into your music for them to feel it."

He was right. We are our own unique sound. Sometimes our

songs were similar and mixed well with others. Other times, our songs were completely different genres. Though, no song was exactly the same; each person played their own tune. And if we could figure out how to make ourselves shine and have that sort of effect on people. On our audience. Then we mastered it.

It was going to take a lot of practice to reach that stage in my life, but it was very encouraging to witness firsthand the power of my gifts. Sometimes in life, it was okay to stand out.

We only have a short time in our lives. And now, knowing that cancer lived inside of me, I was a ticking time bomb because time was working against me. I knew that it seemed a bit wasteful for anyone to just keep their gifts trapped inside. Why would I want to die with my gift unshared? It seemed like such a pity for such talent to go with me to my grave.

I looked towards the sky as I wheeled closer to the main entrance of *G&C*. It was like someone removed the covers I'd been hiding under all these years and turned my power button 'on.' I wasn't going to be one of those cancer victims who was jaded about their own self-worth. I wasn't going to be someone hiding in the shadows. And I wasn't going to put myself down by believing that I wasn't good enough to try. Time was ticking, but I still had *time* to change. If not now, then when?

Now more than ever, I was determined to get into *AMP* and to show the world what I got. I wasn't going to let cancer stop me from keeping my promises or from reaching my dreams. This *was* my dream. It was no longer just a promise to my parents but a promise to myself. I, Emily McGregor, had finally discovered my life's purpose. This was my *destiny*.

Chapter Seventeen

Max quickly ran up to greet me once I wheeled out from *G&C*. The wind brushed across my face; it was so refreshing. The sun felt warm on my skin, like the cozy feeling of being bundled up in a blanket on a cold winter day. But this time, it was an invisible blanket of celebration. I couldn't help but smile. This was absolutely marvelous, and I didn't want this feeling to end. I closed my eyes as Max wheeled me towards his Civic. I turned my face into the wind; I listened to the willow trees rustle in the background, muffling the loud chatter of laughing children.

Was this what a motorcyclist experienced when they road down an open road? The wind in their hair, escaping into the grandeur of the mountains and canyons. Was this the feeling of *freedom*? I was no longer imprisoned in the confines of *G&C* neurology or detained because of something I possessed inside. Perhaps the only way to understand freedom was to understand its opposite. Caged. Constricted. Confined.

I'd seen real prisons before in documentaries like *13th*, which was without a doubt one of the best Netflix prison documentaries out there. It differed from other films that were set in a prison setting because it didn't focus on life behind bars but rather the whole prison system. It was quite unsettling to watch, but as I recalled the series, I knew it was inappropriate to compare a hospital to a jailhouse.

I imagined being constrained to solitary confinement, like at a penitentiary where the country's worse criminals lived in a place of isolation and disparity. They were told exactly when to eat, shower, and sleep. Every moment of their lives was watched closely. That image alluded to a very powerful awareness that we were still free even in the hospital room.

Freedom had nothing to do with geography or physical boundaries. It resided in our minds, our emotions, and our hearts. Our conscience was unchained. Our thoughts were unrestrained. And our hearts were open to see and understand the world as what we wanted to believe. This *inner* freedom, or whatever you may call it, started within ourselves. So, if being diagnosed with cancer meant I could still dream, love, laugh and cry, then I was, and always had been, free. I guess my hospital experience really wasn't *that* bad.

•••

The ride back to Aunt Brenna's house was quiet. Max had the radio on low volume. It was on 97.3 K-Rock. He hummed to Lynyrd Skynyrd's "Free Bird." After the third song on the radio, he clicked it off and pulled over to the side of the road.

"Gosh, Emily, why aren't you talking to me? What's with the silent treatment? We're best friends, aren't we? Friends should be able to tell each other anything. What's going on in your head, Emily? I have feelings too, you know. I'm worried sick about you, and those doctors tell me nothing. This is just killing me," Max screamed out in frustration and anger.

"I'm sorry," I whispered. I couldn't bear to look at him. I didn't want to see how angry Max Miller looked like.

"You're sorry?" Max questioned while uttering other expressions of profanity under his breath.

"Max! It's not that easy, you know. I never asked to have what I have. I never asked for any of this," I cried.

"Asked? That's rich, considering that I never *asked* for any of this too! But you can't just expect me to sit here quietly and play dumb. I care about you, Emily. But I also don't like being left in the dark. How can I help you if you don't let me know what's going on? I know everything sucks now, but we can get through it together if you let me in. Say something other than you're sorry," Max yelled in frustration.

I took a deep breath and looked Max right in the eye. "Cancer. I have cancer. I—"

"Oh my," Max interrupted in shock. "Maybe I should have asked after I got you home," Max said apologetically.

Though Max was right. If he meant anything to me, I had to tell him everything, no matter how much it hurt. He wasn't just *any* friend. He was my *best* friend. And he'd been there for me ever since I got myself into this mess. I wanted to continue talking, but Max held out his hand for me to stop.

"Don't say anymore. I understand. You can tell me the rest when you're ready," Max said with a softer voice.

Max immediately moved back into gear and started driving again. His eyes were fixated on the road, but he seemed distracted. Like he was deep in thought. Max turned back on the radio, raising it to almost maximum volume.

I didn't say anything. I knew he had to drown out his thoughts with the world's second-best medicine, music. First, being laughter, of course, but now was not the time for that. It was hard to joke about something like cancer. Cancer just didn't understand humour.

Max didn't say a word until we pulled up onto Aunt Brenna's driveway.

"Let me get the door and prepare your wheelchair. Just wait here, okay?" Max said softly as his voice quivered.

I guess I'd found the answer to one of my biggest concerns. Max's reaction was not what I'd expected. I'd never seen Max that angry before. Although I had my fair share of curse words that found ways to escape my mouth from time-to-time, it was more like casual profanity. It was rare for me to swear in the company of family, friends, or colleagues. I used profanity more so as a way to mentally vent my anger without physically damaging any walls or hurting someone. But that display of flamboyant language in the car ride home was a far cry for help.

Max was angry. Really angry. And it was strange how one mention of the C-word instantly changed his entire demeanor. It seemed like his frustration stemmed deeper than his anger towards me. It was like he had roots that extended elsewhere that somehow interconnected back to us. Though, I wasn't certain. I closed my eyes to replay the turn of events. My head hurt from thinking too much. Cancer was a lot to digest for everyone involved.

•••

I was scheduled to return to *G&C* in two weeks to discuss my treatment plan with a neuro-oncologist. Dr. Babinski signed me up for chemotherapy and radiation treatment. Although most of my tumour was removed during surgery, he insisted that further treatment would ensure that the remaining mass in my head wouldn't grow back. I was doubtful that any of this could actually cure my cancer, but if I played sitting duck, then I would, more likely than not, be bumped back to square one once again. And trust me, I did not want to go back there. Ever.

I was loopy from the painkillers and steroids. I felt like all the seven dwarfs. Sometimes I was grumpy. Other times, I was dopey. But mostly, I was sleepy.

Dr. Babinski prescribed a medication called Decadron to relieve the swelling and pressure in my brain. The name of that medication just made me think of Geometry. I wasn't sure why.

I was still very weak and felt nauseous from time to time. Doped. Totally. But this wasn't a time to be all macho and not take my medication. Everything about my head just hurt, so there was no way I was going to opt-out of drugs. I took every one of them on schedule. But those drugs turned me into a hormonal, rage-filled beast. I had just as much acne as the number of minutes I slept. And I slept a whole lot. So, whatever was in the candy Dr. Babinski prescribed, well, this was definitely worse than PMS.

After two nights, I felt like I was coming down with a fever. Every time I shivered, it felt like it reverberated straight across my skull and deep down into the centre of my brain. I started wearing socks indoors and spent most of my day bundled up in my warm blanket. I'd found that the best way to control the pain in my head was to press a hand onto my head gently.

Aunt Brenna finally got out of her funk, but she went right back to the grind because her supervisor refused to grant her more personal days off. Fortunately, I was still in the sleeping stage of my recovery, so I was fine being alone at home.

I slept for days and could barely stay conscious for more than a few hours. For the most part, I fell asleep easily but woke probably every two to four hours throughout the night. Sometimes, I even had trouble returning to sleep. While at other times, I felt fatigued throughout the day.

For the first time, I actually appreciated Aunt Brenna's medical advice. I admit, I preferred it over Google, and I was glad she had the answers to my questions. Aunt Brenna assured me that everything I was experiencing was *normal* because it was my body's way of telling me to be patient. So, I kept reminding myself that rest healed all wounds and that I needed to stop and let my body heal. Honestly, it sucked wasting so much time sleeping instead of studying.

Although I had this new determination to 'study hard, play hard,' I had the attention span of a goldfish. I excused myself for not hitting the books or writing music. I listened to my body and stopped obsessing over schoolwork. Admittedly, I was embarrassed to be so lazy. I felt like a sloth. Everything just slowed down to a snail's pace once I got home.

Aunt Brenna eventually gave Max his own house key so he could let himself in to routinely check on me whenever she wasn't around. The thing about Max was that he was able to sweet-talk himself out of trouble any day. His uncanny ability to flatter the ladies meant that he got what he wanted more often than not.

It was so '*un-mom*-like' of Aunt Brenna to grant Max full access privileges. She ought to have trusted him enough not to be some bounty hunter because most parents were sensitive to letting boys into their daughter's room without supervision. It was not like I had the energy to do anything anyway, but having that level of trust was a *big* thing. I was glad Aunt Brenna liked Max too.

Max was sitting at my desk, flipping through my class notes from last semester, when I woke.

"So, you're finally awake, sleepyhead. Who takes a six-hour nap during the day? If you slept any longer, then I would have called Prince Charming to break your sleeping spell. And then charge you for the long-distance fees," Max laughed.

"Ha, ha. Very funny," I said sarcastically.

"If you keep this up, I'm going to have to call you Sleeping Beauty. Though, I prefer watching you sleep than listening to my prof's lectures that put me to sleep," Max joked.

"What? You were watching me sleep for the full six hours?" I asked, shocked.

"No, two. You could have at least given me your Wi-Fi password so I would have other options apart from watching you snore," Max chuckled.

"Max!" I shouted.

"And might I add, you bellow even louder than an elephant's

horn. The doctor should have checked if there was something wrong with your nose," Max snickered.

My face turned red; I blushed with embarrassment. I guess we were now *even* since we've heard each other snore.

"Sorry, Max. You know you don't have to keep coming over if you're busy. You got to keep up with your studies no matter how much you despise it. I'm getting better day-by-day. You can just call or something. I'm fine, really," I said.

"You know I'm just kidding. Loud snoring is completely healthy. It's nothing to be ashamed about. It's not like you pass toxic gas in your sleep. That's by far the worst. Anyway, I probably howl like a hyena in my sleep, so who's to judge," Max said, raising his arms in defeat.

"Sorry. I just don't know what else to say, but sorry," I sighed.

"You can say anything, BUT *sorry*. Okay, Emily? Just stop thinking all of this is somehow your fault. You don't need to apologize," Max said sternly.

"But—" I responded. Max interrupted me and raised his eyebrows. He puffed out his chest and proudly walked to the centre of the room to face me.

"So, since you're not letting me borrow your laptop to watch Netflix, it's time for me to offer you some entertainment. Are you ready for some Dad jokes? They are so bad and so corny that it'll make you cry in laughter because they are so awful. If you hated puns before, you'd love them now. These jokes are so annoying that I guarantee it would make even the brainless smile," Max said with a wink.

"Max, cancer is no laughing matter. It's not funny. It's terrifying. I'm just not in the mood for your jokes today," I huffed.

"Just play along, okay, Emily?" Max whispered as he continued with his comedic showdown.

I knew what Max was trying to do. He was trying to treat my cancer with the world's best medicine. Laughter.

"What kind of music do mummies listen to?" Max paused for dramatic effect before he spoke. "Wrap music."

"Oh gosh, that was just terrible," I chuckled.

"What kind of hat does our brains love wearing most?" Max asked.

I just stared at him, confused. Dad jokes were usually obvious, but my brain wasn't registering this one. I shrugged my shoulders and nodded so he could give me the answer.

"The thinking cap," Max laughed.

"Okay, you got me," I said, laughing.

"Oh, here's my best one. What do you call an epic battle between two starfish?" Max questioned. He looked at me with a knowing nod and yelled out, "Star Wars!" while pretending to hold a lightsaber.

"Seriously," I smirked, "Max, please. If I keep laughing like this, I'm going to tear back open the hole in my head. This is too much," I said, pleading for him to stop his comedic act.

It was true. Laughter really was the best medicine. I felt so much better after Max's impromptu stand up comedy act. Even in the most difficult times, a laugh or a smile could go a long way to making us feel better. Nothing worked faster or more dependably to bring my mind and body back into balance than a good laugh. With so much power to heal and renew, the ability to laugh was easily the best resource for surmounting life's problems. Best of all, it was free, fun, and with Max here, easy to access. I wondered where Max learned all his material from. Max was definitely a multi-talented man. He wore many hats, not just one for music.

Max walked around my room, pacing in circles. Then he stopped in front of my bulletin board and stepped back to take in the decorations in my room.

"Nice wallpaper. Have you been working on it for a while?" Max asked, pointing to the colourful collection of paper airplanes pinned to all four walls of my bedroom.

I'd realized that this was the first time Max was in my room long enough to take in the décor. And I was certain he remembered the paper airplane I hid from him that time at *Amore*. I smiled and took a deep breath. I guess I had some explaining to do.

"Those are my songs," I said.

"All of them? That's a lot of songs, Emily McGregor. You never cease to stop amazing me. You're something else, aren't you," Max said, surprised.

"I write a lot. I've been writing for two years already. You see, I have this fear of being on the stage performing. But I like writing music. There's this special bond I feel when I put pen to paper. Each song is linked to a moment in my life. An emotion I felt. Or something I saw. It's nothing really. I just like posting them on my wall. So I don't forget them. I think a part of me believed that I could one day get over my stage fright and bring life to these songs for the world. I just haven't gotten the guts to do it yet,"

"I figured this much when you panicked under the willow tree that day. Believe me when I tell you that you got good stuff. You should let these paper airplanes soar one day. These songs deserve to see the light of day," he said with a smile.

Max started looking more closely at the paper airplanes on the wall. He tried opening some of them, but I yelled at him for trying to sneak a peek.

"Hey!" I yelled out.

"Can't a guy see some of his best friend's music? I'm just wondering if you wrote any about me," Max said defensively.

"One day doesn't mean *now*, Max," I exclaimed.

•••

Later that day, Max came in with some painkillers. I was getting ready for a nap and assumed that he would leave once I swallowed the medication. But Max just stood there in my room. He looked lost. Like there was something he wanted to say.

I was fighting with myself to stay awake. Then, Max took a deep breath and walked towards my bed. He sat at the far corner and took off his baseball cap, running his fingers through his hair. He grinned and just stared at me in silence. I raised my eyebrows, confused with his sudden seriousness.

Max let out another loud sigh and said, "My Dad had it. Cancer.

In his lungs. Died about ten years ago. He smoked that old pipe like it didn't matter." Max paused to compose himself before he continued. "Smokers have that distinctive hacking cough, so it wasn't unusual to hear Dad coughing whenever he lit up a joint. But one day, he couldn't stop coughing, and then he had trouble breathing. Mom called the ambulance. He never returned."

"Sorry, I didn't know," I whispered quietly. "When you mentioned your Dad left, I thought he walked out on you guys," I explained.

Intuitively, I tried getting up to reach for his hand to comfort him, but my body didn't cooperate. I just sat there in disbelief.

"I don't know exactly what you're going through right now, but I know it sucks. It sucks big time. I know I'm years away from becoming a doctor. And I feel so helpless. I couldn't help my Dad when he got it. And I can't help you now either. What's the point of becoming a doctor if you can't help the people you love? I should be the one saying 'sorry.' All I can offer you now is empathy. Without empathy, nothing works. But I don't think being empathic is good enough to cure you," Max sighed.

"And that's all I'm asking for. I'm not expecting any miracles. You're already doing so much for me. You just don't know it yet. You know what spreads faster than cancer, Max?" I asked.

"What could spread faster than cancer?" Max replied, confused.

"Fear. And I just don't want to fight this alone," I admitted.

"Umm, Emily? You're not alone. You got me, Aunt Brenna, Jimi. I'm sure André is totally in too. And if that's not enough for you, I can find more supporters to cheer you on, but it may not be genuine. It's not strength in numbers. It's strength in here. And here," Max said, pointing to my head and my heart.

I smiled. Max was absolutely right.

•••

After the first week since my return home, my bandages were finally removed. My head looked like the aftermath of a nuclear warzone. There was matted blood in my hair, weird scabs on my scalp, empty patches at ground zero, some bruising, and stitches. My head itched like the time I had chickenpox when I was eight. Worst part. I couldn't pick at it. I wished I could put the bandages back on so it would be less tempting to itch. And as gnarly and frustrating as all of that sounded, Aunt Brenna reminded me that it was very *normal* after brain surgery.

To my surprise, Max reacted quite well to my nasty, scabby looking head. He was never once grossed out by my head. At least he never showed it. Truth be told, I was relieved to know that someone in this world understood my fear of uncertainty in my cancer battle.

The crazy thing was that I could never for the life of me predict how anyone would react. I fully expected Max to walk out on me when he started spewing a year's worth of profanity in the car. But now I understood why the news of my cancer hurt Max so much. I guess cancer *could* hit someone more than once. Cancer truly was a deadly disease. It sucked.

It was times like these when I was fortunate that my social

circle was small. I only owed an explanation to two other people in my life, Clara and Rachel. But perhaps the two of them never noticed that I disappeared during the first half of the summer break. They never once contacted me in July. It was like they fell off the face of the planet.

Later in the week, I conjured up enough courage to call the two of them and invited them over to my house. I had them swear to never tell another living soul of my secret. My cancer secret. There was no way I was going to risk having Clara post something on Instagram without her understanding how private this matter was.

The day when they came over, they acted weird about the whole thing. It was a bit infuriating, but I didn't have the energy to go ballistic on them because, frankly, I had *bigger* things to worry about. They patted me on the shoulder before they left and wished me luck. Never did they offer to stand by my side in my fight to conquer cancer. With their lack of empathy, it was clear that Clara and Rachel just weren't cut out to be someone I could rely on in this fight.

•••

I regained more strength in my second week and had stopped relying on my wheelchair to go to the washroom. I actually had enough energy to walk around on my own, so I insisted that Max stop skipping his lectures and actually go to class. Max still came over often, and on days when Aunt Brenna had an early morning shift at the hospital, Max would sleepover on the couch in the living room.

Despite improvements in my mobility, stairs were a killer. I tried the other day and couldn't stay on my feet for the whole flight of stairs. Max had a meeting with his supervisor, and Aunt Brenna was at work. The doorbell rang, so I intuitively headed towards the door. I took maybe six steps down and had to stop for a fifteen-minute breather. I even tripped on the last few steps of those bloody stairs. Whoever was at the door obviously left by the time I actually made it down. It was quite pathetic. But I assured myself that my strength would eventually return. I just needed to be patient.

After that happened, I stayed in my room on most days to avoid any unnecessary injuries. The one plus to all of this was receiving a free pass from laundry and cleaning duties, which I admit was quite pleasant. Max was right, there was always some positives to every story.

Aunt Brenna made all my meals and labeled them systematically in the fridge so Max could easily reheat them whenever he was over. She even made an identical set on the shelf beneath just for Max. It was Aunt Brenna's way of showing her appreciation to Max for taking care of me. Most days, Max would have already eaten his share before I was awake to have mine. I was intrigued to know whether he enjoyed Aunt Brenna's infamous sandpaper pork chops. Sometimes I felt I was too hard on Aunt Brenna's cooking. Especially since she really was *trying*. Chef Peters actually gave her a B- on her chicken enchiladas last Tuesday.

Although I was on the road to recovery, I was still too weak to hold Jimi. Fortunately, the weeks of rest finally granted me enough strength to hold a pen in my hand. I felt happier being able to write my music again. Whenever I was awake, I either read my textbooks or turned to my Moleskine to songwrite. Music was therapeutic, and it helped calm my nerves whenever fear took over my mind. I thought out loud, singing as I tapped my pen on my notebook to stay in tune.

It was 5 a.m. in the morning, so frankly, I did not expect anyone to be awake. Plus, it didn't help that I was so focused on my Moleskine. Max stood at the entrance of my bedroom with a wide grin. He chuckled, and my head simultaneously moved towards his direction until our eyes met. Was Max standing there all along? I was a little embarrassed that he heard me, but I pretended not to be flustered about it.

"Looks like you're feeling much better today, Emily McGregor," Max exclaimed.

"Well, good morning to you too, Max. Don't you have class today?" I chuckled with an uneasy voice.

"That song was beautiful. Sing it for me again?" Max asked enthusiastically.

"Maybe another day," I said and smiled.

•••

The rest of the afternoon was quiet. Max left for practicum after we had lunch together. So, I took another nap since I felt my body craving for some R&R. By evening, Aunt Brenna returned home from her shift and was waiting by my bedside with the most awesome comfort food—mac 'n' cheese. I could smell the savoury combination of margarine, cheddar, and Monterey Jack. Whatever Aunt Brenna put in that bowl of macaroni could wake any Sleeping Beauty from her deep slumber. I stirred in my bed and rubbed my eyes and gladly accepted the heaping large steaming bowl of mac 'n' cheese.

"Ready for tomorrow?" Aunt Brenna asked as she passed me the spoon and placed the serving tray on my lap.

"Not really," I said with my mouth full as I continued stuffing more helpings of macaroni into my mouth. "Delicious! Aren't you going to have any?" I asked.

"I got a bowl downstairs already. But Emily, I want you to know that you are not alone in this fight. We are going to fight this. Anything less would not be right," Aunt Brenna exclaimed, placing her hand on my shoulder.

I swallowed what was in my mouth and bit my lip. I looked up at Aunt Brenna and spoke with a small tear dancing on the corner of my eye, "I'm glad I got you and Max here to support me. Every now and then, I would get angry at myself for not having answers to all my hyper-specific questions. I'd tried googling, engaging in online support forums, reading blogs. And it just left me more confused and worried. I'm so lucky to not have to fight this alone, but it's just not fair to be in this situation," I explained.

"Maybe fate has led us here. We will never know. But where we are at now is only the tip of the iceberg. Don't be so hard on yourself. You got a long road ahead. You should bottle up all that energy from worrying and make better use for it," Aunt Brenna replied.

Aunt Brenna sounded more and more like my Mom. Her wisdom was like a bottomless pond. She was right. In less than a week, I would learn about my new treatment plan. And like most ailments, it wasn't something that could be resolved overnight. Coming out victorious with the battle of cancer was a challenge that seemed like nothing more than wishful thinking. The real obstacle to positivity was that our brains were hardwired to look for problems that had a perceived likelihood of going poorly. And cancer survival was one of them.

Whenever we contemplated outcomes for situations that had more bad scenarios than good, we would spend months convinced that things would actually *not* turn out. Our mind's tendency to wander through negativity left us with a soured view of reality that would intuitively wreak havoc in our lives.

I tried to remember what Max said last week. About being strong emotionally and mentally. I just had to force myself to remember that these were just *thoughts*, not facts. Just like statistics were just *numbers*. Max convinced me that doctors only use statistics as general guidelines and that statistics could not tell exactly what would happen to me specifically. Medicine had to be treated on a case-by-case basis.

According to Dr. Google, 27% of patients diagnosed with AA would live for five years or more. But for aged 22 to 44, the percentage increased to 49%. I could not find any other statistic on pediatric AA survival rates. But what I discovered was that grade III tumours had a strong tendency to progress to GBM within a two-year period after diagnosis.

I let out a heavy sigh. The problem with Google searching was that we struggled to know when it was best to stop the search. Or rather, when we had sufficient enough information to answer our questions. If I didn't come across that last fact, I would have been fooled that I had a 50-50 chance to beat this thing. It was times like these that I really wished I never googled anything on brain cancer in the first place.

I knew it would take A LOT of work to maintain positivity in these dire times. The more I ruminated on negative thoughts, the more power I would have given them. The next few months was going to be crucial in determining my success rate. No wonder I hated probability and statistics so much. Though, it was pointless worrying over something that couldn't change. I had to be positive. Because whether I liked it or not, I had cancer. All I could do now was to figure out how I was going to deal with it. We all had to.

Doris Siu

Chapter Eighteen

I accompanied Aunt Brenna to work today as I was scheduled to undergo a series of tests to determine if I was healthy enough for chemoradiation. They examined my heart and took more blood (obviously) before I was free to grab a bite to eat. I had a meeting scheduled with Dr. Babinski later in the afternoon—about four hours from now to be exact—so I decided to visit Anna to pass the time.

"Knock, knock," I exclaimed, holding a small gift bag in my hand.

"Emily! Is that for me?" she asked curiously. Her eyes fixed on the gift bag.

"Sure is! Want to meet Lucas?" I asked.

"Yay! Lucas! Yes, please!" Anna screamed with excitement.

I passed Anna the bag, and she quickly tore through the tissue paper before discovering the chubby little plush cactus with a cute top hat, moustache, and dimples.

"Oh my, it's so adorable. Lucas the Cactus! I love it! Thank you, Emily," Anna squealed with enthusiasm.

We spent the next few hours playing tic-tac-toe, doodling, and Concentration 64. Together we repeated, "Concentration. Sixty-four. No repeats. Or hesitation."

Then Anna continued with a smile. "I'll go first. You'll go last.

Category is. Anything."

No matter our age, we all carried our youth with us. It was fun playing classic childhood games with Anna. I loved acting silly and being crazy-care-free. All my worries just melted away. To my surprise, spending time with Anna almost had the same effect as laughter. I finally understood why parents always said that having kids kept them feeling young at heart.

Anna knew little about the economy, the price of gas, and teenagers. Hanging out with Anna meant that I could be like a kid again. I reminisced about my childhood to a time when the biggest issue in my life was deciding what to play at recess, and the hardest test I had to take was a spelling bee. Even Taylor Swift spoke truthfully about this in her song titled, "Never Grow Up."

Children have in them the three I's—imagination, innocence, and imperfections. And these three things were often taken for granted. The irony was that when we were young, we so desperately wanted to grow up. But when we were older, we wanted to be young again.

For every wish chip I'd ever found in my lifetime, I should have wished to stay at the age of seven. If I could be as fearless as Anna, I would be in a much better place now.

•••

Dr. Meyers was the neuro-oncologist assigned to my file. Dr. Babinski introduced him to me and Aunt Brenna during our afternoon meeting. Dr. Meyers was a tall, muscular fellow, likely

6" 6', and looked like a shorter version of Shawn Bradley. He wore a taco patterned tie under his white coat. It seemed like Dr. Meyers had a good sense of humour. I liked that.

My test results confirmed that I was healthy enough to start chemotherapy medication and radiation therapy simultaneously. They suggested daily radiation treatments for six weeks.

"What? Six weeks! I gotta come here every day and get tortured for six whole weeks? What the—" I exclaimed, frustrated before Dr. Meyers interrupted.

"Not *every* day, Emily. It's like school. You'll get breaks on the weekend," Dr. Meyers clarified. "Now, here's a pamphlet to review with your Aunt. You'll be taking a chemotherapy medication called Temodal daily. So on weekdays, you'll take it one hour before coming in for radiation. On weekends, you can just take it before bedtime. Do you follow?"

"Are there any other pills I have to take? I feel like a drug addict," I huffed. "What's the point of all of these pills, anyway?"

Aunt Brenna looked at Dr. Meyers and held up her hand so she could speak. "Please, Emily. Don't be so difficult. You need to take all these medications so the treatment can work properly. Think of these chemo pills as a 'radiation sensitizer,' which would make the radiation '*work harder*.' Okay?" Aunt Brenna pleaded.

I let out a loud sigh in defeat and nodded. As expected, it wasn't just one pill. There were a handful of additional pills prescribed to counteract the side effects of the original prescription. I thought it was stupid, but how could I question science?

Dr. Meyers continued to mention more medication names

that I could not recognize, but when I heard Stemetil I naturally blurted out, "Stem what?"

"Oh hush, Emily dear, it's like Phenegren that people take for seasickness," Aunt Brenna snapped, waving to Dr. Meyers to continue with what she had to pick up from the pharmacy.

"But anti-nausea medication? Are you telling me that I'm going to puke my brains out after each radiation treatment?" I asked in horror.

"Not exactly, but it's typical to take Stemetil with Temodal," Dr. Meyers explained. "Every patient responds differently to treatment, but we cover all bases."

I sighed. I only knew about Phenegren because the lady who sat beside me on a cruise once had a bottle of that medication. I was really young back then and had a slight fascination with learning how to pronounce medical names, so that I could have some conversation starters with Aunt Brenna. I never went on a cruise since, so I would have never expected the term to come up again today when I wasn't at sea.

Well, one thing was certain. Good thing I had a reminder app on my phone. Even someone with impeccable memory would have trouble remembering exactly when to take each medication if they had this many on their list.

Dr. Meyers gave me a couple more pamphlets to take home. I grinned. This was not the type of reading material I fathomed.

"Will you be prescribing any anti-seizure meds for Emily?" asked Aunt Brenna.

I glared at my Aunt, wondering why on earth would she

request more medication.

"Hmm, let me give you a prescription for Keppra," Dr. Meyers responded as he scribbled down some notes.

Ugh, more medication. I hated swallowing pills but agreed to everything because I really had no other *choice* if I wanted to do something about my cancer. Plus, I had more than two unprovoked seizures, so I was technically diagnosed with epilepsy too.

As my Aunt continued to ask Dr. Meyers questions about my treatment, I quietly started flipping through the pamphlets. This time, I actually read all of them so that there wouldn't be any surprises. And I was glad I did. It was relieving to read about the availability of support groups for patients and survivors. It was nice to know that there was a place to turn to if we needed more support outside of family and friends. What a relief!

I made a mental note to investigate the virtual support groups more thoroughly later. It was hard enough to open conversations about living with a brain tumour, but these support groups were a perfect place to feel comfortable because everyone there were or are currently in the same shoes. Our feelings would be mutual.

But what caught my eye was that we were actually *allowed* to exercise. For a moment, I thought I could finally find something in black and white that clearly stated that I was allowed to *not exercise*. Unfortunately, that was just wishful thinking. The pamphlet only said, 'you will probably not feel like you can do 100% of your usual workout program.' Well, I guess that still meant I was scot-free from going to the gym because my usual workout program involved 100% sitting.

•••

I started treatment a couple of days later. I had a radiation planning appointment where I was fitted for a plastic mold, like a body cast, that was to be used during radiation. It was a customized mask intended to keep me in the same position during treatment so that the radiation could be aimed at the same spot every day. Each treatment was much like getting an X-ray, but the dose of radiation was much higher. It was not painful, and the treatment sessions only lasted about fifteen to thirty minutes. Most of the time I spent in the room was actually for setting up the machine, so technically, I only received radiation for a few minutes at most. Surprisingly, it wasn't as bad as I originally thought it would be.

The good news was that I was an outpatient, so I could at least sleep in the comfort of my own bed. Honestly, all I did was sleep. The radiation made me really tired, and it also made me lose my hair in a couple of spots.

I continued to encourage Max to refocus on med school. Although he still skipped, it was at least less often. Max came by to visit on most evenings, but after two weeks of treatment, I didn't want to see him. Actually, I didn't want *him* to see *me.*

First, my hair just thinned. But then it happened. I began losing more hair. I noticed a large amount of hair on my clothes. On the floor. In the drains. I could almost see bald patches on my scalp. I was shedding even worse than a German Sheppard, and

I was afraid to let Max see me so *exposed*.

I cried on most days when I looked at myself in the mirror. I cried A LOT. I eventually asked Aunt Brenna to remove the mirror that hung in my room so that I wouldn't have to see my own reflection each time I looked up from my bed. I was not Emily McGregor anymore. I didn't recognize *her*. This hairless *monster*. I was hideous.

Although the radiation only lasted a few minutes, the side effects were brutal. Tiredness. Nausea. Ugh. That stem medication, or whatever you called it, did nothing to help with nausea. It just sucked.

Still, hair loss. That was the worst for me. But I knew that my hair was not more precious than my life. It was one of those 'out of the frying pan and into the fire' moments. I hated those sorts of conundrums. It was just a tough pill to swallow.

I knew Max was coming over today. He sent me a text after class. I looked disgusting. I lost probably three-quarters of my hair, and it looked like a two-year-old tried shaving it. I leaned a chair against my door to act as a wedge to prevent Max from opening it. About an hour after receiving his text, Max arrived and let himself in. I heard his footsteps approaching, so I hid under my blanket just in case the 'chair in the door trick' didn't work.

"Emily, why won't you let me in? I came by to see how you're doing. Brought your favourite from *Amore*," Max pleaded, trying to convince me to open my room door.

"I'm sleeping. Go away," I huffed.

"Emily, I wasn't born yesterday. If you're really asleep, then you wouldn't have responded," Max reasoned.

"Go away," I cried and erupted into tears as I curled up in a fetal position in my bed.

"It's your hair, isn't it? Emily, I'm aware of the side effects of radiation and chemo. I'm sure you look fine. Come on, just let me in," Max replied.

"No!" I screamed, wiping my tears with the sleeves of my pajamas.

"You're beautiful even without hair, Emily. It's not the hair that makes you beautiful. It's what's inside of you. That's beauty. Trust me. It'll grow back once you finish treatment," Max insisted.

"But I like my hair," I sniffled.

I heard Max knock again at the door. He wasn't going to take 'no' for an answer.

"Fine, you can come in. But no laughing," I compromised.

I removed the chair at the door, and Max quickly entered. I backed away from the door and curled back up in a fetal position, this time in the corner of my room. He quickly set down the coffee cup on my desk before coming over to hug me. I wiggled out of his embrace and sat back on the floor in a pile of my own hair.

I had long beautiful locks that went past my shoulders. They were naturally wavy after a shower, and I never had to worry about volume. Not until now. I knew it was silly to cry over hair, but I'd tried so hard to hide my cancer from the world. It was like a dirty little secret that I wanted to shove under my bed or stuff into the back of my closet. But once I went bald, everyone would know that I was a victim of cancer. I hated being labeled. How many girls do you know go bald just for the sake of it?

Max knelt beside me and picked up a couple of locks of my hair. "You can't spell 'beautiful' without 'BE U,' Emily. You are beautiful with or without your hair. You may not see it, but I do," Max said softly, looking me in the eyes. He flashed a grin like he knew how to fix everything. "I know you're upset. But I also know the perfect thing to cheer you up," Max said with a glimmer in his eyes.

"What?" I shouted out, sniffling. Despite Max's sweet words, I was still upset about everything. I just wanted to wallow in the corner right now.

Max tossed over his baseball cap and smiled. "Well, go ahead. It's yours. At least until I miss it too much, okay?" Max said softly. I placed his cap on my head. I actually *did* feel better. Then I shook my head disappointingly. Why was I so self-conscious about my hair loss?

"Better?" Max asked.

"Better," I replied, wiping away the tears that lingered on my cheeks.

"Would you feel better if I shaved my head too? You'll help my mother save on the water bill. If I was bald, I don't need to shower for weeks. Actually, come to think of it, it may not be a bad idea. With the magic of deodorants, nobody would ever know," Max joked.

I looked up at Max and gave him one of those looks that said 'you can't be serious.' I took off his baseball cap and fiddled with it in my hands before I spoke. "Don't. I like your hair too. Only one of us can be bald at a time. Promise?"

"Okay, but the offer is still on the table," Max said as he pulled me back up on my feet and helped me back in bed.

I placed his baseball cap on my bedside table and whispered, "Thank you, Max."

He walked over to my desk and brought over the coffee cup. Max gave it a long, intense stare before placing it in my hands. "It seems like forever since we were sitting together at *Amore*. A lot has happened since then, eh?"

"Life was much more fun back then," I sighed.

"No. I don't think so. Whether the weather was good or bad, those moments were beautiful. Because every moment with you was, and always will be, beautiful," Max whispered.

Beautiful? How can a storm be beautiful? "Max," I replied while turning my head towards him.

Suddenly, the chorus of Christina Aguilera's "Beautiful" played in my head. Maybe Max was right. Maybe every day *did* shine.

"I, too, miss our days at *Amore*. But in all those moments we've shared together, what I liked most was not the scenery or the weather. It was the company. That's what matters the most in life. The people you surround yourself with," Max said, nudging my right shoulder.

Max held out his pinky finger and said, "Hair or no hair, Emily McGregor, you'll always be my best friend. No *hair* could ever come between us."

I nodded and sealed the deal by locking pinkies with Max. I took a long sip of coffee and smiled. Although we weren't sitting at *Amore*, we were together. And that, I would agree, was *beautiful.*

We spent the next hour hanging out in my room. A couple of months ago, Max's buddies discovered Dude Perfect's YouTube channel, and we became fans ever since. Max enjoyed the trick shot videos the most, but the blooper reels were my favourite. Often, I would find myself watching them whenever I needed an excuse for a good laugh. Today we decided to watch their documentary, *Dude Perfect: Backstage Pass*, which summarized their ten years together of making the impossible *possible.* Cory Cotton's words resonated with me when he spoke about how his support system gave them "the power to try anything." To me, Dude Perfect specialized in the impossible, and their story inspired me to believe that my "impossible" wasn't *that* far out of reach.

•••

Eventually, I decided to shave the rest of my head and accept my new reality. My hair was not more precious than my life. I thought to myself how silly I was to have cried over my excessive hair loss, given the circumstances that I was in.

Surprisingly, six weeks had gone by quite quickly with the help of coffee and Max. Unfortunately, I learned that chemo and radiation were just part one of my extensive treatment plan. I still had a long road ahead. Though, Max insisted that completing chemoradiation was worthy of a celebration, so he came over that evening with a huge bag of popcorn and two cups of coffee from *Amore*.

After flipping through the selection on Netflix, we agreed on *La Casa de Papel* since it received a 91% rating on Rotten Tomatoes. I enjoyed a good mystery series, and after watching *Baby Driver* a couple of months ago, I found heist scenes quite thrilling. I was totally on the edge of my seat when Baby and Debora were running away from the crew of violent thugs. I hoped *La Casa de Papel* met my need for speed in my now sluggish lifestyle. Although I loved sloths, living *slow* was excruciatingly painful, so I craved anything that would pump up my tempo, even if that energy boost was only temporary.

I had another meeting scheduled a week later with Dr. Meyers and Dr. Babinski to discuss part two. But before that meeting, the oncologist scheduled another MRI with neurology to see if my tumour changed. Ugh! Another MRI.

•••

Despite feeling overly tired during the six-week treatment, my MRI results were slightly optimistic. My tumour had not decreased in size yet, but it also remained unchanged. That was hopeful. I guess.

I was fortunate that my cancer treatments started over summer break, so by the time I was in phase two, it was September. Going to the hospital every day for radiation was a painful routine. Though, being stuck at home now wasn't that much better.

September was supposed to be the start of my twelfth grade. Final year at *Glenwood High*. Senior year.

Senior year was the most exciting year of high school. As a twelfth grader, I was basically on the top of the food chain. I mean, I earned the right to feel superior to freshmen, sophomores, and juniors. After all, ever since my first day of freshman year at *Glenwood High*, I dreamed of the day when people would turn to me for advice. Ironically, life was a vicious cycle; next year, if I got into college, I would be a freshman again. It was a bit of a pity that I was already missing out.

Another highlight of senior year was the coveted prom, which was probably the most associated event with senior year, after graduation, of course. Although it wasn't until May, I'd heard from *Glenwood High* alumni that it was one of the *best* nights from their youth. And now more than ever, I needed *something* to look forward to. Literally.

But senior year wasn't all glorious. It was the most *stressful* of all years too. With college applications coming up in February, we were forced to decide on our futures, even if we weren't ready for it yet. Scholarship applications. Community service. Learning a new language. We did anything and everything to pad our resumes.

Our mission for our final year was to supplement our applications. To make them stand out above the rest. I believed that we weren't born just to fit in. We were born to stand out. College applications were the first time we were all forced to put that belief to the test.

I had my work cut out for me if I still wanted to make it into *AMP* for next September. Since I spent more time sleeping than studying now, I started to believe that Miss Penny was right. My dream for early acceptance at *AMP* was too ambitious. At this rate, I may not even get accepted at all. I worried that I would no longer meet the necessary requirements to be eligible to apply for their program. I used to be able to imagine the feeling of my diploma in my hands easily. That feeling of ultimate satisfaction when we'd successfully accomplished a long-term goal. Now, my graduation was not so clear, and I doubted that I would have any opportunities to add some extra *shine* to my application.

My competition. Everyone. I was competing against hundreds, maybe even thousands, of other twelfth graders for a single spot at *AMP*. Well, technically, there were several spots available, but it was very limited, and that was beyond the point. There was a lot to get done this year, and I frowned upon the fact that *cancer* added new complexity to my already stressful life.

Aunt Brenna had a meeting with my school's principal and the board's superintendent once school resumed in September. Together, they devised an online curriculum that was tailored to my needs but still met board requirements for graduation. They stressed that I had to keep up with assignments, despite the flexibility in submission deadlines. Although I did not have to attend classes for instruction, I missed being in the classroom. My teachers posted their lecture notes so I could follow their lessons. I struggled with the material and I wondered if it was fair to blame it on cancer. No matter, school required a lot of concentration. I mean, A LOT. And performing tasks that required that level of focus was something extremely difficult now.

There were days when I was upset at myself for not being stronger. I'd read about some AA cancer patients resuming normalcy about six-weeks post-surgery. I'd also read about many returning to work, albeit in a different role, soon after the first phase of treatment. But I'd failed to match any of these *success* stories. I guess every cancer story was different. Including mine.

•••

I honestly thought I could say goodbye to Temodal after radiation therapy, but part two still involved that drug. Ugh.

"Now, Emily, you'll be taking Temodal for the next six months. I know you're familiar with this drug already, but this time you'll be following a Day One to Five schedule over a 28-day cycle. Do you follow?" Dr. Meyers asked.

"Not really. So, I take it once every five days?" I questioned, confused.

"No, think of it as an inverted spring break. You normally only get five days off of school in March and attend school for the remaining weekdays. But imagine only attending school for five days. That's what we are going to do now. Take Temodal for five consecutive days, and you'll get the rest of the month off. How does that sound?" Dr. Meyers explained with a hint of positivity in his voice.

"Well, it sounds better than before when I practically took it for the whole month. I hate swallowing pills. But there's a catch, isn't there?" I asked, raising my eyebrows.

"No catch, just a new schedule," Dr. Meyers exclaimed, satisfied that he finally figured out how to get me on board with his terms.

But, like most things in life, there was a catch. Always read the fine print. Always. Unlike in phase one, the Temodal really affected me this time around. Perhaps the side effects I felt during radiation were actually from this drug. I mean, what I was experiencing now was ten times worse than before. I laughed at how I used to complain that hair loss was the worst side effect of cancer treatment. Temodal, definitely, was THE WORST. Although I only took it the first five days of each month, it literally took a whole week after to recover.

Honestly, I felt dead for the first two weeks of every month because all I did was sleep. My body felt very stiff and weak. There were days when I felt so tired that I couldn't even get up to go to the washroom, let alone hold a pen to write a report. Admittedly, I had my fair share of bed-wetting accidents because I was too weak to move or do anything. I was certain those incidences were not wet dreams. Though, I mentally blamed it on that because wetting the bed for any other reason was just downright embarrassing for a teenager. It was times like these that I'd wished I was hooked to a catheter.

I was certain that *if* I survived cancer treatment, I probably would have ruined my kidneys from holding my bladder so much. In fact, I started to doubt if my treatment was even effective. I felt worse than before. Secretly, I started to believe that Dr. Meyers was trying to drug me with sleeping pills disguised as Temodal. I even joked with Max that Temodal was code for 'Test Every Minor on Drowsiness & Awareness Levels.' I dunno. But Dr. Meyers had a lot of explaining to do for our next appointment.

To make matters worse, I developed a bunch of mouth sores, which intuitively made me lose my appetite. I had this unpleasant taste in my mouth that never seemed to go away. Thankfully, I discovered that it was best to take Temodal with pineapple-mango juice. I actually spilled my glass of water the other day and reached for the only other liquid within arm's reach on my bedside table. Since then, I'd been trying different juices to figure out the right combination that worked best for me. At least it temporarily masked the foul taste in my mouth from the pill dissolving before I could swallow it whole.

I'd taken iron medication for a good portion of my life, and I could undoubtedly confirm that this drug was even more disgusting than drinking liquid iron. It was like licking a metal lollipop from some ancient statue. Both Temodal and iron supplements had a disgustingly metallic taste to them, but what made Temodal worse was the fact that it totally messed up my taste buds. Foods and beverages that I used to love before cancer treatment had no flavour at all now. It pained my heart to know that coffee no longer tasted like *coffee*. Eating became more of a necessity than something pleasureful.

If I was made aware of this side effect a priori, I would have never agreed to put myself through this sort of suffering. Bravo, Dr. Meyers. Bravo. I couldn't believe I was fooled by a guy who wore tacos on his ties. I always thought it was the quiet ones that were the most dangerous. Lesson learned. Don't trust a doctor with a flamboyant personality.

At my November checkup, I'd protested about these side effects to Dr. Meyers. However, Aunt Brenna lectured me about how I was making everything such a *big* deal. She actually called me a 'big baby' in front of Dr. Meyers. It was so embarrassing.

Dr. Meyers went on to explain that the purpose of radiation and chemotherapy was to destroy the remaining cancer cells that weren't removed from surgery. Honestly, I knew all those things, but what I feared the most was dealing with things where the outcome was unknown.

My palms started to sweat with the thought of exposing my brain to radiation. I wondered if radiation from the sun was analogous to radiation from cancer treatment. How could something like radiation that was apparently dangerous for you be something that can effectively kill cancer cells? I didn't get it, but I was too afraid to ask. If brain surgery already scared the life out of me, I wasn't sure exactly how I would respond during cancer treatment.

I knew everything I was going through served a purpose, but for some reason, I was reluctant to be patient with my cancer. I was constantly at war with it. I always felt that this was all too much for me. So, there were times when I closed my eyes and hoped that someone could just wake me up when it was all done.

I wanted to feel *alive* again. I wanted to have enough energy to walk down the stairs and hang out at *Amore* with Max. I wanted to have enough energy to watch the entire *Aquaman* movie in one sitting for the one-hundredth-and-one time with Aunt Brenna. I wanted to have enough energy to study for school. I just wanted my *life* back.

•••

Despite feeling overwhelmingly tired, I still dedicated as much time as humanly possible on my *good* days to study. I was certain the root cause for my tiredness was the Temodal, but I eventually gave up on fussing about it vocally.

So, I continued following my 'schedule,' like an obedient dog waiting for its owner to give them a treat. What frustrated me was that I lost probably half of every month swimming in my vomit and daydreaming. I hated wasting time and feeling utterly useless.

Time passed by excruciatingly slow. I confused days with nights. And since I was always at home now, I lost track of the days of the week too. In my calendar, there were only three days of the week: yesterday, today, and tomorrow. And that was all my mind could cope with.

Before diagnosis, if I were ever tired mid-afternoon, an extra hour or two of sleep would be enough to renew my energy. But now, rest often *wasn't* enough. Even after a few nights of extra sleep, I found it more and more difficult to complete normal, everyday activities. And it just sucked big time. We were talking about full-blown fatigue.

Dr. Meyers warned me that I wouldn't have the same

bounce in my step once treatment started. But he'd never told me that it would've been *this* bad. Dr. Meyers insisted that I take a temporary leave of absence from school to focus on my health. But I'd refused. I didn't want cancer to be the reason for holding me back from my plans, especially since I was now more motivated than ever to work towards my dream. I had to finish whatever I'd started, even though I was failing very badly.

Chapter Nineteen

Christmas Eve. Fifteen degrees below freezing. It was a beautiful and snowy day in December. And like most days in the latter half of this year, I was sleeping.

I wasn't in the mood to celebrate Christmas this year. Tomorrow was the anniversary of my parent's death. Four years. And this year, the thought of it just made me more bitter because Aunt Brenna refused to drive me to the cemetery.

A week ago, I spoke with Aunt Brenna to negotiate logistics. The cemetery was not wheelchair accessible. The muddy paths were not paved, and there was no easy route to my parents' tombstone without trekking through a field of mud. I was extremely disappointed. Those skinny one-inch tires on my wheelchair were no match for sand, gravel, or mud.

Apart from fatigue, my body moved and felt the way it should. Or at least whatever Dr. Meyers deemed as 'normal.' My temporary paralysis was rarely an issue now, but that didn't mean I had a lot of strength to work with either. Prolonged walking or standing strained the muscles in my lower back and legs. This muscle fatigue made me almost exclusively dependent on my wheelchair for mobility. The only time I didn't need my wheelchair was in the comfort of my bedroom. Here, the distances between the bed, desk, or window were shorter, and therefore much more manageable.

A month ago, Max convinced me to go out for a walk. I agreed because it was winter and, therefore, cold enough to wear a hat without looking too weird. And let me say that it was an *adventure* within an adventure. I mean, Houston, we had a problem. A *big* problem. We got out of the house and just passed the driveway before getting stuck by my neighbour's house. There were tons of dried leaves on the ground, leftover from their poor fall cleanup. Those leaves were all wet from the snow and stuck to the wheels of my wheelchair like bubble gum on the bottom of my shoe. I was left completely immobile. Max had to carry me back home. It was absolutely embarrassing. Luckily, my neighbours weren't home that day, or I would've caused a scene. Since then, I refused to attempt going outside unless it was absolutely essential, a.k.a. to the hospital.

But visiting my parents at Christmas was an exception. It was an *absolute* must. It was a tradition. And it frustrated me that Aunt Brenna didn't understand its importance.

"The doctors said it's too dangerous for you to get a cold at this stage of your cancer treatment," Aunt Brenna insisted.

"But, Aunt Brenna! Please! It'll just be a quick visit this time. Just a couple of minutes. Please!" I pleaded.

"You know I normally would say yes, Emily, but not this time. I just can't let anything else happen to you," Aunt Brenna worried.

"But, Aunt Brenna!" I pleaded again.

"No, buts Emily. No is no! It's fifteen degrees below freezing. And that's without windchill. No way I'm going to let you out in that type of weather. Don't make me explain myself again. No," Aunt Brenna said frustratingly, putting her foot down.

"I thought the treatment was supposed to make me healthier. Not weaker. I'm already more than halfway through phase two. Doesn't that mean I should be 50% healthier?" I questioned.

"Emily dear, it doesn't work that way. An ordinary cold virus can be life-threatening for cancer patients undergoing chemo. And that includes you. The overall goal is to help treat cancer, but the challenge is that the medications that target the tumour cells have negative side effects on the rest of the normal cells in your body," Aunt Brenna explained.

"You don't need to tell me something I already know. I know about the side effects. I'm experiencing all sorts of them. If I didn't have any, then I would have a lot more hair on my head," I retorted, crossing my arms across my chest.

"I don't think you understand the extent of it. Normal cells that are most affected by chemo drugs are the cells of the immune system, which are used to fight infections. So, if you caught something out there, then you can actually die from it. It's serious, Emily. Really serious. You're effectively immune-comprised. You do not have a fully functioning immune system. Don't you get it! I don't know what else to say to make myself more clear. It is not safe enough for you to go outside and brave the cold. No!" Aunt Brenna said bluntly and left the room.

Aunt Brenna constantly worried about me. Deep down, I knew she was right. But I didn't have to agree if I didn't want to. I may have been obedient, following the doctor's orders to take medication and attend appointments, but I was always skeptical of everything they said about cancer. I was not *that* fragile. Was I?

I was determined to get to the cemetery. There was absolutely no way I was going to let *cancer* stop me from seeing my parents. Not on my watch. However, I knew I had to be smart about it. I may have been stubborn, but I wasn't stupid. I started to devise a thorough plan to get there (and back) safely.

Normally on Christmas morning, Aunt Brenna and I would leave the house around 6 a.m., grab breakfast at *Buddy's Diner* and then continue on our journey north to Calgary. But today, I was in on this devious plan alone, so there was not going to be any scheduled pitstops. At first, I contemplated telling Max about my mission, but I was afraid that he would tell Aunt Brenna, or, even worse, take my Aunt's side. I was doubtful that Max would agree to anything that highly jeopardized my cancer treatment. Was I crazy? Probably. But was I determined? Yes. At least the ambitious Emily McGregor still lived inside of me.

•••

Christmas. 4 a.m. Aunt Brenna was asleep, and I was awake in my bed. When all of Glenwood slept, the snow came flying in large white flakes that blanketed the ground. Six full inches of the white stuff. I peered out the window and marvelled at the dazzling whiteness. My ears hearkened to the stillness of the solemn air. As I took in the view, I thought about all the children of Glenwood waking up today on Christmas morning. It was such a beautiful and majestic sight. A white Christmas. The snow laid in the depth of its uncompacted lightness. The scene was beautiful under the dim glow of the streetlights that illuminated the village.

I took in a deep breath and bit the bottom of my lip. I was fearful of venturing out into the darkness.

I spent most of Christmas Eve sleeping so I would have enough energy to sneak out overnight. Aunt Brenna thought I was just tired, so she did not suspect anything was out of the ordinary. I felt weird devising an escape plan on Christmas Day. I mean, people head home for Christmas, not sneak out.

I started to get bad vibes as I stared out my window. I reached for Jimi by the window and hugged him to seek the strength needed to move forward with my plan. Jimi was the only thing I had now to comfort me. And I was terrified about everything. About getting stuck halfway. About compromising treatment. About getting caught.

I could only imagine the look on Aunt Brenna's face when she realized I'd disappeared. I knew there was no way to get back before she woke up because of the physical distance between here and the cemetery. So, I left a note in the kitchen that claimed how Max picked me up for some fresh air. That was the most believable lie I could think of. Anyway, I had to get enough of a head start so that there was no possibility of Aunt Brenna stopping me, even if she tried.

I started to have second thoughts as I placed Jimi back down and rubbed my temples. So, I looked out the window at the starry night sky and tried to locate the brightest one. There in the far distance was Sirius. I closed my eyes and made a wish.

Mom used to tell me that stars were like little holes that peered into heaven. She believed that each star represented a loved one for someone in the world and that even in the darkest hours, we were never alone because these infinite stars united us. I wasn't sure if I believed in it, but I'd grown to love the stars so fondly as I spent many nights just staring into the night sky. When it rained, I'd always looked for rainbows. But in the dark, I'd always searched for stars. And that was when I knew it was time. I took off Max's baseball cap and tucked it under Jimi. Then, I pulled on a thick wool hat and pumped my fist in the air with great aggression.

I changed into my heavy winter gear to brave the elements outside. The adrenaline that ran through my veins made me extremely alert and ready for action. I grabbed my phone by my bedside and stuffed it into the back of my jean pocket. I sat back on my bed to catch my breath. All that movement made me feel a bit tired. I had no idea my natural adrenaline would disappear from my system so quickly.

After a couple of minutes of rest, I lifted myself onto the wheelchair. I snuck out of my room ever so quietly, wheeling towards the stairwell. The floors creaked, so I nervously bit my lip, praying that Aunt Brenna wouldn't hear any of the sounds. Then it hit me. When I made my escape plan, I failed to account for the fact that the stairwell was not wheelchair accessible. I cursed at myself for overlooking this undeniable obstacle in my path. I always had Aunt Brenna or Max with me to help me down the stairs. But obviously, I was on my own today.

Disabled people often had a hard time moving up and downstairs. Whether in a wheelchair or not, it was a major struggle. I looked at the flight of stairs and screamed loudly in my mind. If I actually had hair on my head, I would have already pulled it all out by now. I whispered some motivational stuff that my Mom used to brainwash me with before I got up from my wheelchair. I knew what had to be done. I had to get down the flight of stairs no matter what. I just had to.

As I stood up from my wheelchair, I wobbled like a newborn deer learning to walk for the very first time. I dragged my feet towards the stairway. I had to be careful with how I moved so I wouldn't wake Aunt Brenna up. Cautiously, I placed my strongest leg on the first step while gripping the handrail tightly. I continued moving one foot at a time down the stairs, pausing after each successful step-down. By the time I made it a quarter way down, I had to pause to take a longer break. I breathed heavily and cursed at how excruciatingly painful walking the stairs had become on my own. Something that used to be a simple task was now so deceptively complex. Walking was far harder than understanding the laws of Physics. How was that even possible?

My legs were weak, and it was hard to stand on my feet for too long. But after a forty-five-minute grueling stairclimbing workout, I eventually found myself at the bottom of the steps. All twenty-five steps. Victory at last. But I reminded myself that there was still a long road ahead to get to my destination.

I sat on the last step for quite some time before I had the energy to make it to the front door. I slipped on a pair of ultra-soft shearling boots. UGGs. These were my favourite pair of winter boots. I liked how they kept my feet warm and cozy with every step. I never sacrificed comfort for style. But when I got these UGGs, it was the best of both worlds.

I quietly closed the door behind me and flipped out my phone to dial Uber. As I waited for my ride, I sat on the porch to catch my breath. I was sweating profusely in my five layers of sweaters bundled in a heavy down jacket. Although it was twenty degrees below freezing, I was tempted to remove a couple of layers. That staircase trek was probably the toughest (and sweatiest) workout I ever had. When I was ten, I hiked a 10k trail at Banff with Mom and Dad with ease. I was now almost double that age and the distance for that staircase was probably only about a couple of metres. But, it was no easy task. I don't remember ever feeling *this* exhausted after a workout.

To make matters worse, I really was roasting like a duck confit in the oven. The heat was unbearable, so I decided to remove three of my layers to try to cool off. I leaned against the wall of the house and held my head. I cursed at my poor preparation; I wished I packed some Keppra. Never had I ever exerted myself this much since being diagnosed with cancer, so I was unsure how my body would respond as I continued with my escape plan. I wondered how Jude Law, who played Jerome Morrow, a paraplegic in the movie *Gattaca*, made it up the stairs so quickly when the investigators were coming over to check on him? I made a mental note to watch that movie again once I'd returned from my adventure.

The Uber driver arrived five minutes later. I was in a lot of pain but knew that this was my ticket out of here. I put on a smile and limped towards the car. I was thankful that the ride to the cemetery was long. About two hours one-way without stopping. It gave me time to rest and restore the little energy I had in me to continue on this crazy journey.

I thought to myself how insane I was for going through all this trouble just to follow some stupid tradition of singing to my parents every Christmas morning. Love truly made us do crazy things. Good judgement and patience flew out the window whenever I'd let my heart decide my actions.

I stared out the car window and looked deep into the night sky. Looking up, I gazed into the infinite void above me. The stars seemed to have all disappeared. The vast, seemingly empty, abyss above was dark and full of wonder. Silently, one by one, tiny sparkling diamond-like stars blossomed across the sky. It was beautiful. To me, the night sky was a world of endless possibilities that reminded me of the Wall of Hope that hung on my bedroom wall. Each twinkling star was like my colourful collection of paper airplanes; each seemed to be in its proper place, filling empty spaces, glowing with its own ominous light. It was the perfect display of brilliance. It was mesmerizing. I could only smile as I sank into my seat and rested.

About halfway to the cemetery, I opened the Google Sky app on my phone and tried to decipher the shapes of the constellations above me. Whenever I looked to the stars, I thought about our place in this great, big universe. I wondered which stars were Mom and Dad.

The challenge of any amateur astronomer in the city was the light pollution we encountered from streetlights, house lights, and cars. But as we drove down HWY-2, it was the perfect place to see the constellations in their full glory. I spotted Orion, the Hunter, and his hunting dog, Canis Major. These constellations were the easiest to recognize in the northern hemisphere during the winter. There I saw Sirius again. Only the moon, Venus, Mars, and Jupiter appeared brighter than Sirius in the sky. Blissful. Beautiful. Epic.

It was a dark, serene night. Under the twinkling stars, there was harmony. A harmony that only existed in nightfall. Why were so many things in life beautiful, but temporary? Flowers bloomed but eventually withered away. Rainbows appeared but quickly faded. Smiles could easily be turned into frowns. Perishables perished. People died. I'd always known about the fragility of life, but in the darkness, everything seemed to shine.

I began to forget about all my worries. Being under the stars was invigorating, and I thought of all the people who were sleeping under its magical spell. In a couple of hours, the sun would rise to wake millions of people around the world.

My chest started to feel tight, and I felt overly warm again. I intuitively took off my wool hat to cool down. And that was when I realized what I'd done. My bald head. Fully exposed to the world. Oh my! I quickly pulled back on my wool hat to cover myself. But it was too late. My driver knew instantly that I was a cancer patient. My carelessness totally blew my cover. Could this day get any worse?

I fidgeted in my seat uncomfortably and the Uber driver noticed the movement in his rear-view mirror. “You okay back there?” the Uber driver asked.

“I’m fine, thanks,” I said abruptly.

“You don’t seem fine, Madam. Would you like me to turn back?” he asked.

“No! Please, continue. I need to get to the cemetery. I just need to,” I pleaded.

Fortunately, the Uber driver complied, and he didn’t say a peep the rest of the way. It was exactly twenty-three minutes to eight when we pulled up to the entrance of the cemetery.

“What’s the number? I can drive you closer,” he offered.

I smiled and replied, “Fifty-five, sir. McGregor. On the northwest corner, nestled near the row of rose bushes overlooking the gazebo. Thank you.”

“Fifty-five?” he asked.

“Yes, fifty-five,” I confirmed.

“Isn’t that Roger Mot’s grave? The great Canadian music producer and musician of our time?” the Uber driver asked, intrigued with a small grin on his face.

My Dad worked under a pseudonym. He did that to protect his privacy from creating a level of separation between his personal life and his professional life. Dad felt that adopting the name Roger Mot, which was a portion of his name flipped backwards, was both memorable and powerful in redefining his narrative, and establishing his image in the market. Plus, according to Google, the name Tom McGregor had over 14,700,000 results. Needless to say, there were way too many Tom McGregors for fans to weed through in order to find the right artist. Using an alias, especially for common names, made even John Smith and Jane Doe stand out above the rest.

"Yes, sir. I'm his daughter," I admitted.

"I didn't know Roger had a daughter. Great man. Really. Now it explains why you were so eager to continue heading north after I asked. You know, you could have just told me earlier. Many would move oceans and mountains just to be associated with him," he said.

"I know. But I'm not one who likes special treatment. I didn't want to come across as the daughter of a dead celebrity abusing privileges of the famed and fortuned," I confessed.

The Uber driver just smiled and nodded understandingly. He drove up as close as possible to plot 55. I took up his offer to help me out of the car. I leaned in for support. My legs were killing me, and I was feeling weaker by the minute. When I arrived at my parents' tombstone, he said a few kind words to my parents before giving me some privacy.

I thanked him again and told him that I would likely be a while. He handed over a business card with his direct number before he spoke. "Call when you're ready, and I can bring you back."

I nodded. His engine roared; I could hear his wheels screech and buzz off in the distance. I was finally *here*. Alone with my parents in my sweet solitude. I placed my hand on their tombstone and started to hum a tune.

"Mom. Dad. I'm sorry. I really am sorry," I cried as my eyes welled with tears, endlessly trickling down my cheek.

I collapsed in front of their grave. My shoulders trembled, and my breathing quickened. I could hold back no longer; tears continued to escape from my eyes, followed by my clenched fist meeting the snow-covered ground. I mumbled incoherent things through my hands and choked on my sobs. My bottom lip quivered, and my shoulders dropped in resignation. As more tears came, my mind whirled with guilt, confusion, and pain.

"I know I haven't come by to visit lately. I don't even know where to begin. I have cancer. Inside my brain. The doctors tried removing it, but there's still some there. I'm trying to be brave. I really am. But I'm not that strong. And I'm scared, Mom. I'm really scared, Dad," I cried.

I tried composing myself by mentally humming Andra Day's "Rise Up." Slowly, I controlled my breathing and stood back up.

"Dad, I know you've always told me, 'We can't always choose the music life plays for us, but we can choose how to dance to it.' I want to beat this, Dad, I do. But my gut is telling me that what I have is incurable. That all this treatment is hopeless. And that I'll never get my life back. I'm afraid I'm running out of dances to try, and that my music would soon end. Maybe some promises aren't meant for me to make. I'm sorry I couldn't follow through with my promise to get into *AMP*. I'm really sorry for always being such a disappointment. I really am," I whispered, leaning against my parents' tombstone for support.

As I stood there in silence on the white blanket that masked the muddy floor of the cemetery grounds, I bit my lip to contain my tears. My eyes burned from crying; the tears shimmered over my vision. A blue ocean surrounded me, and the world swam. I felt like I was lost at sea. Helplessly searching for land. I'd never been a good swimmer; I was drowning. Everything was fragmented. My thoughts. My memories. My questions. My emotions. All of it floated above the sea but disconnected in my mind. My spirit was ruined. My mind was destroyed. I just stood there, in front of my parents' grave, broken. Like a shattered panel of glass, and the disappointment cut through my heart a thousand times as I bled with pain.

I was too weak to move and too scared to share more. A cold gust of wind swirled around me; the sky cried with me in a blizzard of tiny flurries. The cemetery was empty. There hadn't been any visitors yet today. I glanced across the field and saw a pristine, untouched, blanket of snow with no other footsteps but mine and the Uber driver's prints.

My body trembled, and I shivered uncontrollably. I started to feel chills, but my head felt very hot. I fumbled to grab my phone in my back pocket. I had to go home. I had to rest. I searched my jacket pockets for the Uber driver's business card, but my fingers started to tingle awkwardly. I was feeling nauseous and lightheaded.

"Ahh!" I wailed out in frustration. "Keep it together, Emily.

Just keep it together," I muttered under my breath.

I felt very sick and started to regret making the trip to visit my parents. My heart told me that I needed this today. To be here with my parents. The heavy weight I carried on my shoulders always felt lighter each time I visited the cemetery. However, my body told me that I was stupid. Very stupid. Honestly, I was indifferent.

Suddenly, my phone buzzed. It was Max. I trembled. Chills. I was certain I was having a fever. My phone continued to vibrate and I felt lightheaded. I finally accepted the call and slowly raised the phone to my ear.

I whispered, "Max?"

"Emily! Where on earth are you? Aunt Brenna is having a panic attack right now. She thought you were abducted from her home. She saw your wheelchair abandoned, clothes all over the floor, and the front door was left slightly opened. She called me immediately when she saw a note in your handwriting that said you were with me," Max exclaimed with worry in his voice.

"I'm just out," I said faintly.

"Emily! Tell me where you are, and I'll come get you. You can't be out in this type of weather. You'll get sick," Max insisted.

"Just let me die, okay? Just leave me to die in peace," I pleaded.

"Emily, don't you dare say something like that! You can't be serious! Tell me where you are, or I'll search every nook and cranny in Glenwood just to find you. Tell me!" Max threatened.

"I'm not going to get better, Max. I'm not that lucky to be blessed with a medical miracle. I don't know what to believe in now. But just let me die so that you and Aunt Brenna can have your lives back. Every day I wake up, I try to convince myself that I'll get better. That this is just the necessary evil I need to go through to win this battle. But I'm tired, Max. I'm tired of struggling every day to fulfill my promises. I'm tired of fighting. I'm tired of not having the strength to do the things I love. I'm just tired of being a failure," I sobbed.

"Emily, get a hold of yourself! What has gotten into you? Just the other day you were telling me about your dream to be at *AMP* next September. So, what's all this about? You're just giving up? That's not like you. You've been fighting this for several months now and you're just going to run away before you reached the finish line. There's a cure for all cancers, Emily. You just have to believe it to find it. Now tell me where you are so I can take you home," Max exclaimed.

"No Max, there isn't," I said, defeated.

"Emily McGregor, you're the one who told me that you'll release those paper airplanes one day. You got to be alive to do it. So don't pull this joke on me and tell me where you are!" Max screamed, frustrated.

That was when it hit me. My paper airplanes. My Wall of Hope. My music. There was still time.

I sighed and quietly trembled, "I'm not in Glenwood. I'm at Netherspring Cemetery."

"In Calgary? Why on earth are you at a cemetery on Christmas morning? That's like two hours away. Are you out of your mind? I'm telling your Aunt, and I'm getting you back home now," Max yelled angrily.

I immediately screamed a reply, "No! You can't tell Aunt Brenna."

My head started to burn like a volcano about to explode. I felt extremely weak and my breathing quickened. "Just promise me you won't tell her where I am. Just tell her that you found me at Clara's or Rachel's. Just please don't tell Aunt Brenna the truth. I won't forgive you if you tell her. Please, Max," I pleaded desperately.

"Just stay put and don't move," Max insisted.

I weakly spoke. "Max, I—" But I cut off mid-sentence. It was getting harder and harder to breathe and my vision blurred.

"Emily? Emily? Emily? Talk to me. I'm coming, okay. Hang in there," Max yelled into the phone.

The world spun around me. There were lots of bright colours swirling, and my eyes glossed over. I shivered uncontrollably, and I gasped for air. I thought of Aunt Brenna, Max, and Dr. Meyers. The looks of disappointment in their faces. Wagging their fingers and shaking their head in disbelief that Emily McGregor would do something so incredibly stupid.

I cried out in pain and dropped to my knees. My head started pounding as I desperately pressed my phone tightly to my ear. The clouds above were darkening, obliterating the sun. I felt like fire on the icy ground, burning everything beneath me. The cold wind harshly brushed against my face as I saw the ground inch closer and closer by the second.

My eyes closed and the last thing I heard was Max's voice,

"Hold on please, Emily!"

I whispered, "Max."

Chapter Twenty

Max dialed 911. The Calgarian paramedics found me unconscious on the snow-covered ground in front of my parents' grave. I was admitted to the ER at Calgary Children's Hospital, where they treated me immediately. I had a fever of 40 ^{0}C, which was a telltale sign of a serious infection. Because my immune system was compromised from cancer and chemotherapy, getting a fever related to infection was life-threatening.

I was barely conscious by the time Max made it to the hospital. I zoned in and out of consciousness as my fever reigned in my head. I was in isolation, so I wouldn't be exposed to any new infections while I was being treated. There was a huge window facing my bed for visitors to peer in; I vaguely recalled seeing Aunt Brenna there with Max too.

The doctors started me on antibiotics through my IV before they arrived. By midday, the doctors were still scrambling to determine the source of my fever. They continued to draw more blood and urine samples to check for bacteria in my cultures.

Before cancer diagnosis, a fever was just a sign that my body was working and trying to fight off an infection. It was nothing to be concerned about unless it was dangerously high. But today, I'd realized that fevers were not the same for cancer patients.

By the evening, my breathing slowed, and my heart actually

stopped momentarily. The doctors were, fortunately, able to revive me. Afterward, they hooked me to a ventilator to help with the breathing. I thought I heard Aunt Brenna screaming in the background. I also thought I heard Max repeatedly calling my name. I wasn't sure, though. Everything was a messy blur.

But, as Aunt Brenna and Max feared for the worse, I whisked away to a strange world where pigs spoke pig Latin, humans had tails, and the roles of our extremities were reversed. It was a strange *Alice in Wonderland* type of dreamworld.

I suddenly woke, screaming, "ickenchay oupsay!" That was pig-Latin for '*chicken soup*.' Then, I began hyperventilating and I trembled uncontrollably. And with one glimpse of Aunt Brenna and Max through the window, my body began convulsing again. I had another seizure.

I returned to the company of darkness, but this time I saw my parents. Mom and Dad were sitting by my bed, singing Michael Bublé's "White Christmas." It was a magical moment. Mom was braiding my hair, and Dad was humming while looking out the window. A loud bang sounded, turning my dream into a nightmare. Mom screamed; my braids had all fallen off my head. My bed was covered with hair. My hair. Dad then turned to face us, but he had no eyes. Then suddenly, water started pouring into my room. I stood up from my bed and walked closer to my Dad. But each motion forward brought forth more rain.

And by the time I made it to him, the water was so deep that my Dad disappeared. I turned back to my Mom, and she was gone too. Then a giant monstrous hand pulled me into the pool of water. I gasped for air, and then the water instantly transformed into a frozen wonderland. I peered down into the hole that I arose from and saw the ocean filled with human corpses. Then the hole crystallized, and I was back in my room, in front of a mirror. Before I could see my reflection, a layer of smoke blinded my eyes. I hit my head against the mirror, and my head broke open on the shattered glass. My brain fell out of my head, like egg yolk, and started sizzling on the broken shards. Finally, I jolted awake.

My throat hurt from being intubated. I wanted to scream at the top of my lungs, but the endotracheal tube that was in my mouth was uncomfortably in the way. I looked around to make sure I still had my eyes. I touched my head to make sure it was still intact. I thought to myself how vivid that dream was. That nightmare. I decided not to dive deeper into analyzing my nightmare but instead tried to comprehend what was currently going on.

Max noticed that I was awake. He was waiting patiently outside the isolation room from the viewing window. I could tell that he was waiting for quite some time. He looked disheveled, and his eyes were full of worry and pain. He had a slight five o'clock shadow, and his hair was a mess. He knocked on the room window and waved with a goofy smile. I wanted to respond but couldn't. Although I was angry at Max, it was nice to see a familiar face that wasn't half-dead or ill-ridden. Max should have just left me to die with my parents. But I knew that it wasn't my time. Fate somehow wanted me to be alive still.

Aunt Brenna ran to get the nurse while I laid there helplessly. Beads of sweat dripped down my forehead. I felt a bit better now that the antibiotics kicked in. My fever started to drop a couple of degrees, and I began to breathe more regularly.

•••

After another day in the isolation room, I was transferred to the ICU. The doctors wanted to ensure that I was stable enough for transport. They monitored me overnight, and if I survived the night, I would be transferred to *G&C* by tomorrow afternoon.

Max entered the room to speak with me. I turned my head away from him, frustrated that it had come to this.

"I know you're probably not going to forgive me, but I had to Emily. I had to tell your Aunt. She was the only one who knew all the details about your medical condition. And seeing that you had a fever, I don't regret what I'd done. Fever and cancer are a totally different ball game. You didn't just have a seizure. You almost died back there. You can hate me all you want, but I couldn't risk it. I couldn't risk your life," Max explained.

"How could you?" I whispered angrily.

My throat hurt. It was still swollen from the tube. My voice was scratchy, and I whimpered helplessly. In normal circumstances, I would have been throwing a temper tantrum and screaming obscene profanity to get my point across. But I didn't have the energy for that today. Not now.

I was just disappointed. I felt betrayed. The thought that my best friend, Max, betrayed my trust by telling Aunt Brenna my dirty little secret. The act of sharing secrets with anyone, without permission, completely violated the loyalty and respect that were the cornerstone of a close friendship. I was shocked. I'd never ratted to his supervisor about his disappearances from school. I'd never told his Mom that he scratched the paint off the passenger seat's door of her car from parallel parking too close to the curb at *Amore*. I'd never told Aunt Brenna that Max stole chocolate chip cookies from her emergency stash in her room. Then why was it fair for Max to leave me hanging this time? The pain of betrayal burned inside, and I closed my eyes to compose my emotions.

"Go. Just go," I whispered with tears in my eyes.

Max did not try to fight my wishes. He cautiously approached me and squeezed my hand to say goodbye. "Sometimes we need to break promises to look out for others. Take care of yourself, Emily," Max said softly as he backed out of the room with guilt and pain that rested heavily on his shoulders.

•••

That evening, my breathing slowed, and I found myself waking up gasping for air. So, the doctors put me back on the ventilator for another night until my breathing stabilized. Two days later, I was transferred to *G&C*, where Dr. Meyers spent an entire afternoon explaining why I must heed the advice from my medical team. He stressed that I could not rely on luck to save me. If I failed to follow through, then I would be willingly letting cancer defeat me.

Dr. Meyers worked with Dr. Babinski over the next few days to devise a new treatment plan under the new circumstances of my medical situation. I'd developed an infection in my lungs. Pneumonia. My chest X-ray confirmed the diagnosis. Just another part of my body that *wasn't* working normally.

I was reacquainted with Zita but had a smaller room down the hallway in oncology. Being back at *G&C* brought with it many painful memories. It was a trip down memory lane, but not of the good variety. The curtained walls haunted me, but I could not remember why. I wistfully thought of Max to put my mind at ease. I felt lonely and lost without him.

This time I was the one on the receiving end of the silent treatment. Max was surprisingly distant. I knew I hurt him for being angry at him for saving me. If we ever fought over something, we usually forgave each other by sunrise. I really did hurt Max this time. I felt really bad about it. I frowned and let out a loud sigh.

"Hey beautiful, did you do this all to yourself just to see me again?" Zita joked.

I shook my head. I wasn't in the mood for jokes. It only reminded me more about Max. I started to cry, choking on my tears.

"Emily, I know you don't want to be stuck here again. But you must take these warnings seriously. You must recognize that there's a lot of things you need to hold off on for a while until you're feeling stronger. You must be patient and hope will find you. Though, it's not helping if you keep adding more layers of complexity," Zita warned.

Aunt Brenna came by that night to check up on me. At first, she yelled at me until my ears bled. Then, she burst out in tears after admitting that she thought I was a goner back in Calgary.

"Emily, why won't you just take your cancer seriously. You're a smart girl. But you're sick. Very sick. I don't understand why on earth you would sneak out behind my back to see your parents? Your Mom and Dad know that you love them. You don't need to go to the cemetery to prove it to them. They know. And wouldn't they feel worse knowing that you could have *died* from doing all of this," Aunt Brenna screamed.

I remained silent. I wasn't going to agitate her. We cannot spell 'smother' without 'mother.' And although Aunt Brenna wasn't my mom, she was the closest thing to a 'mother' for me, and she had every right to lecture me on my rebellious actions. She was doing what any parent would do for their children. To give them a wake-up call when things got out of hand.

Aunt Brenna continued with her rant, "You're grounded once we get home. The world is a very hard and cruel place. That's why we have something called black coffee. If the world was all roses and fairies, then we'll be serving iced tea in cocktail cups with little plastic umbrellas all the time."

"I'm sorry," I said. I sounded like a broken record. 'Sorry' was all that I said nowadays.

"Emily, I'm not looking for an apology. It would really serve you well to wake up and smell the coffee, and to quit acting like a teenager," Aunt Brenna scoffed.

Even the smartest people have done stupid things. This was my *stupid* thing. The reality was that I was unable to rewrite the book that I called life. My early chapters in my life story were already written in black and white. I could not change it, no matter how hard I tried. Some things in life were just out of our hands. But there are three phases in life. Past. Present. Future. And what mattered most to me now was the ending to my story. My future. And that ending was still up to me. Max was right. You have to believe in a cure to find one.

Aunt Brenna eventually forgave me for my shenanigans. But only if I promised to start putting my health first on my agenda.

I feared the uncertainties that lied in my path ahead. I was afraid to walk alone. But I knew that alone or not, I had to keep up with the fight. My heart swelled in pain as I looked out the window. There was an explosion in the back of my mind. Like one wrong word could cause a war. Like one gasp of air could save a life. There in the corner of the room was Max's baseball cap by the window. I was certain that was Max's cap. It was red and black, with a gold rim and a gigantic G symbol in the middle. The G stood for the *Glenwood Broncs*, the baseball team Max's Dad played on during the prime of his career.

I tried to collect my thoughts. I was certain that I left Max's hat under Jimi before I left for the cemetery. How on earth did Max's hat get here?

I called out to Zita. Almost instantly, Zita appeared at the door and checked my monitors for any issues. I assured her that I was feeling a lot better, and I only called her to chat. She let out a sigh of relief and sat down on the visitor's chair in the corner of my room. She nodded to let me begin.

"Zita, did I have any visitors?" I asked.

"Your Aunt came many times. She even visited during her breaks," Zita exclaimed.

"I know about my Aunt, but did anyone else come by when I was sleeping?" I hinted.

"That young man. What was his name? Ah yes, Mr. Miller," Zita said before she quickly covered her mouth. I could tell from her reaction that she revealed something that she wasn't supposed to mention.

"I knew it!" I screamed out, relieved. Max wasn't giving me the silent treatment intentionally. He was giving me space. But why?

"Oh, Emily, I'm sorry. You weren't supposed to know. Mr. Miller told me not to mention anything about his nightly visits. He said that it would upset you," Zita apologized.

"Nightly? Upset me?" I questioned.

I took a moment to piece everything together. I assured Zita that I would not tell Max what she told me. Zita smiled and left after she gave me another dose of antibiotics.

Guilt overwhelmed me. Deep down, I knew that Max was just looking out for me. He didn't mean to hurt me by going against my wishes to inform Aunt Brenna about my whereabouts. He was just doing what was right. And if I didn't make amends soon, then I would have driven him away for good. I didn't know where to begin. Unfortunately, coffee didn't seem like it could fix it this time around.

A tear formed in my eye. I had to fix this. I had to do something. True friends should never let their differences come between them. I couldn't lose Max. I just couldn't.

Chapter Twenty-One

January. It had been just over six months since I was first admitted to the ER. The taste of *Rue 143* that night still lingered in the back of my memory. A night that felt like one of the best nights I'd ever had turned out to be one of the worse. Bittersweet. Life was truly bittersweet.

Today was my eighteenth birthday. January 13th. And looking at where I was today, there was no denying that everything sucked. But life never promised to be fair.

Being diagnosed with cancer had taught me a very valuable lesson. There was no consistency in life. We really do ride life's roller coaster and bite our lip every time we plummet down those near-ninety-degree drops. The secret for survival? To be fearless.

Yesterday may have been terrible. And today, we probably still felt terrible. But tomorrow. Well, that was unknown, and it was okay. Because there was absolutely no way, we could feel good *all* the time with cancer. I reminded myself that I had brain cancer, not heart cancer. It took several months for me to finally *get it.* To finally embrace myself and accept what I had. If there was one positive in all of this, it was that I was still breathing. I wasn't a vegetable. And I was still *alive*. Wasn't that worth celebrating?

I knew that if I just put my heart into that *one* good thing about my cancer story, then that little fire burning inside of me would be kept alive. *Hope*. And hope was a very powerful thing.

There were three categories of truth—personal, political, and objective. And the interesting thing about objective truths was that it was true no matter what. Today I was a year older, maybe even a year wiser. And my wish to myself was to turn the *one* good thing in this cancer to be an objective truth. To believe that every single day I was still alive meant another opportunity to keep fighting. Today was my birthday. And every day after would be a *bonus*.

"You look amazing today, Emily. Happy Birthday, sweetie!" Aunt Brenna cheered as she walked into my room with a tray of all my favourites—pancakes, chocolate chip cookies, and coffee. She put down the tray of food on my desk and ran over to give me a tight hug.

I smiled at Aunt Brenna. It was really sweet of her to surprise me with breakfast in bed this morning. She always knew how to make me feel special. I was a bit disappointed, though, that I couldn't really savour the food like the way I used to. But I'd come to terms with a lot of the side effects I'd been experiencing. I kept reminding myself that the most important thing was that I was still *alive*.

"Thanks, Aunt Brenna," I said, smiling. And yes. I was smiling. I haven't really smiled since the day I was discharged from *G&C*. But even then, that smile was more like relief rather than happiness. I'd come a long way since then. We all had.

"Max plans to swing by later today. I mentioned your birthday to him. Maybe you want to freshen up after breakfast?" Aunt Brenna hinted.

“Max? But, I haven’t heard from him much since the incident,” I sighed.

“Max hasn’t forgotten about you, sweetie. He’s a big boy with a big heart. I’m sure he put all of that behind him. He said that he’s coming. Trust the guy, okay?” Aunt Brenna said reassuringly.

“Okay, I’ll change into something nice,” I said blushing.

After that grim day, when Max said goodbye to me at Calgary Children’s Hospital, I haven’t seen him since. I tried contacting him once or twice after I was discharged from pneumonia. But he’d elected not to return my calls. We only exchanged a couple of text messages in-between. His messages were all terse. I missed him terribly. It was awkward not seeing him. Just the thought of him coming by today warmed my heart.

Aunt Brenna was happy to see my spirits up today. I felt like a new person. Well, perhaps it was typical for eighteenth birthdays to feel this way. Turning eighteen was considered a milestone in our lives. Like a right in passage. I was now officially and legally an adult. Me, Emily McGregor, an *adult.*

•••

As promised, Max came by to visit later in the afternoon and he snuck upstairs quietly to surprise me. I actually was asleep when he arrived, so it was definitely a surprise to be awoken by song. A soft, but catchy tune played in the hallway. And then there was a knock at the door.

“Knock, knock,” Max whispered.

“Who’s there?” I exclaimed. My face lit up from the sound of

Max's voice.

"Max," he replied.

"Max, who?" I played along.

"Max Miller, you silly birthday girl. Don't tell me you forgot me already?" Max chuckled. The door swung open the moment he finished his sentence, and there stood Max, holding a beautiful bouquet of a dozen red roses with El hanging across his left shoulder.

"Sorry for being a bit distant lately. As you can see, I had a lot of things on my mind," Max said with a smile.

Max played a beautifully written ballad for me on his guitar. I'd only seen El once or twice before, so this performance was extra special. I could tell that he poured his heart and soul into this moment.

Acoustic guitars are attractive instruments by nature. Their curves. The shiny strings. The beautiful wood. The energy Max radiated with El was electrifying, and he wasn't even playing an electric guitar. I stared into his emerald eyes as he took to stage in my room. The twangy sounds. The little quiver in his voice. His song was unpolished, but I appreciated those imperfections. They were so meaningful. Max was swelling with emotions, and as we connected through song, I felt like our hearts were beating at the same beat. The passion in his voice created a beautiful aura around him. He really was a beast on stage. And it was magical.

♪♫♪♫♪♫♪

Baby call me crazy
Everything's worth your love
Don't hold back anymore

There's no explanation
Why we're a perfect harmony
My heart decided on you

So give me a chance
Give me your heart
Give me this moment to say, 'I love you'
Give me your hand
I'll never let go
Give me a chance to be with you

♪♫♪♫♪♫♪

I grew up in a family where music was the glue to everything. It was our language when we couldn't talk verbally to someone. It was our heart when we had something meaningful to share that would have been too difficult otherwise by words alone. Music was like braille. We had to *feel* it to connect with it. Almost like magic. And when we played music, it was like bringing light into the darkness. Like when the clouds clear on a gloomy day. Like the transformation of our heart into one note. One voice. One song.

Max placed El beside Jimi and then walked over to close the distance between us. He was inches from my face; I could feel the heat from his breath. Max acted as though nothing happened between us. There was no uneasiness. No awkward pauses. It was just Max. Which was what I preferred anyway. But there was something different that glimmered in his eyes.

I still wanted to apologize. For the things I said. For being angry at him for caring about me too much. For putting my well-being over anything else, even if it hurt our friendship a little. I wanted to tell him that I missed him. I wanted to tell him to stop avoiding me. But each time I tried to speak, he put his finger over my lips to silence my plead. I could tell that Max had something to tell me, and he wasn't going to let me change the subject.

He pulled me up from my bed, off-balanced, so that I fell against him. He lightly lifted my chin and held my face to stare into my eyes. And suddenly, everything just stopped.

A tear trickled down my cheek. I couldn't help it. Max's serenade was beautiful. And I was breathless. He reached out to hold my hand. I blushed, and my heart skipped a beat. I leaned in closer and laid my cheek against his shoulder. I felt the warmth of his skin on mine. My heart instantly melted.

For the next few minutes, we just stood there in silence. It was almost as though our prolonged silence was making up for all our lost time for weeks of neglect. I didn't say anything. I didn't want to ruin this moment. Max was a *gift*. And I didn't know what I did in my life to deserve someone like him.

Sometimes the things we loved the most hurt the most too. I definitely had a crush on him after our rocky start. I already analyzed every inch of him. What it meant when he smiled, who his friends were, and always kept tabs on his whereabouts. I was guilty of it. And after hearing his song, I was positive that Max was guilty of this too.

Max placed his hand over mine. We sat back down on the edge of my bed, still holding hands as he spoke softly. "Happy Birthday, Emily! These past few months have not been easy, and honestly, I'm so grateful to be here by your side. You're the best thing that ever happened to me. You've rekindled my passion for music ever since we met. Each moment I spend with you, I find that I'm constantly falling. Falling in love. And I like the direction that I'm heading," Max declared.

"Max—" I blurted out, unable to complete my sentence. I was at a loss of words. It was clear that Max was smitten with me. That night when we celebrated at *Rue 143,* I felt the chemistry between us. Max really made an impression on me. And when he complimented my dress, I was awestruck. Our relationship had merely been platonic. He'd flirted with me on several occasions, but that was just Max being Max. The thought of having something *more* with Max made my entire body tremble. I was scared. I was confused. And my heart was vulnerable.

"Emily, please hear me out, okay?" Max pleaded.

I bit the bottom of my lip and nodded.

"You see that look you're giving me right now? Like you think I'm nuts. I love that too. I love that you get a little crinkle above your nose when you're angry. I love that you are so committed to your promises and do whatever it takes to keep them. And I love that I smell like coffee after spending the whole day with you. You're a strong girl. Woman. You're just as committed to school as you were prior to getting sick, and that sort of dedication just blows me away. Ya, you have your moments. When you think everything in life is horrible and you come crashing down. But I don't mind picking you up, and being your pillar whenever you need the support. If I were just half the person you are, I would be a much better man than what you see here today. You're my best friend. And if you let me, my life partner. And I hope that's okay," Max confessed.

"Are you for real?" I said, staring at him blankly.

"Very real," Max replied and planted a kiss on my forehead.

Max smiled and said softly, "I don't expect you ever to accept me. Especially after all the times, I'd hurt you. But watching you battle every day the past few months changed the way I looked at you. When we argued in Calgary, I really thought it was over. I knew you were really angry at me. You felt betrayed. And I get it. But let's not go there again, okay? I love you so much, Emily, and I could not see a world without you in it. I had to fight for you when you didn't want to fight. When I left the hospital, I thought I was going to lose you before I had a chance to let you know how I really feel. I actually came to visit you at *G&C*. But I didn't have the guts to confront you then. Every day I waited for you to be asleep before I came in to visit."

I opened the drawer of the bedside desk and tossed back his baseball cap. He caught it in surprise, and I spoke. "I know. You got to do a better job not leaving any evidence."

Max chuckled and continued. "No, you can have it. Looks like you need it more than me."

We both laughed as Max placed his cap on my head.

He held my hand and continued, "I know what you're going to say. That I shouldn't love you because you have cancer. But I'm not afraid to love someone with an illness. I'm not afraid of the burden because there is none. You deserve to be loved just as much as anyone else in this world. And I want to be the one deserving of your love. Having cancer would never change my affection towards you."

"But I don't want my cancer to hurt you," I cried.

"It won't. I won't let it. My only regret was not telling you sooner. I want to stop running from my feelings. I want to slow down my pace and walk alongside you in life," Max said. I couldn't help but smile. "Is that a smile I see, Emily McGregor? Well then, I'm going to keep saying, 'I love you,' until you find it in your heart to give *me* a chance," Max whispered heartedly.

"But I'm afraid, Max," I replied.

We'd reached a point in our friendship where the boundary between friend and lover no longer functioned as a boundary. It served only as a reminder of a line that once divided space. These blurred lines scared the life out of me. Romantic feelings for one another could either be something that ruined our friendship or the thing that transformed it into something bigger.

It was a risky business transcending the friend zone. Max was the very same guy that I'd shared all my secrets with. Well, *almost* all my secrets. And he was the very same guy who knew about all my pet peeves, my fetishes, and my music. I feared that taking things to the next level would only disappoint. I'd run out of surprises. And taking care of me would be more of a chore than a blessing. I couldn't do that to someone I loved.

Maybe I was selfish. I still felt that it would be better if I denied my true feelings just so we could retain our friendship. I was afraid of the risk of losing it all. I knew that we both deserved to be in love, yet there was that bond of friendship that was seemingly holding me back. I was apprehensive. Love was a source of ambivalence; our future together was now a path riddled with confusion. And it was absolutely terrifying.

•••

The rest of my birthday flew by like a breeze. Max ordered a cappuccino cake, and Aunt Brenna decorated it with my name across in yellow icing. It was a nice intimate birthday party. Just me, Aunt Brenna, Max, Jimi, and El. André even stopped by in the evening for the cake cutting.

As a kid, celebrating my birthday was a BIG deal. Everything from the location, to who I was going to invite. Even the cake and decorations had to be exactly the way I'd imagined it. But on my first birthday, after my parents' passed, I told Aunt Brenna that I didn't need her to set up a birthday party anymore. All

I wanted was a cake, some candles, and maybe some chocolate chip cookies for good measure. Maybe.

Sometimes birthday parties had too much hustle and bustle. I loved celebrating life and usually was the one who would get excited over any excuse to celebrate. But there was also nothing wrong with just taking it easy for the day, capturing silly pictures, and doing absolutely nothing in the comfort of my pyjamas. Well, that description sounded quite like my current day-to-day life, but I didn't mind. Lounging around in pyjamas was totally okay.

Today had already proved special, and I couldn't wait to blow out my candles.

"Make a wish!" Aunt Brenna cheered as she hugged André.

I closed my eyes and held my breath. I'd always looked forward to blowing out the candles on my birthday cake. Legend had it that birthday wishes were very powerful. And I believed it. On my seventh birthday, I wished for a new bike. It happened a week after. On my eleventh birthday, I wished that I stopped having cavities. I haven't had once since. Today, on my eighteenth birthday, I wished to be cancer-free. It was a lot to ask for. But I was glad that I still had the strength to blow out my own candles to (hopefully) make my wish come true.

•••

It was a pleasant evening spent in an intellectually intriguing conversation with Max, followed by a short jam session on our guitars. It was nice having the energy today to strum Jimi. But like most nights, all good things had to come to an end. I suddenly felt very tired, so I closed my eyes to rest them for a bit. Max furrowed his brow and instinctively ushered me to my room.

In my room, Max held my hand briefly as he helped me to my bed. The warmth of his touch made my head spin. He gave my hand a tight, reassuring squeeze before letting go.

"I had a lot of fun tonight. But it's late. You probably should get some rest," Max said as he placed El back in her carrying case and started packing up his belongings. He walked back to my bed and removed his baseball cap from my head so I could lie down more comfortably. I blushed and turned away from him, trying to hide my face. I felt slightly embarrassed that Max had to see my bald head up-close.

"Don't do that," Max lectured.

"Do what?" I asked, confused.

"Stop looking so embarrassed, Emily. Bald is beautiful. When I'm fifty and bald, I hope to wear it as beautifully as you do," Max exclaimed. He paused for a moment and asked, "Do you know what I see when I can catch a rare glimpse of this?"

"Cancer?" I said bluntly, not understanding the point of Max's conversation.

"Hope, Emily. I see *hope*. Hope that not all is lost. Hope that they will find a cure," Max said, smiling. Then he joked, "Well, maybe the only thing that's lost is just a little bit of hair," Max chuckled.

Max held my hand and gave me a reassuring squeeze. I couldn't help but smile back. That was probably the sweetest thing I'd ever heard anyone say to a cancer patient. Max was right. Bald really was beautiful. And the more I thought about it, the more I embraced my new look.

Feeling good about myself during cancer treatment was challenging. Especially since my body went through a lot of physical changes. Cancer and its experiences were very isolating.

When I first lost my hair, I couldn't look at myself in the mirror. I felt like I lost my identity. It wasn't until a couple of months later that I realized how hair did not define me. Whether we had hair or not, the reality was that people make presumptions and apply stigmas around hair and the identity of the person connected to it. If she was blonde, then she was dumb. If a guy had long hair, then he was a hippie. Anyone who dyed their hair an unnatural colour was either goth, punk, emo, or crazy. And the most obvious one, if you were bald, then you had cancer. But were these labels real?

I was never into wigs. They were so uncomfortable, incredibly scratchy, and way too warm in the heat. I used to wear my headwrap in the house. I just didn't want anyone, and I mean anyone, to see my bald head. Until one day, it slipped off during my nap, and Max came by to visit. He saw my exposed head. I panicked. He just smiled.

If Max could still see me as Emily McGregor, then so could I. Sometimes, we really are our own toughest critics. I'd finally understood that. Because no matter how we decided to wear our hair, it does not define who we are. We define ourselves. And we should never let anyone else tell us otherwise.

Although I wasn't fully ready yet to go out in public without covering up my head, I felt much more comfortable wearing my baldness after Max's sweet words. But those cancer patients who were brave enough to go bald publicly were setting more than just a statement about defying social expectations of beauty. I silently took a bow to all those ladies who proudly showed off their bald head. My baldness may have encapsulated cancer's realities of life and death, but it also promoted strength, empowerment, and beauty for anyone battling cancer. It was a part of me. And for the first time since I lost my hair, I surprisingly didn't *hate* being bald anymore.

Although it really was getting late, I longed for Max to stay. Plus, it didn't help that Max was still holding my hand. I squeezed back before softly whispering, "Max?"

He sat back down and turned to face me. We simultaneously leaned closer into each other, and I felt his hand encircle mine again. I stared into Max's eyes, longing for our lips to touch. His smiling eyes searched mine before glancing quickly at my lips. And while I clasped my hand around the back of his neck, our lips tenderly touched. And at that moment, I felt like I was in paradise. Like I was frozen in a moment in time, and all I could hear was the rhythmic beat of Max's heart. I felt this surge in energy overpower me. It was almost indescribable. That feeling when our lips locked for the *first* time.

A smile set on my face as we disconnected our lips for a moment. Max ran his fingertips up my forearm, leaving a trail of goosebumps before resting his hand on my shoulder. It was like magic. The way his lips connected with mine so perfectly. My lips trembled. My heart soared, and the world seemed to stop. I knotted my fingers in his hair as he moved his hands to caress my cheeks. I felt a tingling sensation whenever he touched me. I closed my eyes to savour the moment.

My *first* kiss. *Ever.* And it was spellbinding. It was soft. It wasn't that long. It was nothing like the kind of kisses I'd seen in the movies, but it was wonderful in its own way. Romantic kissing scenes were too Hollywood. It seemed to last for *eternity*. But that was clearly staged. The 'first kiss' experience was a jolting concoction of emotions, racing heartbeats, nervousness, and happiness. It was an exciting moment of closeness and intimacy.

I'd envisioned many times how my first kiss would be. And this was nothing like what I expected. The way Max's gaze locked onto my lips, moving up and down like he was already touching them. That sort of intention in his eyes, his pupils swirling in the pool of excitement, almost like his eyes were giving off an expression to foreshadow a kiss. It was exhilarating and awkward all at the same time. But it was so perfect. It was better than I would have ever expected.

We both smiled at each other before we started giggling. I knew I was officially an adult today, but I honestly felt like a little schoolgirl right now, all giddy from eating an entire bag of sweet and sour gummies.

"That was amazing," Max whispered as he pulled me in for another quick peck on my lips.

"You're amazing, Max," I whispered. I fidgeted in my bed and bite the corner of my lip before admitting, "But I'm afraid I was quite bad at it."

"Impossible!" Max whispered, placing his right index finger on my lips. "But if you would like more practice, I could help," he chuckled.

I let out a small giggle and smiled. I felt like the luckiest girl in the world. This moment was of total admiration. I was the only thing that mattered in the entire world to him right now. Max was mine. And I was his. It was incredible! The sensations of a new journey together warmed my heart. It was like Max's love turned my 'flicker' of hope into a fire that burned inside because I now had so much more to hope for.

"Stay curious. Take risks. And beautiful things will happen," I whispered.

"I couldn't agree more. Thank you for giving me a chance," Max whispered back.

We sat there holding hands, side-by-side for a couple more minutes before Aunt Brenna walked in with a box of four slices of birthday cake for Max to take home. He waved goodbye and promised to call me in the morning.

Max stole my first kiss and my heart. If I could bottle up the feelings from that moment and experience it over and over again, I would in a heartbeat. Getting lost in the feeling of his lips for what seemed like an *eternity* would never get old.

Chapter Twenty-Two

The next morning, I still remembered Max's lips capturing mine. I was on cloud nine and was full of this *new* energy that flowed through my veins. Aunt Brenna came in with breakfast and instantly knew something was different about me today.

I just put on my biggest smile, and Aunt Brenna smiled as though she knew all the gory details of what happened last night.

"Yes?" Aunt Brenna asked.

"Yes," I replied, smiling back.

She couldn't stop screaming and grinned ear to ear. She held both of my hands and waved my arms frantically like we just won the lottery. It was nice to share in the moment with my Aunt. Her excitement reminded me of the day when she told me about her newfound relationship with André. It was great to know that both of us were now *complete*.

"I'm so happy for you, Emily! This is wonderful! You and Maximus! You two are so perfect for each other. I feel another scream coming on again. I'm going to make a batch of cookies before I head into work. And maybe an extra batch for you to share with Max later? How does that sound?" Aunt Brenna smiled, placing her arm on my shoulder.

"Delicious!" I replied with a giggle.

•••

Fear and anxiety typically accompanied a cancer diagnosis. I fell into that trap too. But once I embraced who *I* was and what was *inside* of me, it forced me to understand my own value. Me. I began to appreciate the little things in my life. And to appreciate love. Although many of those little things were now taken away from me, I appreciated what I still had. And my attitude about myself changed. I felt more confident. More beautiful. And just happier being me. My fear no longer controlled me.

My life had new meaning. A new motivation. We are the promises that we keep. And it was that sort of motivation and commitment that should define us. I had more failures than successes in my life. But anytime I did anything, I was always fully committed to see things through.

My battle against cancer should be no different. And now with things *different*, I wasn't just fighting for myself. I was fighting for Max. With Max. If just a small change in my attitude could bring such a positive influence, then perhaps changing the way I looked at cancer as a whole could improve my chances at the battlefield. My life had finally reached a point where the only direction I was going was up.

Intuitively, with this new perspective, chemotherapy no longer seemed so bad. I was still tired, to say the least. But I recovered faster between Temodal days and had more energy to get my schoolwork done. I stopped complaining about having low energy and started pushing myself more whenever I felt like I had nothing left in me. I knew that I should stop confusing my bad days as a sign of weakness. Feeling *bad* was the only way my body could communicate to me that it was working at its hardest.

And through it all, as I progressed through treatment and school, Max called me every morning and visited every night. We had indoor date nights whenever Aunt Brenna was at work. We studied together, but at my home, so it was sort of like old times. And we even went camping under the stars in my backyard on a couple of occasions.

We were sitting outside under the stars one night when Max shared some news about his friend in New Zealand. He told me that he too had found the love of his life. I was happy to hear that everyone was finding their rainbows.

Max brought over his thermal sleeping bags to make sure I was warm enough inside the tent. We gazed into the dark void above us and sat under a million glimmering stars that sparkled like diamonds. I rested my head on his shoulder, and he placed his hand on my thigh. We shared a bowl of buttery popcorn and watched the night sky like it was some sort of foreign silent film.

"You're my worst distraction, Emily McGregor," Max whispered.

"And you are mine," I replied.

Max picked up Jimi, who was resting inside the far corner of our tent, and started singing The Cure's "Friday I'm in Love."

Soon enough, I drifted off to sleep. It was just Max and me, and everything was *perfect*.

•••

In movies, falling in love was always portrayed as something slow and beautiful. Being in love always looked so easy and effortless. Even Aunt Brenna and André, made it seem that way. And it was true. However, the 'keeping it together' part was much more complicated. My mood swings. My mental breakdowns. My highs. And my lows. I had fallen victim again to this vicious cycle that cancer followed in my mind. And the mix of highs and lows repeated again, and again. I was foolish enough to believe that the only direction I was heading was up. Life could never stay on a high note. Even in music, we needed rests that sometimes interspersed with the melody.

The first few months of our relationship were loaded with fun, surprises, and constant communication. We were both lost in the haze of romance. But like many important things in life, we needed time for it to nourish and grow. Love was no different. Our relationship started progressing faster, and I began to scrutinize, analyze, and overanalyze all the things Max would say and do. And that was what scared me. I started to doubt my heart. There were nights when I was unsure if I was doing the right thing.

But if love was truly blind, then why could I still feel it in the darkness. Love was like wearing a pair of sunglasses at night. It was all-seeing and accepting. For all our flaws. For all our bad habits. For all our fears and insecurities. It was finding ways to work around all those limiting factors so that they would not be *limiting factors*. It was patience. It was devotion. And it was comfort. It was never perfect because it was real. And it was never blind because it allowed us to see more than what others were able to see. It never relied solely on our eyes. But constantly relied on our minds and our hearts. Love was fantastical, but it required a lot of work to maintain. And it was worth it.

•••

Walt Disney was one of the most powerful media giants in the world. It was an empire that created key trademark masterpieces like *Cinderella* and *Fantasia*. They owned the rights to Pixar, Marvel, and Star Wars. And defined themselves as a household name. Disney unanimously taught children to believe that it was possible to live in a fairy tale full of magic and dreams. When you wished upon a star with Disney, *anything* was possible. Sometimes I missed that portion of my childhood. Growing up wasn't all that it was cut out to be. As a child, we simply didn't stress that much about our future.

"Max, what if I can't get into *AMP*? What if—" I asked, worried, staring at the letter that Aunt Brenna left on my desk before leaving for work.

"It's not a question of *if*, but *when* Emily. You're not one to just give up on your dreams that easily. The Emily McGregor I know doesn't let anything get in her way," Max interrupted, speaking confidently.

"Save your flattery for someone else! But thanks for the inspirational spiel," I laughed.

"I'm serious, Emily. I speak the truth. You've been working on this dream for a while. You're totally dedicated. *AMP* would be blind not to accept someone of such high calibre," Max insisted.

I was able to complete the necessary requirements to apply

to *AMP*, but my grades started to slide a bit as my treatment prolonged, threatening my already late application. I submitted my application at the end of January. That was when the first round of acceptance letters for North American applicants should have been sent out. It was March now. I had a late application and knew my chances were already slim. So, as I held the letter from *AMP* in my hands, I had a gut feeling that this letter would mark the end of my dream.

Max assured me that it was not a rejection letter because he was certain those didn't come out until May or June. I took a deep breath and tore open the envelope. I closed my eyes and bit the bottom of my lip as I opened the letter. I quickly glanced over the letter, and a small smile crept onto my face. My face was flushed with triumph and success.

"No way! I got conditional acceptance! I did it!" I screamed in relief and satisfaction. I jumped up from my seat and grinned ear to ear. I turned to Max and waved my letter frantically in front of him. He gave me a quick peck on my lips and pumped his fists up in the air.

This was a proud moment. All those years of struggle to keep up my grades totally paid off for this one moment. All those days when I fought with my body to stay awake and study just a bit longer. For this one moment. I was thrilled about my acceptance letter, and I couldn't wait to see the reaction on Miss Penny's face the next time I marched into her office to give her a piece of my mind. Well, rolled into her office. But close enough.

•••

Congratulations Mademoiselle Emily McGregor!

On behalf of the President and the Board of Trustees, I am delighted to announce your conditional acceptance to the *Académie de Musique de Paris* as a candidate for the Paris campus, Bachelor of Music Degree, Guitar, September, fall semester.

A new door has opened, and a new chapter begins in the pursuit of your life's passion. Your acceptance to the *Académie de Musique de Paris* is a privilege reserved for those we determined to be bold, creative, passionate, and elite.

These qualities resonate with our community, and we have identified that you are a candidate that has the potential to thrive. We expect that you will engage with us to your fullest.

We look forward to welcoming you to the *Académie de Musique de Paris*. The Head of Guitar, Matthew Alexander, will be contacting you within the next few weeks to discuss your audition.

Yours in music,

Cane Thomas
Dean of Undergraduate Admissions
Académie de Musique de Paris

•••

"I'm so proud of you, Emily! You totally earned this moment. Now all you got to do is keep your grades up and start preparing for your audition," Max exclaimed.

"Thank you, Max," I said softly.

"For what? It was all you, Emily. I didn't do anything," he insisted.

"But you did. I couldn't have done any of this without your support. It really is a dream come true. My parents would be proud of it too. I can't wait to tell them," I cheered.

In the corner of my eye, I saw Max fidgeting uncomfortably. "Was it something I said?" I asked.

"Emily, that day. On Christmas. When you went to visit your parents. Why did you end up at the cemetery instead?" Max asked.

"My parents passed away four years ago. Car accident on Christmas Day. They were buried in my hometown, Calgary. That's where I grew up before I came here. I wanted to see them on the anniversary of their death," I explained.

Max looked shocked. I walked up to him and squeezed his hand. His face turned pale, and then a look of shame appeared on his face. It may have only lasted for a brief moment, but I could tell that Max was hiding something from me, but I just couldn't put my finger on it. Max shook out of his trance and walked towards the window.

He stared out of the window to take in the view before turning back to speak with me. "We should celebrate your acceptance letter tomorrow. How does that sound?" he asked.

"I have an MRI scheduled for tomorrow and a meeting with Dr. Meyers late afternoon. I'm usually really tired after all those medical appointments. Rain check?" I asked, a bit disappointed.

"Oh, don't look so disappointed, Emily. Celebrate, we will. We got just over four months before September, so we got plenty of time. We will do it the next day you're available. My schedule is always open for you. Your meeting with Dr. Meyers is important. Now that you've finished your treatment, it'll be good to get an update on your prognosis," Max reassured me.

"Max?" I asked.

"Yes, Emily," he responded.

"Is there anything else you want to tell me? Before you—" I asked, but Max interrupted.

"It's nothing," he insisted.

Max and I sat in silence. He seemed fine and placid on the outside, but he couldn't fool me. Although Max appeared like nothing was bothering him, I knew there was something wrong. I started to think back about the first time I'd ever mentioned *AMP* in his presence. It was the day we met. I tried to remember our conversation, but it was like a broken puzzle with missing pieces. And my brain just couldn't fill in the gaps.

Then it hit me hard. I knew exactly what was wrong. Max was a very analytical man. I had always been grateful to him for forewarning me about many of life's problems. Although being forewarned did not necessarily prepare me for how my life would change, it was still nice getting the heads up from time to time.

I was certain that Max spotted this earlier but was afraid

to follow through in fear of stealing my thunder from today's exciting news. I had spent almost every waking minute, hanging out with Max once we met. Our longest separation was a three-week span between Christmas and my birthday a couple of months ago. And that was before we were a *thing*. We shared almost everything together, so was relocating to Paris for *AMP* a sign of disrespect to our relationship?

We'd just started our journey together, and with cancer, things got quite complicated but survived. I now felt a tad bit guilty for submitting my application without consideration of Max's feelings.

I knew that Max did not want to lose me again. Ugh. I should have just kept my doors opened for that ultimate French boyfriend.

Chapter Twenty-Three

Today was another big day. I had been taking MRIs every three-months since treatment started to monitor the tumour in my brain closely. I'd finished my last round of *Temodal* to close off my final 28-day cycle of chemotherapy last week. Phase two was officially complete. I worried about the scan though. I felt better towards the latter half of the treatment, but still had occasional episodes of seizures, headaches, and numbing pain.

I decided to visit Anna before heading over to oncology to cheer myself up. As I approached room 55, something seemed different today. Mabel saw me wheeling down the hallway of the ICU and stopped to give me a warm hug.

"Good morning Emily! I've missed you. Though, I'm sure you didn't miss me that much 'cause it's never a good thing if you saw too much of me, eh?" Mabel laughed.

"I missed you too, Mabel," I said. We spent some time catching up. I told her that Max and I were now official, and she was ecstatic that the two of us finally kicked it off. We chatted about the latest news, recommended a list of new Netflix series to watch, and after all of that, I asked her about my friend, Anna.

"Ah, yes, Anna Minor. Our latest medical miracle. She woke up one day with all the fluid drained from her lungs. She'd been in a clinical trial for over fifteen months, and then one day, she wakes up and is almost cured. Her lungs were clear of fluid. She didn't feel weak. And although she still needs a cannula for extra oxygen, she remained stable for a whole month, so the doctors discharged her. Her mother came to pick her up last night. Sorry, you missed her. She's still an outpatient. You may see her around the next time she's in. I'll let her know that you were looking for her," Mabel explained.

I was thrilled that Anna could finally leave *G&C*. Though, a part of me wished she was still here. I loved visiting her every time I was at the hospital. But I was happy that her wish finally came true. I whispered under my breath, "Hope."

"You don't mind if I just take a peek in her room?" I asked.

"Go right ahead, dear. I'll be clearing it out later this afternoon for a new patient, so you better take a look while everything's still there," Mabel insisted.

"Thanks, Mabel. I won't be long," I replied.

I walked down the hall to room 55. It was strange opening the door and not seeing Anna's cheery smile on the other side. Her room was still filled with her drawings. She only took George and Lucas home. I rolled up to the side of her bed and used her abandoned IV pole for support. I made my way to the wall where her drawings hung and began taking them down, one by one. I'd noticed that a couple were missing. They were the drawings that I'd drew for her. That made me smile. I sat down in her visitor chair to catch my breath. Standing for too long was still a struggle for me. I only hoped that once the chemo drugs were out of my system, then I would regain more strength in my body.

I got back up to finish removing the last few of her drawings and placed them in a neat pile on her bedside table. Mabel came in soon after as I wobbled back over to my wheelchair.

"You keep them. I was going to toss them anyway. If she wanted them, she would have taken them when she left," Mabel said.

I nodded and flashed a small smile.

Mabel picked up the pile and walked over towards me. She began flipping through her artwork until she stopped at one that caught her eye.

"See something you like, Mabel? Anna's such an amazing artist for a seven-year-old. She got a lot of talent that girl," I said fondly.

"Emily, you got to see this," Mabel said. She moved the photo of interest to the top of the pile and placed the whole stack onto my lap. "That's you with the guitar. And it looks like that's her with her stuffed teddy bear. I think you're all outside under the stars in a desert or something. I see a cactus."

To everyone else, this drawing was like all the others left behind in room 55. There was nothing unique about it, except that it had someone who resembled me. But in my eyes, the drawing was more than a sketch. It was a message from Anna that said both 'thank you' and 'goodbye' all at the same time. She wanted me to know that she was safe and that we would all meet one day again under the stars. Anna always wanted it to stop raining. It finally did.

●●●

I was in a good mood going into my meeting with Dr. Meyers. Now that I was eighteen, Aunt Brenna didn't have to accompany me to my meetings with the doctors. It actually made it easier for her since she didn't have to switch shifts to accommodate my schedule. Although she insisted on accompanying me for moral support, I assured her that I would be fine today. The past MRIs were all the same. Unchanged. Stable. Nothing new to report.

But the little *high* that I was riding on wasn't enough to stop me from hitting the ground hard. Dr. Meyers entered the room and showed me the MRI scan. The truth hit me hard, and it was too hard to handle. All these months, I'd been slightly disappointed about my MRI results showing no significant change to my tumour size. But I'd failed to recognize the positives of stability. And now I faced the worst news of it all.

"It appears that your tumour has progressed," Dr. Meyers said with a sigh.

"Progressed?" I said, alarmed.

"Yes, Emily. There's no easy way to say this. But your MRI results show an increase in your tumour's size. As you see here, there's a distinct appearance of a tumour where the center is necrotic, which is characteristic of glioblastoma multiforme. You see, glioblastoma tumours grow so quickly that they outgrow their blood supply, which is why you see a bunch of dead cells right here in the center and a lot of swelling and inflammation. It's about acorn sized. Unfortunately, treatment could not control the growth of your tumour. It has already spread to an area of your brain that is inoperable, so I am unable to attempt removal," Dr. Meyers explained.

"Where exactly?" I asked.

"Your tumour has spread deep to parts of both the frontal and temporal lobe, which control your movement and speech respectively. Surgery could cause irreparable neurological damage, so I advise against it," Dr. Meyers said solemnly.

Now I knew exactly how Gord Downie felt when he learned of his prognosis, even without watching his documentary. GBM was stage IV. And there was nothing more the doctors could do for me, except to offer me comfort in my dying days. There was no such thing as stage V. GBM was the most malignant of all brain tumours. My cancer really was incurable. And I had a ginormous squirrel monster living inside my head.

I backed up in my wheelchair. The news was too hard to handle. I held back tears and bit my lip until I tasted blood in my mouth. I kept shaking my head. I didn't want to believe what Dr. Meyers was saying.

"No, you're wrong. It's a lie. It's all a terrible, terrible lie," I screamed, my voice shaking uncontrollably. I struggled to contain my emotions.

"You have some very difficult decisions to make in the coming weeks. I'm sorry, Emily. Let me give you a moment, and we will discuss our options," Dr. Meyers said as he got up from his desk and left the room to give me some privacy.

I'd entered the world of denial again. I'd survived brain surgery. I'd been stable throughout radiation and chemo. I'd beat this once before. Even pneumonia didn't kill me. How was it possible for so much to change since my last MRI?

I finally had everything I'd ever imagined. An amazing boyfriend. *AMP* acceptance. And my Aunt was no longer single. I still had so many more big moments that I wanted to experience. As I recounted my most recent big moments, there was a grim realization that the joys from all those big moments were no longer there. News of GBM stripped away my dreams. My future was now blurry again. What was supposed to be *big* was now inconsequential because I had *bigger* things to worry about. I didn't want to accept my fate. I wasn't ready to die. Not yet. Not like this.

I curled up in the seat of my wheelchair and closed my eyes. I pulled my knees tightly into my chest and screamed loudly from the inside. I hung my head low and buried it under my arms. My first tear broke free, and the rest followed in an unbroken stream. I cried until I had no more tears inside of me. I did it again with the crying. I was a mess. I was a pathetic mess. All I could hear now was Green Day's "Boulevard of Broken Dreams" playing in an infinite loop.

•••

Dr. Meyers returned to the room after my fifteen minutes of solitude. I felt better, just slightly, after releasing the anguish and fear that was bottled up inside.

"How long do I have? Before I die?" I asked bluntly. I didn't want to know the answer to this question, but I knew knowing would help me prepare for the inevitable and tie off any loose ends that needed my attention.

"Less than a year. Fifteen months at most," Dr. Meyers replied.

"So, do I just sit here and wait to die? What are my options?" I asked, trying to be mature about the whole situation.

"Unfortunately, glioblastoma is a terminal illness. But we would like to run some tests to see if you qualify for one of our new clinical trials. We are constantly researching new treatments to cure cancer here at *G&C*, and I want to offer you some options to prolong your time. We can see from your previous treatment plan that the more standard treatment methods used for brain tumours were not effective at managing your tumour. I am considering anti-angiogenic treatment and immunotherapy this time. We can discuss this once we see if you qualify for these clinical trials. Or we can consider some new radiation techniques for GBM like stereotactic radiosurgery. And if all else fails, we will do our best to make you comfortable and offer you space in our palliative care unit," Dr. Meyers explained.

"I understand. Thank you, Dr. Meyers. Thank you," I said solemnly. I had no more tears in me. The meeting room suddenly felt claustrophobic. I just wanted to get out of here as quickly as possible, so I could breathe.

•••

There was no cure to GBM. There were medical miracles, but even those were few and rare. There are over a hundred different types of cancer that could be found almost anywhere in our bodies. Not every cancer patient matched the textbook definition of the cancer they'd been diagnosed. Even the way we responded to treatment was dependent on the individual. And technically that totally made sense because everyone even reacted to mosquito bites differently. Doctors are supposed to devise a treatment plan to tackle reality, not some perfected version of it. With every situation in the textbook, we were bound to have outliers. I only wished I could be an outlier.

Treatment of brain cancer was always complex. But new therapies for cancer were being developed all the time. When they showed some promise, researchers then tested those therapies in labs before finding volunteer cancer patients to be the lab rat. Although clinical trials posed a risk of not being proven to work for everyone, I liked how it offered me some hope.

If GBM were a death sentence, then I would prefer to be the marathon runner trying to extend my finish line to life's race. Ironically, a couple of months ago, I wanted to die so badly. Now, I wanted to live so badly. Life really was unfair. And now, no one would even dare to promise my victory in this cancer battle. How could I remain hopeful if I was a lost cause?

Chapter Twenty-Four

Glioblastoma. Glioblastoma. Gosh, what did I do to deserve glioblastoma? I don't even know how to pronounce the name of this disease that has taken my brain as a hostage.

Ten missed calls. Fifteen unread text messages. Max. I wanted to be alone. I was going to die alone, anyway. And I just needed *time* to digest everything. I appreciated Dr. Meyers being direct with me instead of sugar coating the statistics. In some ways, this outcome was better than how my parents ended their stories. At least I know. I actually had the chance to say goodbye. Gosh, I hated goodbyes.

•••

Life liked to toy with my mind. Whenever we heard the truth, we wished we had not. Yet, before the truth was told, we were dying of curiosity to dig it out. We wasted a lot of *time* trying to predict or know our unreliable future while the present was slipping away from our hands. As Dr. Seuss once said, "Today I shall behave as if this is the day I will be remembered."

Time. *Time* was now my true enemy. It wasn't just the enemy within. It seemed like the whole world was against me now, and there was little I could do in the face of such a powerful adversary. Resistance to treatment still remained a huge challenge. Cancer was complicated, with too many unknowns. I'd already tried chemotherapy alongside surgery and radiation. These treatments were the mainstay of modern oncology, but my tumour remained stubbornly incurable. Any gains were blown away when my tumour progressed to its final stage. Despite the multitude of drugs in an oncologist's arsenal today, the knife still cured more cancers. But now, going under the knife again was not even an option. I felt stuck.

Cancer was a disease to be feared, only to be mentioned in whispers. A diagnosis of brain cancer was tantamount to a death sentence. There was no prevention. No cure. It wasn't even clear what actually caused it. Was it our lifestyle? Our diet? Our environment? Was it preventable? Was I born with it? Or was it induced by stress? It could have been a combination of all those things (and perhaps *other* things). And I would never know.

•••

I sat outside *G&C* at my safe haven under my lonely willow tree. There was a splendid feeling I got in silence. Surrounded by the quiet hum of the wind under the warmth of the sun, it gave me an opportunity for reflection. Something I really needed right now. It would be absurd to speak to our inner voice in a noisy realm. The two just did not go well together.

I continued sitting under the willow tree until the sun set in the horizon. And when the stars illuminated the night sky, I sat there to take in the beautiful spectacle above me. As I watched the gradual transition of day to night in the sky, I thought about how picturesque the contrast was between the dreary hospital room, the vibrant sunset sky, and the sparkling starline. If nature was always this beautiful, I should have become a geographer instead of a musician. I soaked in the last few rays of colour before the sky turned pitch black with speckles of light. Ten more missed calls. Six more unread text messages. Aunt Brenna and Max.

I let out a loud sigh. I didn't want to face them. I didn't want to tell them. How on earth do I tell someone I love that I'm dying. How? Do I just mention it casually, like 'Hey, by the way, I'm dying,' or was I supposed to be more sensitive?

A disease that I'd been fighting for almost a year had taken a turn for the worse. Dr. Meyers had brought up palliative care for the first time. So, he wasn't kidding when he said it was terminal. There was no single right way to tell someone about my impending death. Although I did not want to believe it, death was near. No right time to break the news. No proven method that would result in the least amount of pain.

People often felt uncomfortable around the subject of death. I know. I felt that way, too, when my parents died. I was terribly hurt about how I couldn't give them a proper goodbye. So, maybe this was fate giving me a chance to redeem myself.

I was hurt when my parents died so suddenly. I wished I could have been there with them to hear their last words before they disappeared from this world. Not many eighteen-year-olds could say that they empathized with both sides of the spectrum. Even today, I'm still a victim of grief. Death doesn't make us disappear completely from this world. Remnants would forever remain in the hearts of those we touched.

Decisions. Very tough decisions. I had one foot already stuck in the grave and had absolutely no idea which way I should look for support. How I decided to face death was a profoundly personal decision. My mind was swirling, considering all options. I tried to play out each scenario. But none of them were really all that good. Then again, how could death be good?

If I stayed hush, I would face this alone. I would hurt those who wanted to be there for me. But a silent goodbye would spare Aunt Brenna and Max (and maybe even me) of despair and the pain of a tearful goodbye. I continued to contemplate my options to devise a game plan.

If I told the truth, I would be accepting my fate. But I would not have to face this alone. It would give those I loved a sense of closure with my final days encompassed in their love. Though I dreaded the idea of being drenched in their tears, and I did not want to burden them more than I already have.

I looked to the sky, as though it had all the answers. I feared death. But I also feared the distress my death would cause to those closest to me. What to do? What to do? This shouldn't have been such a hard decision. Deep down, I knew that whatever I decided to do, I had to be content with that choice. I should not spend my precious time second-guessing myself. I had to make a choice. One choice. And then just go with it.

So, I closed my eyes and thought of the first thing that came to mind. I was sitting at *Amore* in the corner booth. There was Max, Aunt Brenna, and André. We were on a double date. Laughing.

Having fun. And enjoy a cup of coffee together.

I knew what I had to do. I had to be straightforward with them. I just had to.

My phone rang again, and I opened my eyes. It was Aunt Brenna. I swallowed hard and decided to pick up this time.

"Where are you, Emily? You have to stop scaring me like that! When are you coming home? You need to rest. Is something wrong, honey?" Aunt Brenna asked.

She sounded relieved that I picked up the phone, but also frustrated about me being MIA. Ever since my pneumonia scare, she'd been keeping tabs on me and have been extra cautious with everything.

"I'll be home soon. Just tied up at the hospital still. I would have called earlier. But you know," I said, unwilling to say more.

"Oh, Emily, you should have told me you were still there. I would have waited for you. Wasn't your meeting with Dr. Meyers at three in the afternoon?" she asked, concerned.

"It was delayed, and I went to visit my friend in the ICU. I'll be home soon. We can talk more then, okay?" I replied.

"Sure, Em. See you soon. Love you," Aunt Brenna exclaimed.

"Love you too," I said and then hung up.

Then a familiar voice echoed from behind me. I bit my lip and swiveled my wheelchair around to look. And there standing directly in front of me was a very handsome and sweaty Max Miller with a mischievous grin that always made my heart swoon.

"Emily!" Max exclaimed, catching his breath. He looked like

he just ran a marathon in his suit. "I've been looking all over for you. And might I say, you're quite hard to find. It's like looking for 'Where's Waldo' without any clues."

"And you are quite hard to hide from," I chuckled.

Max walked up and planted a soft kiss on my forehead. I placed my hand on his cheek and wiped some sweat off his brow.

"You know, they make sweats and tracksuits for a reason. Didn't know that you dress professionally for a jog, too," I joked.

"I didn't plan on jogging today. I got worried when you didn't return my calls, so I came by after practicum to see if you were still at the hospital. I was on a wild goose chase until I saw Mabel. I love that lady. Quite the talker. She told me about her new car, about Anna, and even about how you've been sitting under this willow tree for over five hours. What gives?" Max explained.

Mabel must have noticed me when she was preparing room 55 for her new patient. Curse her impeccable eyesight.

"Emily, it's either your MRI went so well that you already started celebrating without me, or there's something that's really bothering you. And if I know you well enough, I think it's the latter, isn't it?" Max said, cupping my face so he could take a closer look at my puffy eyelids, red eyes, and blotchy face. "You've been crying, haven't you?" Then, Max noticed my bloody lip and alarm spread in his eyes, "Did somebody hurt you? Let's go inside and get you cleaned up."

Max started to quickly wheel me towards the hospital, but I screamed, "Stop!"

Max stopped in his tracks, and his hands dropped to his sides.

I turned my wheelchair to face him as my lips quivered. Max quickly kneeled beside me and pulled me into a tight hug.

"Max, I—" I started, but a lump formed in my throat. My breath stuttered, and another tear trickled down my cheek. I tried my best to hold back the seething avalanche of tears that had been building up since I came outside. I just had to tell Max. I just had to.

"I think I'm going to decline my offer to *AMP*," I said.

"But Emily, that is your life dream. One audition, and then you got it. I thought we already made plans to tape a copy of that acceptance letter on Miss Penny's office door next week. What's with the sudden change in heart?" Max asked.

"I can't go," I replied bluntly.

"You're going to love it there, Emily. I know I wasn't as excited for you as I should have been yesterday, but I was just scared about losing you. I'm sorry if that gave you second thoughts. I thought about it a lot when I left, and I was wrong to raid on your parade. I should never be the one stopping you from fulfilling your lifelong dreams. Being in a healthy and strong relationship means we should support each other, talk, and compromise. We do things together and talk things out until they are right," Max explained.

"But Max," I interrupted.

"Emily, accept it. I'll find an internship over there, and we can still be together. I was talking with my supervisor today about some options. I know the area well. There's a nice coffee shop that I'm sure you'll love on the north side of the campus too. It's quaint. They don't make double-shot espressos as good as *Amore*, but their cappuccinos are to die for. I'm not going to let my girlfriend get away from me that easily," Max said with a smile.

I was confused. Why was Max doing all of this for me? What have I done in my life to deserve such an amazing boyfriend? I felt even more terrible about what I was about to say. But then, it suddenly hit me. How did Max know so much about *AMP*? Only people who lived in a place before would be aware of hidden gems within the city. Paris was a big place and Max never mentioned that he was an avid traveller. Did Max react yesterday to my letter only because he was afraid of having a long distance relationship? I was unsure. But it seemed like we all had our secrets. We all do.

"Max?" I interrupted again, but Max put his finger on my lips to let me know that he wanted to finish what he had to say.

Max's shoulders dropped, and he let out a sigh before he continued. "It was me. I was the lone *Glenwood High* graduate who got accepted to *AMP*. But I dropped out in my second year, returned home, and started med school. Let's just say I was a much-maligned *beast* on my guitar. Alexander was probably relieved about the whole thing. He always told me that my unwillingness to learn how to pick with my hand floating would handicap me in his program. I never understood the great debate to anchor or not to anchor. Alexander disliked how I rested my wrist on the bridge, arguing that down picking anchored restricted my movement and speed as a guitarist," Max confessed.

I raised my eyebrows. Shocked. No wonder Max was bitter when I mentioned *AMP* the day we first met. Max may have been what he referred to himself as a 'much-maligned beast' on his guitar, but his music had tremendous spirit and imagination. He was definitely the stronger guitarist between us. Even if Alexander just needed some time to warm up to his tunes, Max didn't seem like one to just give up on something he loved that easily. I tried to piece everything together in my head, but some things just didn't add up.

"It was you?" I blurted out.

"Ya, it was me," Max said, slightly embarrassed.

"All this time, you never said anything. Why?" I asked, confused why he kept it a secret for so long. There was nothing wrong with dropping out of a program if it didn't match his needs.

"You never asked," Max said defensively.

"Why med school after? Doesn't seem like you really like it there," I asked.

"Mom wants me to be a doctor. I didn't listen to her. Applied to *AMP* anyways. So, when I dropped out, I thought I listen to her for once. She probably knew that *AMP* wasn't for me when I first applied. You know, the whole bloodline thing. Maybe that's why she'd always been insisting that I become a doctor. Like it's my calling or something. That or an athlete like my Dad," Max explained.

"I appreciate that you're telling me all of this. I really do. But the thing is, I'm not declining because of *that*. Don't get me wrong; I did consider it. I thought you were upset about me leaving and that doing so meant that I didn't value our relationship. I really didn't mean to hurt you in any way. And I felt guilty about doing that to you too. About forcing you into a long-distance relationship without any consideration of your feelings. You're really important to me, Max, and I couldn't imagine a life without you," I admitted.

"I can't imagine a life without you too, Emily," Max replied.

It was a comment like that which made what I was going to say even more difficult. But I continued. "I'm blown away with all the trouble you went through to find a compromise. I couldn't ask for a better boyfriend, and I'm so glad I have you. But—" I stopped, choking on my tears. I paused to compose myself. I just had to tell Max. I promised myself that I'd tell the ones I loved. I had to follow through.

So, I closed my eyes and squeezed my hands tight into a fist. Tears endlessly trickled down my cheek. I bit my lip really hard again; I could taste the blood in my mouth.

"Emily? What are you doing? You're going to hurt yourself!" Max gasped. He rubbed the small of my back to try to help me calm down.

"You see, I'm dying, Max. And you can't turn something terminal into a joke. It's very real," I confessed.

I said it. I finally said it. My heart ached. Why did my reality hurt so bad? And after I saw the pained expression on Max's face, everything hurt even *more*.

"But you were getting better. This must be some mistake. No. You're kidding, right?" Max said, unwilling to accept what I had just told him.

"GBM, stage IV. It's a death sentence," I admitted.

"No, it just. No, it's not. No," Max repeated.

I reached for his hand, but he pulled me into a tight hug. Max shook his head and spoke. "I'm not going to accept it. We are going to keep fighting, okay? Let's get a second opinion. No way I'm going to accept this. There's still hope, Emily. I know it. We're going to kick GBM out of your noggin. Trust me on this one, nothing is *impossible.* Even the word impossible has '*possible*' in it. There's still hope."

•••

Max drove me home after cleaning me up in the hospital. The car ride back was in complete silence. Max didn't even turn on the radio to listen to tunes, which never happens in Max's car. Never.

As we pulled up onto Aunt Brenna's driveway, I let out a huge sigh. It was time to tell Aunt Brenna. I had to.

And right on cue, Aunt Brenna rushed out of the house the moment we pulled up onto her driveway. She hugged me and told me that she saved a huge bowl of lasagna for me on the stove. Max gave us a nod and restarted his car. I wanted Max to stay, though. I needed his support now more than ever.

I looked towards him and asked, "Aunt Brenna, can Max stay for dinner?"

"Maximus is always welcomed at our house. I'll get the plates ready," Aunt Brenna cheered as Max turned off the car engine.

He got out of his car and walked up behind me. Aunt Brenna smiled and Max wheeled me inside the house.

The lasagna was delicious. Aunt Brenna was getting better at cooking. I only wished I had more time to taste all her improved dishes. Ah, good ol' fashioned lasagna. A pasta dish that was like the pasta version of shepherd's pie, made with pasta instead of potato. It was a gloopy, cheese feast that just hit the spot and stood on my plate sturdy without a bunch of meaty, tomatoey sauce oozing outwards across the plate. Aunt Brenna truly perfected this all-time classic. I was really proud of her. André would be in good hands when I leave this world.

After Max cleared the dishes, we sat down in the kitchen where I eventually told Aunt Brenna the grim news. Aunt Brenna broke down in tears. She started blaming herself for all that had happened to me. Which was absurd because she wasn't the one who gave me the brain tumour. No one would ever wish this sort of thing onto anyone. Not even for our worst enemy.

"I failed to take care of you, Emily," Aunt Brenna muttered between sobs.

"No, Aunt Brenna, you'd never failed me. Cancer just chose me because it thought I was up for the challenge," I said.

I held Max's hand tightly as I spoke. And I told them *everything*. I told them about my MRI. About the squirrel living inside my head. About the grim prognosis. About my remaining options. Even about my struggle to tell them all that I knew.

Life never promised to be fair. Life never promised to be easy. This was probably *the* biggest and toughest thing I'd ever faced in my life. Being on the short end of the stick. I finally knew how my story ended, but the number of pages it took before I reached the end was still unknown.

How are we to face death? At such times, the profound importance of family was reasserted, underscored, and brought into relief. Out the door was the arguments, the indifferences, the misunderstandings. Death brought everything into focus. It purified. It clarified. It was an awful reality, yes, but not as awful as we made it be.

In my denial of impermanence, I felt like I was trying to clutch running water with my open fingers, only to find that I could hold very little of the liquid in my grasp. Clinging onto our lives when our days were outnumbered had that very same feeling. Death was the inescapable part of life. And it was what made life so important.

After getting everything off my chest, I felt the weight lifted off my shoulders. Although I was never a strong swimmer, I was no longer drowning in my melancholy and fears. I was somehow floating, albeit in the middle of the ocean, in search of land. And here in front of me presented an opportunity for extraordinary growth.

Before Max left that evening, he serenaded me with Martina McBride's "I'm Gonna Love You Through It." This song was coined the 'cancer song,' written for women suffering from breast cancer. The words were empowering. And having Max sing it to me made me feel like I wasn't alone. Music was a very powerful thing.

His voice sang sweetly as he strummed the tune on Jimi and gazed into my eyes. It was a beautiful moment between Max and me. And it was at that moment I'd realized how much Max meant to me. When we're diagnosed with cancer, everybody else around us was diagnosed as well. This *was* the toughest part to accept, apart from the possibility of death, of course. We all were afraid. The reality was insurmountable. But the support I'd received from Aunt Brenna and Max was incredible, and I was so lucky to have that type of support system. They'd showered me with love. But more importantly, they never made me feel like a burden, even though I sometimes thought I was. I knew they loved me, but I had no idea *how much* they loved me until I got really sick.

I was no longer afraid for myself or for any of us. When the darkness comes, as it must, I can only stand in front of the shadow and understand that I was now on the other side of the light.

Although I believed in truth and wanted to protect Aunt Brenna and Max, to deceive them was to exclude them from the recalibration of the inner self. Not just for me, but for all of us. Loss and change were inevitable. For Aunt Brenna and Max, the worst part of grief wasn't that I was dying. It was the part of me *inside* of them that made dying so hard. I'd realized why the death of a loved one hurt more than the pain and suffering we saw in the wider world. Compassion hurt. It meant suffering with and caring deeply about someone we loved. To love someone was to hurt for them as well. Death hurt. For me. For Aunt Brenna. And for Max. Cancer affected *all* of us.

Chapter Twenty-Five

I grappled over the possibility that my days were outnumbered. Although it seemed pointless for me to continue school or to try out for my audition, I still went through with everything. It was business as usual. I spent many days reflecting on the part of me that would go on living even after I was dead. My legacy. I did not want to just give up on life. Cancer could take away my *time*, but it could not take away my *spirit*. We are the promises that we keep. No matter how hard life may get, I had to finish what I started.

My mind swirled with a plethora of questions as I attempted to seek some measure of peace and consolation as I faced life's final challenge. I was still saddened that although *destiny* had pulled Max and I together, it was destiny that was also pulling us apart. I desperately longed for my eternity with Max. Although I'd accepted my fate, I wasn't ready to leave when my journey with Max had just begun. We had so much more to share with each other. So many more songs to write together. So many undiscovered places to still explore. And I was going to die a virgin too, but who's counting. *C'est la vie.*

In the next few weeks, I underwent several tests at *G&C*. Max accompanied me to all of them. He was my pillar of support, helping me through many difficult moments in my life. Max really was my strength when I thought I had none left in me.

Unfortunately, the size of my tumours were too large for clinical trials and Dr. Babinski was doubtful that my body was strong enough for gamma knife surgery, which was my only hope in helping to reduce my tumour size and qualify for the clinical trials. The risks of gamma knife surgery were too high. Plus, I was excluded from most clinical trials anyway because I'd already had radiation and chemotherapy too. Many trials required the patient to be newly diagnosed. So, after weeks of testing, Dr. Meyers eventually prescribed some medication to make me more *comfortable* and told me that he would prepare my application for *G&C*'s palliative care unit and assign me a social worker for mental support. The truth hurt. But today, I handled it better with Max by my side.

As Max wheeled me out of *G&C* towards the willow trees, I looked up to him and reached out for his hand. Max stopped and placed his hand over mine. We stood there together under the silent whisper of the wind brushing against the leaves of the willow trees. He swiveled the wheelchair around so I could look at him. We both put a small smile on, and Max leaned in to give me a soft, passionate kiss. Our noses pressed against each other as our tongues twisted a million different directions, dancing inside our mouths. It was so natural, smooth, and unexpected. My heart pounded, and I warmed from head to toe. It felt like a lucid dream. It was a beautiful connection.

"I could have millions of years with you, and it would still be *too soon*. I don't want to leave you. I don't want to die. I love our life together, and it hasn't been long enough," I blurted out.

"Me too, Emily. Me too," Max said softly.

•••

My hair ended up growing back once I stopped Temodal. It wasn't like my normal hair. It was thin, fuzzy hair that started covering the surface of my bald head a few weeks after my last chemo treatment. From a distance, it was invisible as it was thin, and it grew back as patches, so my head looked unruly at times. It was weird seeing my head with hair again. I admit I'd gotten used to my bald look.

As my hair grew, Aunt Brenna and I started contemplating about different short hairdos that matched the shape of my face. She was even thrilled about being able to book hair appointments together again as it was one of the few girlie things I used to do just with her. And for Max. Well, he was thrilled to get his hat back. Though, I borrowed it from time-to-time still just for good luck.

I met with Dr. Meyers later in the week to ask him about whether I was healthy enough to travel. My audition was scheduled in two weeks, and Alexander already sent me details about the day's events.

A month ago, I'd become completely reliant on my wheelchair. I used to only use it for times when I left the house or on days when I felt very weak, but that was no longer an option. I lost the strength to stand up on my own. Walking just a few steps to transfer myself from the wheelchair to bathroom necessities became an excruciatingly painful chore. I hobbled. I crawled. I cried.

I remembered the very first time I lowered myself into a wheelchair was back in the ICU. I fantasized about a world of Paralympian glory and how easy they made using a wheelchair look. But boy was I wrong. I managed maybe just a couple of metres from the doorway before my arms seized up and I had to stop. After a few attempts, my hands blistered. I never complained if someone offered to push me. Especially since, more often than not, many places were not wheelchair accessible, and the extra help was welcomed. Inside the hospital, though, I never got the weird and uncomfortable stares. But outside, I got the odd gawp. I was tired of being called 'the bald lady on wheels,' and surprisingly, their eyes were more hurtful than any of the name-calling.

Although my body was deteriorating rapidly, I was not one to give in to defeat so easily. I knew my cancer was invading for more territory inside, and I was on the losing side of the battle. But I had to do something. Anything. To put up a fight.

I challenged myself intentionally every day. I needed a way to tell my body, 'No!' Not yet. Not now. Not never. So, I fought with myself every morning and every night. I pushed myself to walk from my bed to my desk without any assistance. I fell on several occasions. I got bruises. I scraped my arm. I banged my knee. But each time, I got up, I continued. And I kept going and going until I reached my destination. It was the least I could do to encourage myself in my battle. If I could learn to walk again, then there was hope.

More often than not, we faced our challenges alone. I was fighting with myself every day. I couldn't let my cancer control my life. By challenging myself to fight in my dying days came this incredible *strength* to move forward in life. Bit by bit. Day by day. I simply could not subsist in the status quo of just 'getting by' and *surviving*. Our greatest flaw is our tendency to just give up. Success always came if we tried just one more time.

In truth, not a lot of people know what it was really like to be me. Or what it was like to be in *that* chair, with all the extra things I had to think about and do because of my cancer. Sometimes, I'd like to be *normal* and do everything a *normal* person would do. So, on my good days, although there were few, I added more songs to my Wall of Hope, went on dates with Max, and made chocolate chip cookies with Aunt Brenna.

Dr. Meyers, obviously, did not give me the green light to travel to New York, where *AMP* auditions for North American applicants were being held. And after my pneumonia scare last Christmas, I wasn't going to risk anything this time around. So, unless I was going to be blessed with some sort of medical miracle, *AMP* was no longer in my immediate agenda. It wasn't like I'd actually given up, but I knew I had to pick my battles, and *AMP* was no longer feasible in my current condition. But I still wanted my audition. It became more of a personal thing for me. To tie loose ends. To finish what I started. So, I sent Alexander an email to request for other options.

"I told Alexander about my situation. Well, not the terminal part. But enough for him to understand that I could not travel until September. At least that was what I told him. Alexander agreed to a video audition, but I'll need to borrow some equipment from my Dad's studio. Do you mind driving down to Calgary this week? I can show you my Dad's studio," I asked.

Max didn't respond at first. He was looking out my bedroom window, deep in thought. Then he turned around to face me and nodded. "I'll be happy to help, Emily," Max agreed, leaning down to kiss me. "So, does that mean I scored front row seats for your lucrative performance?" Max asked, with a glimmer in his eyes. Max's awe-filled expression was accompanied by his widened eyes and raised eyebrows. He flashed a mischievous grin before chuckling.

"Ha, ha, ha. Very funny, Max. If you're going to watch me perform, then just promise me that you won't put on that grin you have on your face right now, or I'll get distracted and mess up my performance. Behave, okay? Having you there will help with my nerves, but you're also a bit of a distraction," I confessed.

"Emily, it's all in your head," Max said, pointing to my noggin.

"I know. That's why I have cancer. I probably think too much," I joked.

"No, really, Emily, stage fright is all in your head. Just imagine yourself wearing a helmet. Does your Aunt have one in her attic? Perhaps you should practice singing this week while wearing one," Max suggested.

"A helmet? How would that help me overcome my stage phobia? Don't people usually suggest imagining everyone in their underwear. I actually tried that and it doesn't work. I end up laughing instead. What do you know, undergarments are just so funny," I laughed.

"Underwear, eh. Bet you can't guess what colour mine is," Max chuckled.

"Max! Stop changing the subject," I giggled.

"And you claim that *I'm* the distraction. You should speak for yourself, young lady," Max joked.

"So, this helmet you speak of. Please enlighten me," I insisted.

"Well, if you're not naturally comfortable on stage, try putting a helmet on so you don't have to *see* it. You know, your audience. And then somehow you get from nothing to something. You'll stop fumbling over your words. You'll stop pausing unnecessarily. I'm certain that you won't feel intimidated by their presence because you won't see any of it. You'll get so used to being in the *zone* that when you actually remove the helmet, performing would feel less of a daunting task, and you would feel free to develop your own sounds," Max explained.

"That actually seems plausible," I admitted.

"Then let's give it a try then," Max said with a smile.

Later that day, we asked Aunt Brenna about the helmet. Max found her old goalie helmet from her time on the Glenwood Grunts in her senior year of high school. I would have never considered Aunt Brenna as the athletic type.

The helmet was simple. It was painted all black with a silver star on the front. I felt weird wearing it at first, and it was a bit constricting on my head. It was like riding a three-legged horse. It wasn't as comfortable, but it still got us to our final destination.

With each day, jamming got easier and easier. That by the end of the week, I actually willingly took off the helmet and just played like a *normal* guitarist. The goalie mask no longer muffled my voice, and my music now vocalized the confidence I'd gain from the whole experiment. All Max could do was smile.

"You're ready, Emily. You're ready," he said proudly.

•••

I spent the weekend writing the song I wanted to perform for my audition. I considered singing one of the songs already written in my Moleskine notebook, but because this was going to be my first, and likely last, performance, I wanted to make it count.

Now my biggest challenge was no longer the audience. It was finding enough strength for a thirty-minute audition. I spent most of the day sleeping to ensure that tiredness was not going to be my limiting factor tomorrow on my big day.

Max came by to visit in the evening to sort out travel logistics. He knocked on my room door and surprised me with a bouquet of a dozen red roses.

"Oh, Max, you shouldn't have," I blushed.

"For my beautiful Emily, even a dozen roses aren't enough to show you how much I love you," Max exclaimed.

"Max, don't be silly. They are lovely. I don't need a dozen roses. Even if you came with just a dandelion you picked off my front lawn, I would still love it because it was a gift from you," I said sweetly as a wave of exhaustion crept up on me after his grand entrance.

Max placed the bouquet on my desk and sat down beside me on my bed. He leaned in, and as our lips touched, our tongues passionately danced together before we gasped for air. It was like Max could read my mind. I was totally awake now. Max always had a way of getting my undivided attention.

Max flashed a mischievous grin and winked while placing his hand in his suit pocket. What was Max up to tonight? He removed a tiny box from his pocket and smiled as he stole a quick peck off my lips.

“I want you to accept this necklace as a token of my love to you. You are my beauty, and I am your beast. This necklace will now rest around your neck so I can continue protecting you even when I’m not around. Mom tells me that it’s lucky, like my hat.” Max said with a smile as he put the necklace around my neck.

The necklace was beautiful. It was sparkling silver and had a star-shaped diamond pendant that glimmered in the moonlight. It was like Max picked out one of the millions of twinkling stars in the night sky and sealed it into this necklace. I thought of the many nights we laid together in my backyard under the stars. Each star, a twinkle of hope.

“Max, I can’t accept something so valuable. You’re a med student. You don’t need to buy me expensive things, Max. I’m just going to keel over any time soon, so save your money for your future girlfriend,” I smiled weakly.

“Emily McGregor. There is no other. My heart belongs to you and only you. Why can’t I get it through that thick head of yours? You can lose all your hair, be super sick, and even dying, and all those things won't change the fact that I love you. No illness is going to stop me from loving the woman of my dreams. I find myself falling in love with you, again and again, every day. You're the only one who could ever keep me up all night," Max confessed.

"Only? I thought coffee was your sweet confidant," I teased.

"Even Emily McGregor tops coffee on my most favourite list," Max insisted.

I couldn't help but smile. Max's hand grazed over my lips; my hands shook slightly as I blushed. Slowly, Max grasped my hand, lacing our fingers in a way that made my heart beat faster. It was just Max and me. No boy had ever said he loved me like the way Max did right now. Max pulled me in closer; our bodies touched. His breath was on my lips, and I quivered a bit. It was like we were about to have our first kiss all over again. Max intensely stared into my eyes, and without another moment to spare, our lips pressed together in a slow and sweet kiss.

After what seemed like an eternity, we pulled away. His eyes were still closed, as though he was savouring the taste of our passionate kiss. When his gaze returned to mine, we sat there together on my bed, enjoying our contentment.

"I love you, Max," I said softly, leaning my forehead against his.

Max smiled and placed his hand gently over my hip to move me closer towards him. He whispered, "I love you too, Emily. I love you too."

•••

It was almost midnight, and although I loved Max's company, my body was aching for me to go to bed.

"Max, I don't think I can stay up much longer," I said.

"I better get going, or I'll disturb my sleeping beauty. I'll be here at 6 a.m. sharp. We should probably arrive earlier to set up and get you settled in," Max suggested.

"I already called Dave about our visit. He booked us a studio room for the full hour, just in case, it runs longer than half an hour," I explained.

Dave was my Dad's, right-hand man. When my Dad died, he left behind a multi-million-dollar music production business and several budding stars. Ownership was transferred to Dave according to the partnership agreement they had in place. Without a doubt, my Dad's studio was in good hands.

I probably visited Dad's studio once or twice in my lifetime. But even on those rare occasions, it was always at really odd hours, so I never got a chance to see anyone else who worked there. But Dave was like an Uncle to me. He had no family in Alberta. He immigrated in his thirties to Canada with just his guitar and the shirt on his back. My Dad found him jamming outside of his studio on the streets, took him in, and watched him grow. Dad had a knack for finding raw talent. He saw something that day in Dave, and for better or worse, Dad gave him a chance, and Dave had never disappointed him.

Occasionally, when Mom and Dad had business trips to

attend, and Aunt Brenna was unable to schedule time off work, Dave would take care of me. I rather liked the fellow. About six-foot-tall with round spectacles. He had a high-top fade haircut that reminded me of *Fresh Prince of Bel-Air*. But his humour was like Steve Urkel.

Dave wasn't just Dad's colleague. My Dad trusted him dearly with everything. Also, Dave wasn't just my Dad's best friend. He was family. Dave joined us for every Thanksgiving, Christmas, and Easter dinner when my parents were still around. I felt a bit guilty that we only got back in touch because I required his services at the studio.

Dave reached out to me a couple of times when I was grieving, but all I did was respond with a terse reply. I hoped my silence did not damage the relationship Dave had with my family. But knowing how Dave went out of his way to arrange space for my visit tomorrow, I knew deep down that Dave was still the same Dave from my childhood.

"Dave?" Max asked nervously.

"Dave Sanders. My Dad was the President and CEO, while Dave was the Vice President and General Manager. They made a good team, flying across Canada, searching for talent to join their studios. You would have loved it there," I exclaimed.

"I did," Max muttered quietly under his breath.

"You did?" I asked, confused.

"I did not know your Dad had such a successful music production company. I thought we were picking up equipment at your old home and setting up there. Too bad you didn't figure out how to manage your stage fright earlier. You would have definitely excelled in your Dad's studio," Max exclaimed.

"Thanks for the boost in confidence, Max. But even if my Dad were still around, he wouldn't have allowed me to work in his studio. Dad taught me that the only way to be truly successful in your life is to earn your stripes, not just to be given them by birthright. Dave was one of the few who knew about me," I said as I let out a loud sigh. I leaned forward to give Max a peck on the cheek as he fidgeted uneasily.

"You got a big day ahead of you. Less talk. More sleep," Max said, helping me back onto my bed. He tucked me in and gave me a very long and sweet goodnight's kiss.

Although we'd kissed many times before, every kiss with Max still filled my stomach with butterflies, like that feeling you get after taking a shot of espresso for the very first time, but less jittery. It was electrifying every time and I felt a bit sad that this sensation was only temporary.

"I'll see you tomorrow morning at six. Sweet dreams Emily," Max whispered.

"Sweet dreams, Max," I replied. "Thank you."

Chapter Twenty-Six

It was six in the morning, and Max was already in my room. When I woke, I saw him staring at my large collection of paper airplanes hung across my bedroom walls. He didn't hear me wake; he was too absorbed in thought as he glared at the flamboyant display.

I quietly lifted myself from my bed, and with all my strength started walking over towards my desk where my wheelchair rested. After a few steps, my knees buckled, and I fell forward awkwardly on the ground. Max suddenly turned and ran towards me. I put my hand up to usher him away. I had to do this on my own. Just like all those other days of trial and error.

Max watched as I pushed myself closer and closer to my desk. I tripped a couple more times. But I got right back up on my own. Max held back upon my request, but I could tell he was hurting inside, watching me struggle alone. After several long minutes, I made it to my desk. I leaned forward, breathing heavily, using the table for support. Then, like always, I plopped myself onto my wheelchair and started my morning wake-up routine. By the time I finished getting ready, Max already loaded the car with Jimi and my bag. Aunt Brenna left some snacks on the table for us to take on the road. She was always so sweet and thoughtful.

I wheeled up to Max, who returned to study the walls of my room.

"Like what you see?" I asked while nudging him to bend down for a morning kiss.

"Why do you call this your Wall of Hope?" Max asked.

"Because I hope to one day share all my music with the world. Each paper airplane acts like a wish. A wish to one day find the courage to sing to the world. It is like the stars in the sky. Fearless. And available to everyone," I explained.

"Why not today? I mean, you've come a long way since the beginnings of your preparations for this audition. Why wait to share your talent? Let today be the start of your musical career Emily," Max said encouragingly.

I reached out to hold his hand. The two of us stared in silence to take in the energy that radiated from my wall. I closed my eyes and thought about what Max had just said.

If my music could impact just *one* person, then that meant that I'd done something right. Sometimes, it doesn't happen right away. Maybe a year. Five years. Ten years. And sometimes, it doesn't happen at all. But I wouldn't know if I never tried. It was always better to have tried and failed than to have failed to try.

"Okay," I said with a nod. "Today."

One by one, Max quickly removed the paper airplanes from the wall by my bedroom window, placing them into a reusable shopping bag.

"That should be enough for today. We got to keep some here for you to look at," Max said with a smile.

•••

As we drove to my Dad's studio in Calgary, Max and I took turns to karaoke. Halfway there, we stopped for gas and a bite to eat. My live video audition was scheduled for noon, and it was still T-minus three hours before my gig.

We stopped at *Glenmore Reservoir* on the southwest side of Calgary before heading to Dad's studio. It was windy today, perfect for flying kites and paper airplanes. Max parked the car and helped me into my wheelchair. I remembered coming here as a kid for picnics. Mom would pack a basket full of peanut butter and jelly sandwiches. We would race along the trails, chase butterflies, and count the number of sailboats that passed by. They had wonderful bike trails that stretched along the Elbow River, surrounded by wetlands and excellent views of the Rocky Mountains. It was nice coming back here today.

We stopped at the monument commemorating Calgary's Centennial in 1994. There was a picture of a compass rose with the quote, 'May the joy of nature inspire your direction in life.'

Max gave me a knowing nod, and we began to arrange my paper airplanes on top of the monument carefully. And with one huge gust of wind, my songs touched with the wind. And just like that, my paper airplanes took off. They soared endlessly across the river, towards the mountains, and into the clouds. It was a beautiful sight to see. The bright colours swirling in the sky. It was like seeing stars in the daytime. I guess Max was right; anything was possible.

•••

We arrived at the studio around eleven. Max was acting awkward once we parked and started to fidget in his seat, frantically looking around the parking lot like he was afraid of being seen.

"Max, is everything okay?" I asked.

"I'm fine. I just need to stretch my legs after a long drive. You don't mind if I grab a coffee after I wheel you to the door. You can get settled with Dave first so I don't delay your preparations. I can meet you in the studio room," Max suggested.

"Sure. I guess you can meet Dave after my audition," I said, a bit disappointed.

"I really need that cup of coffee. I'll be back as soon as I can," Max said reassuringly and gave me a good luck kiss at the door.

Max disappeared into the streets while I wheeled inside to check in with the receptionist at the front door. I clutched the necklace Max gave me for good luck and whispered a few words to Mom and Dad.

"Hi, I'm Emily McGregor. I have a room booked for noon," I said.

"The pleasure is all mine. I'm Jennifer. You must be Roger Mot's daughter. Dave told me all about you. I haven't seen you around here before. I'm a big fan of your Dad's work," Jennifer exclaimed excitedly, shaking my hand.

Jennifer wore a graphic tea with an outline of a mermaid on it. Her nails were painted jade and she wore black coloured lipstick. I took in her outfit and smiled. Mom and Dad were watching, I was sure of it.

"Is Dave here?" I asked.

"He's setting up your room now, so he'll be up in a minute. Or would you like me to help you find the elevators to the lower level so you can meet him there," Jennifer asked.

"Elevators would be fine. Thank you," I said.

I followed Jennifer as she led me to the elevators.

"Oh, I came here with my boyfriend. Can you let him know where to go when he arrives?" I asked.

"Most definitely, Emily," Jennifer said with a smile.

The elevator doors closed. I pressed the button for the lower level and wheeled down the hallway to studio 3B. It was strange walking through these corridors. The very same corridors that my Dad used to walk through when he was at his recording studio. Dad spent a lot of time at the studios. He recorded his own music. He recorded his clients' music. He even recorded his students' music. This was a place where he poured his sweat, heart, and soul to create beautiful music for the world.

We get thrown off emotionally almost every single day. From petty annoyances to deep-seated anxieties, I'd been guilty of over-analyzing my past and incessantly worrying about my future. Like being caught in an endless loop.

No matter how well our lives go on the surface, this endless loop slowly eats us away from the inside. I'd always had trouble taming my emotions, and today was no different. Being in the very same place where my Dad spent most of his life creating music was overwhelming. Everywhere I looked, I tried imagining what he would be doing, what he would be saying, or what he would be hearing. There was so much I didn't know about him. There was so much he had yet to teach me. And because he wanted me to live freely without the burden of his shadow, this place was like Pandora's box. And being here today only meant I was treading in deep waters.

As I continued to walk down to studio 3B, a weird feeling bubbled in the pit of my stomach. I was certain it was my nerves, but my brain was sending me mixed-up messages, and I had no idea how to respond. I closed my eyes momentarily before continuing down the hall.

I thanked Jennifer for her help and wheeled into the room to find Dave. I searched the room to find him, and then suddenly, a loud voice echoed from behind me.

"Emily! Oh, look at how much you've grown. Do you still remember Uncle Dave?" Dave said with a sincere smile. He gave me a big bearhug and put his hands on both of my shoulders.

"I missed you too, Uncle Dave. Though I haven't grown much. Not vertically at least, maybe horizontally," I joked.

"Oh, Emily, just like your Dad. Learning to crack jokes, aren't you?" he said.

"Well, a lot has changed since we've last hung out. I actually learned most of my stand-up comedy from my boyfriend. He'll be here shortly. You would love him," I said.

"Well, if this fellow you talk so fondly about makes you happy, then you have my blessings," Dave acknowledged, winking.

"So, is everything ready for noon?" I asked.

"Yes! If you sit here, then the camera will be directly facing you. We got headphones here that you can use, a mic, and you can adjust lighting over there if that's necessary for your performance," Dave explained.

"Thanks, Dave! I really appreciate how you pulled all of this together so last minute," I said.

"Emily, your Dad would have been very proud of you today. I know," Dave said softly.

"I know, too," I replied. Then I asked, "Dave, do you miss him?"

"Of course, I do. We all do. He was the true mastermind in this place. I know your Dad wanted to protect you by keeping you from this place, and I would honour his wishes to my grave. But Emily, once you've made a name for yourself at *AMP*, don't forget that you're always welcomed here," Dave insisted.

"Thanks, Dave," I said with a tear in my eye.

"Why don't I give you some space to practice. Come by my office when you're done. We can catch up over a cup of coffee. Jennifer will show you where to find me," Dave said as he placed his hand on my shoulder before leaving the room.

I took a deep breath and started some fingering exercises on Jimi. My fingers felt a bit numb, but I pleaded to my body to cooperate. I whispered to myself, "Just hold on for about an hour. That's all I'm asking for." Then, I warmed up my vocals with some scales and stretched my arms in the hopes of improving blood circulation to my fingers. Not now. "Pull it together, Emily," I repeated to myself.

I glanced at my phone and started to sweat profusely. It was 10 minutes to noon. Where on earth was Max?

Like right on cue, I heard footsteps coming down the hallway. Max knocked on the window and entered the room.

"Sorry about that. There was a long lineup at the coffee shop. You're right about Calgary being a much bigger city. It's like quadruple the size of Glenwood," Max said.

"I'm about ready. Umm, Max. My fingers. I'm starting to feel numbness in my fingers. If anything happens, take over, so I don't scare Alexander, okay?" I explained.

"That's what I'm here for, but don't let it bother you. Focus Emily. You got this," Max exclaimed.

At exactly noon, the video feed from studio 3B went live. I was face-to-face with Alexander, who first quizzed me on theory and musical history. I whizzed through all the questions easily. Fortunately, music and studying were both my forte.

"Excellent work, Emily! I am quite impressed," Alexander said, very pleased.

"Thank you," I responded politely.

"Now Emily, I would like you to understand because of your late submission of your application, you forfeited the possibility of entrance scholarships. However, depending on your performance today, I may exempt you from this," Alexander explained.

"Thank you. You won't be disappointed," I said confidently.

Every piece of music tells a story. About our lives. About our hearts. So, if music were ever devoid of the heart, then it technically would have no meaning. When I was deciding on what song to sing for today's audition, I thought to myself about all the emotions I'd been experiencing and all the things that I hold dearly in my heart. I wanted my first (and perhaps last) performance to be something worth sharing with everyone. So, this was it. This was my big moment. This was *my* life story.

My *AMP* audition marked my first live performance in front of a *real* audience for 'Emily the Brave.' I took a deep breath, closed my eyes, and imagined my goalie helmet. I imagined being outside under the darkness of the night sky. I imagined my willow tree. And as I sang, the sky slowly turned brighter until it was filled with millions and millions of stars. My voice quivered a bit, but it was still powerful. My fingers hit some wrong notes a couple of times, but I was hoping no one noticed. After all, I decided to play my own song, which worked to my advantage in situations like these. Alexander could not judge my performance to the original because my piece was *original.* I was completely satisfied that I was thinking ahead.

♪♫♪♫♪♫♪

I see a rainbow, outside my window
When the rain clears in the sky, I soar like a butterfly
Stars all around me, that's when I feel free
When the darkness hits my eyes, I still feel alive

I hope to be, more than a memory

I hope to beat, cancer that's inside of me

And even if it seems impossible

And even if the world says 'no'

That's hope

That's hope, that's love

That's what I'm thinking of

That's hope, that's love

That's what I'm thinking of

That's hope, that's love

For me

That's hope, that's love

That's what I'm thinking of

♪♫♪♫♪♫♪

After my performance, I was so relieved that my body held up its end of the bargain. Max gave me a thumbs up and had a ginormous smile across his face. I did it. I finally did it. I couldn't help but smile too.

"That was amazing, Emily. What a heartfelt performance. We could use someone with your talent at *AMP*. You passed the audition. Pending you keep up your grades, we look forward to having you as a member of *AMP* this September. Congratulations!" Alexander cheered.

"I passed? I passed!" I screamed before composing myself.

"Thank you so much. I look forward to the opportunity," I said excitedly.

"I will notify admissions to send you a thorough package on preparations for international studies this fall. Excellent job today, Emily. We will be in touch," Alexander explained.

After Alexander signed off from the live feed, I screamed at the top of my lungs with excitement. I couldn't wait to give Max a celebratory kiss, so I quickly got up from my seat only to fall back from a wave of tiredness. I suddenly felt very weak, my heart raced, and my breathing quickened. Max rushed towards me and helped me back onto my wheelchair. I bit the corner of my lip and closed my eyes. Max brushed his lips on mine and held my hand tight.

Although I was thrilled about passing my audition, my high note was only temporary. I was thrilled to have accomplished my dream of getting into *AMP* and for fulfilling the promise I made, but my body was getting weaker. I could not escape my reality. Music lived inside of me, but it was not enough to fuel my heart and soul. I could not fool death. I was dying.

Whether I liked it or not, I was fading away. I felt like an Olympic gold medalist who won the title, only to have it stripped away because of a positive drug test. It was a golden moment to finally reach something that used to be almost unattainable. To succeed in something that I'd been working on for the past four years. To overcome all the anxiety that I'd ever endured whenever I stepped up on stage. It was a defining moment in my life that marked the beginnings of my career. A proud moment only to have it all taken away from me because I wouldn't be *alive* to live it.

I cried in Max's embrace. I cried until my eyes were tired and sore. I cried until I had no more tears in me. And now, I was ready to go home. My dream was a dud, just like Dad's. I wondered if I'd ever have a chance to sing my song of hope to the world again.

•••

As Max wheeled me back upstairs to the lobby, a part of me wanted to forgo my meeting with Dave. After the whirlwind of emotions down in studio 3B, I longed to be elsewhere. But, a part of me knew that I owed it to my Dad to stay a bit longer. To at least say goodbye to Dave, my Dad's closest friend.

Although I tried encouraging Max to join me, Max excused himself by claiming that he would only be the third wheel in my family reunion. Before I could respond, Max disappeared out the door to wait in the car. I sensed that Max was acting very strangely today. I was certain that there was something wrong. He usually wasn't so distant.

I met with Dave in my Dad's office, which was now his office. There were three cups of steaming hot coffee waiting on the table. I guess he assumed Max would be coming too. Over the next few minutes, Dave and I talked about many things, including a brief discussion over which Jimi Hendrix song was the ultimate all-time best. We talked and talked until our conversation gone grave when I mentioned the whole part about me dying.

"You McGregors need to stop hurting Dave's heart. And for a

moment, I thought your return today meant the beginning of our new partnership together," Dave sighed, worried about the turn of events.

"I'm sorry, Dave. But I thought you should know," I said.

"I'm glad you told me. When I saw you in the wheelchair today, I thought you just hurt yourself from some school track and field event. Uncle Dave remembers that you were never really good at sports, and all high schools force kids to participate in a whole bunch of activities. But I really had no idea. How's your Aunt handling all of this?" Dave asked.

"She's surviving. I'm still trying to convince her that all of this was not her fault. No one could have predicted this. I thought I had many more years of music in me too. I worry about her. I really do. But after losing Mom and Dad, I'd realized that death is probably just as tough on those around me than myself. I also learned how important it is to say goodbye. I wouldn't want to miss my opportunity like how I did with my parents. Goodbyes hurt. But they are sometimes necessary," I said softly.

"You really have grown up, Emily. You really have," Dave exclaimed.

"Promise me you'll continue looking after my Dad's studio?" I asked.

"I wouldn't have it any other way," Dave said with a smile. Then, he got up and exclaimed, "I got something of your Dad's that I think he would want you to have."

"What is it?" I asked, intrigued.

Dave headed to my Dad's bookshelf and began searching

carefully. I followed closely behind him. As he was searching for this mysterious book, I noticed the frames on the walls. There were many pictures of my Dad. There was one of him and Dave. Another of him receiving an award at some sort of black gala event. There was another of the three of us. It was the only family picture in his office. Dad was holding me with Mom's arms around him. I had no recollection of that picture. I looked at most five to six months old. I scanned the rest of the photos on the wall before stopping at the last one that hung in the corner of the room. But wait! It was my Dad with his arm draped around a young boy. I didn't have any cousins, so who was he? A student? But those eyes. Those emerald green eyes. This boy seemed vaguely familiar.

"Dave?" I called out, interrupting his search. "Do you mind if I ask who the boy is in that picture?" I asked, pointing to the last framed picture hanging on the wall.

"That's your Dad's top protégé. He was so proud of his talents. I remember him telling me that this kid was going to be the next Elvis Presley. He was certain of it," Dave explained as he continued searching the bookshelf. "I wonder what happened to that boy. He disappeared without a trace after your parents died. What was his name again?"

Dave suddenly pulled something out of the bookshelf. My face lit up when I saw the book he held in his hands. "This was your Dad's Moleskine. He held his most precious songs in this book, and I'm sure he would have loved to share them with you," Dave insisted, placing the book in my lap.

"I don't know what to say. Thank you, Dave. Thank you for everything," I said softly.

As I tucked the book into my bag, I put my hand over Jimi and closed my eyes like I was giving my Dad a salute. I thanked Dave again as I headed towards the door. Then suddenly, Dave blurted out.

"Ah yes, it was Max Miller," Dave said, as though a lightbulb just turned on in his head.

"Max, what?" I asked, unsure if I misheard the name.

"Max Miller," Dave repeated.

What?!? Max! The very same Max that stole my heart? The very same Max that is waiting outside in the car right now?

The details of Max's past were revealed in this lone photograph. All this time, Max hid this truth from me. But why? And for what? The way he looked at my guitar when we first met. All those times, he acted strangely when I mentioned my parents. *AMP*. The cemetery. Even today.

All of these fragmented memories came together like pieces of a puzzle. There was a piercing pain in my heart. It felt like I was being stabbed a thousand times in the same spot, each time chipping away my trust. I felt betrayed. How could Max hide something like this from me? He had several chances to tell me. Why did he continue to fool me?

My breathing quickened, and I struggled to comprehend all the details of Max's mysterious past now exposed. Like the final brushstrokes of a painting, everything now made sense. Max was avoiding Dave. That was why he insisted on grabbing a coffee upon arrival. And why he insisted on waiting in the car right now.

I clutched the pendant of Max's necklace in my hand. I felt this burning pain around my neck and fire burning in my eyes. Why? Just why?

I closed my eyes and breathed in and out to calm myself. Suddenly, I thought of Anna. She was singing a children's rhyme, but it wasn't her usual 'rain, rain go away' tune. Anna sang, 'cross my heart and hope to die, stick a needle in my eye,' then she looked up at me and disappeared.

I immediately opened my eyes and gasped for air. I always wondered why children's rhymes could be so gruesome. I guess I just got 'poked in the eye,' and this was my wake-up call. Clearly, I was emotionally blindsided by my heart.

As I slowly wheeled myself towards the lobby, I tried to comprehend the turn of events. How could I face Max now? And yet I still loved him. I still loved him with all my heart. How could I be so stupid to love someone who hurt me so much?

Chapter Twenty-Seven

Max got out of the car as he saw me wheeling out of my Dad's studio. He rushed over and gave me a quick peck on my lips. But I didn't reciprocate.

"Is something wrong, Emily?" Max asked, unsure why I looked so upset.

I refused to say anything. If I were to survive the car ride home, I had to stay silent.

"Emily, don't scare me like that. Did something happen inside when you were with Dave? Say something. Tell me what's wrong. You can trust me," Max insisted.

I wanted to stay silent, but Max's last remark burned the remaining sanity that was holding me together. I exploded.

"*Trust*?" I screamed.

"Emily, what's the matter?" Max asked.

"How could I *trust* somebody like you? You've been here before Max. You've been here many times before, haven't you?" I yelled, tears streaming down my cheek.

Max's face hardened. He knew exactly what I was referring to. Max reached for my hand, but I squatted it away. I shook my head and bit the bottom of my lip.

"Emily, I can explain," Max pleaded.

"No, just bring me home, Max. I don't want to hear another

word from you," I exclaimed, firmly crossing my arms across my chest.

All this time, I was living a lie. After my fiasco at the cemetery, Max was fully aware that I was the daughter of Roger Mot. Max and I gone through a lot together, to say the least, and I thought our relationship has grown enough to be open to each other. If I never discovered Max's secret from Dave, would he have always kept it hidden away? Why did he not tell me? It hurt whenever someone else exposed the truth. I was such a fool to believe someone like Max would not intentionally lie again. I closed my eyes, unwilling to open them; I did not want to see the face of deceit.

•••

Whether on a road trip, a flight, or a bike ride, the journey back home always felt shorter than the way there, even though the actual time elapsed was exactly the same. But this time, my two-hour journey home felt like an *eternity*. I kept my eyes closed all the way back. Even when Max stopped for gas, I kept them closed. I refused to look at the guy who broke my heart. I refused to let my eyes deceive me and let him back into my life.

I remembered a time when Max told me that there were always *two* sides to *every* story. I guess he was referring to himself. And Max did a very good job hiding the other side of his story from me. I felt like everything we built together was now crumbling. I was broken. And I just wanted to get out.

It was just two hours from midnight when we arrived back at

Aunt Brenna's. We pulled up and parked behind Aunt Brenna's Mazda. I knew she must have switched her night shift to be home to celebrate my successful audition. It was rare to see her car on the driveway on a Friday night. Those nights were either reserved for work or dates with André. I felt disappointed in myself for not seeing through Max's lies. I felt disappointed in Max for not having the courage to speak the truth. And I also felt disappointed that I was no longer in the mood to celebrate my accomplishment. Why do so many of my mountaintop moments fall into the bottomless pits of the deep blue sea? I really should have learned how to swim as a child. Constantly staying afloat was getting too tiring.

I was turned away from Max, still staring out the window, when I spoke. "Goodnight, Max," I said coldly. "Thank you for driving me today." I turned to grab Jimi from the backseat and reached for the door.

"Emily, don't do this. Please, just hear me out," Max pleaded, grabbing my hand tightly.

I turned to face him. I looked into his emerald green eyes. The very same eyes that I fell in love with now stared at me with great regret. It pained me to know that there were probably many more lies that were yet to be revealed. How could I love someone that I could no longer recognize or trust? I closed my eyes. I didn't want to see him. I didn't want to hear his voice. All I wanted to do now was hide in my room and cry myself to sleep.

I whispered, "What more is there to say? You lied, Max. We've known each other for over a year. We had our disagreements, misunderstandings, and fights. And through it all, it came down to one thing. This one thing that distinguishes you from me. This very thing that could actually come between us. That's honesty, Max. Honesty. And you downright suck at it."

"But, Emily!" Max cried.

I ignored his pleas and continued, "Honesty is the foundation to any relationship Max whether we're just friends or life partners. We have to be *honest* with each other. And you know what really bothers me about all of this? Is that you seem to think that it's okay to just lie about something. It's not okay. You think it's a joke to play with my emotions? What were you trying to do? Get close to me to get back at my Dad? I don't get it Max. Why couldn't you tell me about your connection with my Dad? Did you think I was too weak to hear the truth? Actually, you know what, I don't need to hear it."

My head hurt almost as much as my heart; my breathing was heavy as I reached for the door again. Max was still holding my hand, so I pulled at it for him to let go.

"But I don't—" Max said before I interrupted him.

"But I don't get it? Is that what you're going to say? It doesn't take a genius to understand that deception comes with great costs. It's not like I was wearing an atrociously frilly top with bellbottoms, and you lied by saying that I looked lovely. It's not like you lied about not being tired, so you could stay up a couple more hours to finish helping me study. This is different, Max. Lying about knowing my Dad when you knew how much I wanted to reconnect with him. This is a completely different level of dishonesty that goes well beyond this car," I explained.

"I'm sorry, Emily," Max whispered.

"I'm sorry too, Max. I'm sorry for ever believing you," I said as I bit the bottom of my lip really hard. I took a deep breath and continued, "I want the truth. I don't care how much it may hurt. Because I'll tell you that the truth hurts, big time. I know. But I don't need to be entertained by your lies. If this relationship means anything to you, then tell me why you hid this from me for so long?"

"I swear. I was going to tell you. But the timing was never right," Max insisted.

"Timing? There's no *right* timing for the truth Max. You just say it! I thought you loved me enough to be truthful about everything. It seems like it's only one-sided in our relationship. I loved you enough to tell you the truth about my diagnosis. I loved you enough to tell you about my parents, my Wall of Hope, my deepest fears. I even loved you enough to tell you the truth about my feelings. And it absolutely sucks right now because the truth is, *I* no longer know if you love me *enough* to do the same?" I cried.

I felt a wave of sadness overcome me, and the feeling of emptiness inside. Max reached out to touch the side of my face. His fingers grazed my cheeks as he wiped away my tears. His touch that once warmed my heart and soul felt cold.

We both sat in Max's car in awkward silence. Not saying a single word sometimes speaks volumes in a heated argument. The silence was a very powerful thing. And my patience for Max was growing extremely thin.

Max shifted his hand away from my face as he turned to face the window. He couldn't even look at me in the eye to tell me the truth. "I didn't intentionally lie to you. I just thought. Umm. But it's just. Umm. I just didn't want," Max said, struggling to speak.

"You just didn't want me to find out, right? Save it, Max. I don't need this tonight. I'm going inside," I said, letting out a loud sigh.

I opened the car door and placed one foot out the door. I put my hand around the pendant of my necklace and angrily yanked it from my neck. I threw the necklace back at Max; I heard it clatter as it hit against something inside his car. Max suddenly turned towards me and screamed out my name.

"Emily! No! Just, please hear me out," Max pleaded.

My heart told me that Max deserved a chance to explain himself. But my mind told me that he had more than enough chances already. Lost. Conflicted. Confused. I pulled my foot back into the car and slammed the door shut. "Fine. But you only have 60 seconds to convince me to listen. So, make it worth my while," I said impatiently.

"I will, Emily," Max said with a nod. He took my hand and caressed it gently as he spoke. "When we first met at *Amore*, I felt this strange connection to you. Your guitar. I was certain it was Coach Roger's. It was almost identical. Except your Dad's guitar had a deep scratch on the body, right below the bridge. And yours was like brand new. But you said it was a gift from your Aunt, so I passed it off as being just a coincidence. I was, at first, drawn to you by my curiosity. When I saw you again at *Amore*, I thought studying with you would help me find the answer I seek. But then it happened. The more I got to know you, the more I couldn't stop thinking about you. I fell in love. What started off as a desire, turned into something more."

Max paused momentarily, pulled my hand up to his lips, and kissed the top of my hand softly. He rested my hand now on his lap and continued. "That night after *Rue 143*, I wanted to ask you if you were related to Coach Roger. But then you wounded up in the ER, and I got tongue-tied to say anything," Max explained.

"Okay, you got me there. But you could have told me later. Why did you keep this from me for so long?" I asked.

"Emily, you don't understand. Your Dad was the best thing that ever happened to me in my childhood. Hooking up with you had nothing to do with me seeking revenge," Max insisted.

"Okay, I'm listening," I said, impatiently.

"When my Dad died, my Mom temporarily switched to the management department at the hospital to spend more time with me at home. She was way too smothering though. So, I signed up to deliver the local paper to get some space. But delivering the paper every Monday after school was boring, so I always made sure my iPod was loaded with songs to make things more entertaining. At first, I only hummed the tunes, but I quickly memorized all the lyrics and started singing along out loud. I guess singing was like my thing because I was never embarrassed if anyone heard. After a couple of weeks, the seniors along my paper route actually started sitting outside on their patios to wait for my arrival, just so they could submit a song request for next week. I thought it was fun, so I complied," Max explained.

"I don't see where this is going," I said, raising my eyebrows.

"I'm getting to the part where I meet your Dad next," Max replied before continuing with his story. "One day, your Dad was sitting with Senior Rico when I was delivering the paper. Rico introduced me to your Dad who was visiting him for his birthday. You see, Rico was a bit of a depressed fellow ever since he became a widower and his grandchildren moved out. I decided to treat Rico to some tunes from his favourite singer Elvis Presley. Not knowing who your Dad was, your Dad immediately handed over his business card after my performance, offering me to come by his studio for guitar lessons. I thought your Dad was one of Rico's relatives or something, but apparently Rico's granddaughter was one of his former students. I took his card and joked that he was wasting his time because I had no background in music. I remembered him responding with 'Son, you got some raw talent there and with enough guidance, you can go far in the music industry.' Your Dad offered to show me the ropes, and if I liked it, then I could continue learning from him as long as I promised to study hard and get into *AMP*," Max explained.

"So, my Dad took you in like how he did with Dave. That sounds just like him," I said.

"I wasn't completely sure if I wanted to learn music, but it was essentially for free. I figured that I would give your Dad a chance since it was too good of an offer to pass up on. My Dad, being an athlete, knew firsthand about seizing opportunities.

He spent many games in the dugout and rarely got his chance to play. He taught me to seize *every* opportunity because *missed* opportunities are *not* like library books. You cannot keep borrowing them, renew them, or put them on hold. You either take it or you don't. So, I stayed with a friend in Calgary that summer so I could learn at your Dad's studio. I never told my Mom, though. She just thought I was doing some medical summer camp in the city. And that summer I learned everything there was to know about music. He even bought me a refurbished guitar," Max exclaimed.

"I don't get it. Why stop then? My Dad could spot talent even with his eyes closed. He was rarely wrong. Why did you just give up?" I asked.

"I didn't lie about dropping out of *AMP* in my second year. But I wasn't fully honest with the reason why I left either. When I heard the news about your parents' accident, I felt like the music died inside of me. I was devasted. Coach Roger was the only one who ever believed in my gift. My Mom almost disowned me when I told her I was going to *AMP* instead of some prestigious medical school in the States. And with all the people who were most influential in my life now gone. My Dad. Coach Roger. I was overwhelmed with the fear of never being able to live up to your Dad's dream. I just had to get out, so I dropped out. I returned back home to Glenwood, broken, and ashamed. I felt like a complete failure," Max admitted.

As Max continued to open up about his past, I began feeling just a tad bit guilty for calling him out for his lack of integrity.

Don't get me wrong, I was still upset that he was dishonest, but I was also empathic with what he had to endure during his childhood. Clearly, my Dad's death had a stronger impact than I could ever imagine. Max was a victim, too, just like me.

Chapter Twenty-Eight

The truth hurt. The truth sucked. It was sort of like *tough love*. Someone had to say it. Sometimes we needed it. But no matter how the truth eventually came out, we had to accept it. Our lives are what we made of it, and the only person who controlled what we see as the *truth* was within ourselves.

The most common human error in research was unconscious bias. What we decided to believe when conducting research was often biased. When we found things that went against our own beliefs, we tend to reject them. Likewise, when we found things that supported our pre-existing beliefs, then we would often accept them. Decision making was based on an intellectual judgement of one's perception.

In short, our world was doomed if we only viewed it through rose-coloured glasses. Doomed of this ignorant bliss that clouded our minds and fooled our hearts. What we do not know cannot hurt us. Or so it may seem. We are all stupid to believe that there are no *bad* things in this world. Or that we were not flawed. But for a couple more moments, I wanted to be *ignorant* because the truth hurt a little bit too much.

•••

I left Max's car, not knowing how much of the *truth* I was willing to accept. I told him I needed some time to digest everything. I just needed some space. And to my surprise, Max did not fight me with this. He nodded and told me that he would respect my wishes; no matter how long it took, he would wait.

As Max helped me out of his car, he looked at me and said, "Your Dad always told me that 'there's always time for music.' And at first, I thought he meant physical time. But not until I left *AMP*, I'd realized what he really meant. Music is like breathing. You don't make time for breathing. It just happens. You can't escape from it because it's like a flame burning inside of us. My flame was weakened, but it was never out. I thought that without his guidance, I could do nothing. That was until I met you," Max said softly, squeezing my shoulder as we rolled closer to the door.

"But, I didn't—" I said, shocked.

Max swiveled the wheelchair around to face me. He placed his fingers on my lips, and I trembled. "Meeting you has rekindled something inside of me. The more we spent time together, the stronger that flame got. And I don't know how, but you'd made my flame so strong now that it's going to take a category five hurricane to blow it out. I am not Coach Roger's best protégé. Emily, the best protégé your Dad could ever have was you. Coach Roger's daughter, the most beautiful and talented Emily McGregor," Max said proudly with a smile.

"Max, I think you're wrong," I said sharply. "My Dad never believed in me. From what I see, he put all his faith in you. I could have never lived up to my Dad's dreams. And I'd never won the critical acclaim I'd sought for many years. I only dreamed of

AMP because I knew he wanted all his students to get there one day. He always said, 'To be the best, one must learn from the best.' My Dad knew about my stage fright. He was embarrassed that I was nothing like him or Grandpa. Sometimes, I thought that the only reason why he kept his personal life so private was because he was ashamed of letting the world discover me. His protection could have been genuine. But I would never know. I promised my Dad that I would get into *AMP* because I wanted to prove myself to him. To prove that I was worthy of being his daughter. And look at me now. I'm nothing but a broken dream. You're crazy to even compare me to my father at the same level of greatness," I said sadly, hanging my head in shame.

Max placed a finger under my chin and tilted my head upwards. He stared into my eyes and spoke. "You're right, Emily. You're right that you're nothing like your father. You're better."

He kissed my forehead and wheeled me the rest of the way to the front door. He let go of my wheelchair and walked away in silence. I was afraid that this kiss might have been a kiss goodbye.

Max drove off as I sat outside my front door, surrounded by the silence of the night under a million stars. The magical awe of the dark void above me used to bring me peace. But not today. It only reminded me of Max. And I wanted to get inside before I lost control of my emotions. While holding back tears, I turned my key to enter the house. Aunt Brenna was already standing on the other side. She pulled me into a tight and comforting hug.

"I know Emily, I know. You don't need to say a thing," Aunt Brenna said reassuringly as I cried in her arms.

When Max first spoke of the truth, I was resentful about it. I struggled to filter through his words to distinguish between what was the *truth* and what was a *lie*. But as I reflected upon all that was said, my heart shattered. Although I wanted not to believe it, it was true. Sometimes the people we loved the most end up being the people we trusted the least. Love really was blind. And it was eating me from the inside.

•••

At some point in our lives, we have all, unfortunately, been the victim of a lie. Whether it was a lie by our partners who were caught double-dipping with another, or a global corporation being sold out when promised protection. Or even finding the snack compartment empty when there was only one other person in the house. Some lies were easier to spot than others, and it was easy to get upset whenever someone lied to us. But there were many shades of dishonesty and many motivations to lie. Just like there were many ways to react to lies too.

Throughout my life, I'd struggled with forgiveness almost as much as I struggled with goodbyes. I felt insulted at being the target of deception, but my emotional reaction to dishonesty sometimes brought more harm than good. The truth could be taxing when it inflicted a wound on someone's ego. Perhaps before I accused Max of lying, I should have given him a chance to explain himself first, rather than the other way around.

My mind whirled with confusion. On one side, I understood why Max distorted his reality because he was unwilling to accept the truth. But on the other hand, I felt betrayed because I thought we reached a point in our relationship where we could be open and honest with each other.

As I thought about it more, Max's lies were driven by insecurity. Many of our lies are the product of insecurity. Lies were often motivated by fear, temporarily protecting the liar's ego. And I knew how egotistic Max was, so this should not have been so much of a surprise. Still, how could Max lie to me like this? After all we've been through together, this was disappointing, no matter how many different ways I tried to slice it.

•••

Days passed. There were no missed calls. No voicemail messages. No unread texts. It was like Max Miller disappeared off the face of the Earth and flown away to some remote planet in another galaxy. I did tell Max that I needed space. But I didn't mean to push him away. Perhaps this was the best for both of us. That way, whenever I faded into the stars and exploded like a supernova, Max would be spared from the inevitable pain of grief. Maybe to love someone so much was to let go while there was still time to breathe. I sat in my room all day, staring at the remains of my Wall of Hope. All I could think about was Max. I was miserable.

When someone we cared about hurt us, we hold onto anger and resentment. For some people, it took a *long* time to move forward and embrace forgiveness. *I* was one of those people. Throughout my childhood, I'd been a constant victim of emotional abuse. My Dad constantly criticized me while growing up. Friends sabotaged school projects. My parents died. My prognosis was less than a year. And Max broke my heart.

I didn't have the energy for vengeance, nor did those moments spark any spite. But it did leave me with wounds and the lasting feelings of bitterness. I was a grudge holder. Those negative feelings already began crowding out the positive ones. All these things sucked then, and thinking about them sucked now, albeit to a lesser degree.

The problem with this conundrum was two-fold. I not only had to find it in my heart to forgive Max but also to forgive myself. I knew Max sincerely regretted his actions, but forgiveness did not necessarily guarantee it would not happen again. Lies severely eroded the trust in our relationship. And I could not just absolve Max of his actions. The more I told myself to stop being angry, the angrier I got. The more I tried to let it go, the more it haunted me at every turn. After experiencing so many *ugly-bad* moments in my life, I should have been an expert by now at forgiveness. But in reality, I was as clueless as a young teenager trapped in a grown-up twilight zone.

Forgiveness was a *choice*. Not just on the surface, but deep in my heart. For once in my life, *I* was in the driver's seat. I was solely accountable for my emotions and thoughts and ultimately responsible for forgiveness.

To move from suffering to forgiveness was a commitment to defining my life through compassion and understanding. I was not ready to simply '*forgive and forget*' or '*let bygones be bygones.*' But after days of solitude in my room, I was ready to acknowledge the tiny glimmer of compassion in my broken heart. I called that *humanity*.

Being terminal has made me more aware of the wounds in the world. I'd become more patient with people and become more aware of others' pains. Everyone in this world walked wounded. All the time. But it was the stronger ones that did not let pain control them. I had to be one of them. Life would be much happier, stronger, and more fulfilling if we could swallow our daily dosage of pain in just one gulp before we started each day.

•••

I laid in my bed, unable to sleep. I looked out the window, desperately searching for an answer. I'd realized that forgiveness had everything to do with relieving myself of the burden of being a victim. If lies could get bigger when I believed them, then so could truth. But how could I forgive when it felt impossible?

My head felt tired, but I desperately needed something to put my mind at ease. I suddenly remembered Dad's Moleskine that Dave gave me before I left the studio. I crawled out of bed and rummaged through my bag. I was so distraught after returning home that night that I forgot all about this little book of wonder. I pulled out my Dad's Moleskine and held it close to my heart. I quietly whispered a prayer as though I was asking my Dad for permission to read his words. His music.

I took a deep breath and opened his notebook. It was like reading a novel for the very first time. There was this 'old book' smell that I inhaled as I turned each page of the book. My finger slowly moved horizontally across the page like it was absorbing every word my Dad written with my fingertips. The thrill and excitement I got as I turned each page, wondering if the next song could be even better than the last. It was like Dad was singing to me. And I loved it. By the time I got to the very last page of his notebook, I felt a bit sad because I knew that no matter how many times I went back to page one, reading it all over again would never be the same.

I closed Dad's Moleskine and placed it on my desk. I let out a loud sigh and whispered, "Thanks for sharing this with me, Dad. I may never be as good as you, but if you're watching, I hope you're proud of what I'd accomplished. Seems like you knew Max better than me. I wished you were here to guide me."

I could feel the onset of a headache, and my eyes felt tired. The past few days have been emotionally and physically exhausting. It was already well past midnight; I knew I had to rest. Though, I knew that I would have plenty of time for sleeping later when my time here was done. I felt the urge to read through Dad's Moleskine one more time. I picked back up the notebook, but suddenly, my head throbbed intensely. Then, my hands trembled and Dad's Moleskine fell onto the ground. I looked to the ground, only to find a loose sheet that fell out of place. I tried stuffing it back into its proper position so that the pages would align neatly in a crisp line. But the stubborn page was calling for my attention. It refused to go back in.

I opened Dad's Moleskine to the loose page, and there I saw a song that I must have missed upon my first round of reading. The song was titled "Forgiveness."

♪♫♪♫♪♫♪

I truly am sorry

Don't turn your back on me

Open your heart to forgiveness

I was wrong

But can't let things be

I really mean it

My apology is true

If anger wins

We both lose

♪♫♪♫♪♫♪

I sat on the floor, in front of my desk, and stared at the open page of my Dad's notebook. And after several more minutes of mulling over pointless thinking, something changed. Like someone just switched the lightbulb inside my brain, allowing me to see beyond the haze.

It was like Dad was advising me on my next course of action. His song spoke to me. His words were like my inner voice, trying to help me break free and make peace. Once again, I'd felt the power of music. My heart started to warm and I thought of Max.

I had to stop pointing fingers at the lies I'd been led to believe. And I shouldn't waste my time letting the question of '*why*' chase me to my grave. It was pointless to torture myself to try to make sense of what didn't make sense.

The worst wounds are the ones that bled internally. Max had a lot of emotional baggage. And frankly, that was okay. I did too. I was wrong to allow his past define our relationship. I lost focus of the bigger picture and was unwilling to let go of things that happened before we met. It was clear that I was caught up in the eternal blame game, and I'd failed to recognize how scars could only heal if I allowed them to.

It was no longer a question of why Max lied about his past. Because it didn't matter. There comes a time in our relationship where we shouldn't have to prove ourselves anymore. When the trust should outweigh any baggage brought in from the past. If I refused to forgive Max, I would have given up on my chance from living a better present, and more importantly, a better future with him. Was I ready to say goodbye when I still had time to spare? To be hopeful for a future together, I knew I had to forgive. And I was ready to take back control of my life. I wanted my happily ever after.

Love could hurt even the strongest of couples, and if I loved Max enough, I had to be willing to accept him for him. The more I thought about it, I'd realized that Max loved me enough not to be silent. He could have ended the evening without saying a word, but he didn't. And now I was the one pushing him away. I remembered back to our first argument. Love wasn't just *one* thing. Love was acceptance and believing that we should not just *give*, but also *forgive*.

I pulled out my phone from my pocket and bit the bottom of my lip. I wanted to call Max, tell him that I was sorry, that I forgave him, and that I didn't want to spend my final days fighting with him. But I was still afraid and felt terrible for pushing Max away. I could not find the courage to talk.

My entire body trembled, and my head spun as I pushed myself to my feet, dropping my phone on the ground in the process. I closed my eyes and focused on my bed. I had to lie down and rest. The pain throughout my body intensified as I pushed myself closer to my bed. No! The *monster* inside of me was waking up in my head. Not now. I wasn't ready. Although I'd spent months battling cancer, I was still a terrible warrior. It was a losing battle, and my battalion was weak. But I had to put up a fight. I just had to.

The pain was becoming harder to bear. I dropped to my knees by my bedside and reached for my medication. I heard my phone buzz, but I had to focus before it was too late. I grabbed it, frantically trying to open the bottle. My hands began to tremble uncontrollably, and the pills spilled all over the floor. I fought to keep my eyes open as my vision blurred. I reached for a pill but grabbed air instead. The *monster* inside had taken over. I dropped to the ground, convulsing in an awkward jolting movement before the world went dark around me.

•••

My headaches were unbearable. Brain cancer caused me to lose most of my strength and mobility. But I was fortunate to have not suffered memory loss. For better or worse, I still had my memories. I was thankful for that.

I'd heard about patients getting lost in their own neighbourhood where they had lived for years. I'd heard of patients forgetting the names of their children and having to relearn how to do simple day-to-day activities, like brushing their teeth or washing their hands. When my brain functioning was at its worse, I would drop down and begin to seizure. There were times when I was unconscious for several hours. At most, one day. But, this time, everything felt different.

Brain cancer affected everyone differently. We each had our own timelines, treatment plans, and prognosis. But I now wondered how much longer my body was willing to give.

Aunt Brenna found me on the floor, unconscious the next morning. She screamed very loud, but it wasn't enough to wake me from my coma. She called for an ambulance, and I was taken to the ER. The scene was vaguely familiar, but this time Max wasn't there. I was admitted to the ICU once again at *G&C*. Though, this time, I feared that I would never come back out.

I stayed in deep slumber for several hours. My hours turned into days. I always heard voices. Like people were talking to me. But I couldn't make out who they were. There was music. Lots of music. Some I'd recognized. Some I'd never heard before. Being in a coma was strange because it was like being asleep, except I couldn't wake up. And after three days, I woke from my slumber, disoriented and confused, gasping for air.

"I'm dying!" I screamed, muffled by the tube that connected me to the ventilator.

"We're all dying, sister. Tell me something I don't know," a voice echoed from nearby.

I panicked. Sister? I was an only child. I looked around and saw nobody in the room. Where was I? Where was that voice coming from? Was I already dead?

The monitors were blaring loud beeping sounds, grabbing the attention of the staff. Mabel rushed into the room and soothingly told me that everything would be okay. I looked around the room and saw a curtained wall, then a visitor chair, and a window with my lonely willow tree sitting right outside. Slowly, I calmed down and began breathing at a regular pace. I knew exactly where I was. In room 55, ICU, *G&C*.

As Mabel worked the machines, I peered through the tiny sliver through the curtained wall. I saw a patient sitting upright in their bed, not too far from me. She wore dark sunglasses and had a white cane propped by the wall. I inferred that my roommate must have been blind.

I wanted to say hello. After being asleep for so long, it would have been nice to have some social interaction. But it was difficult to speak with a tube down my throat.

"Sounds like someone is awake. Say something that isn't a scream or a muffle. You've been doing that the past few days. I'd been just dying to meet you," the voice spoke playfully.

I weakly tapped on the side of my bed to let her know that I awake. It was too painful to speak, and Mabel told me to stop fidgeting.

I zoned into and out of consciousness, but I thought I heard the mysterious lady speak. "So, it's Morse code, eh? Don't tell me you are speech impaired. Why do they always pair me up with the most boring patients? Ya'll just trying to be difficult, aren't we?" she huffed, crossing her arms across her chest.

I looked up at Mabel, and she shook her head. "Emily, you have other things to worry about now. Lisa can wait," Mabel insisted as she tried to restrain me.

So, her name was Lisa. I laughed at the thought that in my dying days, I would be stuck with someone who already understood darkness. Maybe we would be good friends.

My head felt like a Thanksgiving turkey that swelled to twice its size from being bloated with extra stuffing. I could not remember how I got here. I kept my fingers crossed that it wasn't a sign of short-term memory loss.

Suddenly, in the corner of my eye, I caught a glimpse of something. I thought I saw someone wearing a baseball cap. Was it, Max?

"Max?" I whispered weakly.

"Oh honey, I haven't seen that boy since you got in. Stop worrying your pretty head of yours. I'm going to tell your Aunt that you're awake," Mabel exclaimed.

During the whole coma, I dreamed many dreams, from the surreal to the mundane. I dreamed of going about my daily business at *Glenwood High* and *Amore*. I hallucinated that I was walking out of the ICU, and then suddenly, the walls turned into stars. I thought about being trapped in a completely white room, but unable to leave because I was paralyzed and couldn't walk. I had a nightmare of evil squirrels chasing me with sharp teeth that oozed green slim. I even dreamed of my Dad with one arm around me and one arm around Max. We were all smiling and having a good time.

●●●

I longed to see Max. I wished that I was with Max at *Amore* right now enjoying my favourite double-shot espresso with a hint of cocoa and cinnamon spice.

Honestly, I was the happiest at *Espresso Amore*. Just sitting in the coffee shop, sipping coffee together with the man I love. I needed nothing more, nothing less. *Amore* was where Max and I first met. It was also where we shared hundreds of coffees together. And it was where we both desired to be when I was bed-ridden. Coffee would never be the same without Max.

Time went by slowly when I was asleep. It felt like months had passed, even though it'd only been three days. By evening, I was stable enough to be taken off the ventilator. Aunt Brenna was allowed into the room. She rushed in, her eyes swollen, and held my hand tight.

"I wished there was more I could do," Aunt Brenna cried.

"Aunt Brenna?" I called out to her.

"Yes, Emily dear," she replied.

"What did the doctors say?" I asked.

"It's not good," Aunt Brenna said solemnly.

So, we sat there in silence, enjoying each other's company. I looked at Aunt Brenna. She looked exhausted. The burden of my illness had finally caught up to her. For all these months that I'd been fighting cancer, she had never seemed fazed by my illness, until today.

"I'm ready, Aunt Brenna. Don't be sad. Everything's going to be ok. You've done more than I could ever ask for," I whispered as tears trickled down the side of my face.

"I'm sorry, Emily. I'm sorry," Aunt Brenna cried.

"There's nothing to be sorry about. Just promise me that you and André will be happy, okay?" I said softly.

"Okay. But always remember that you may not have my eyes, but you'd always be in my heart. And no cancer could ever take that love away," Aunt Brenna exclaimed as she closed in on a tight hug.

"Love is hope, right?" I asked with a smile.

"Definitely," Aunt Brenna said, smiling back.

In these unprecedented times, having hope was very important. Hope was what sustained me and Aunt Brenna, even though I found myself challenged to readjust what I'd hoped for.

That evening, Aunt Brenna brought some items I'd requested. Jimi. My Moleskine. And a stack of colourful paper.

It was hard to write with my head pounding, but I knew that once the stars aligned, I would disappear into the perpetual black hole of oblivion and become a part of the night sky. I could not forgo my last opportunity to say goodbye. With whatever remaining strength that was left in me, I wrote like a madwoman. My eyes felt strained, but I opted to sacrifice sleep because frankly, I was going to be *sleeping* soon for a *very* long time.

There was something very calming about writing. When life hit me, in all its random unfairness, the only thing left for me to do was to reach for pen and paper. I was running out of time. The pain in my head was indescribable. Something felt different this time and I was afraid. I looked out the window to my willow tree. The more I loved, the more my heart ached.

Although I'd been preparing to leave this world ever since my prognosis worsened, I was not going to leave without one last fight. Even though there was no magical wand or witchcraft I knew that could change the inevitable. Unfortunately, there was no spell that could go 'poof' and make cancer just magically disappear. But I kept telling myself that there was absolutely no way I was going to leave this world without seeing Max one last time.

Doris Siu

Chapter Twenty-Nine

GBM was a horrible disease that only knew how to take. It took my strength. My mobility. And very soon, my life. It took so much from me, without ever once asking for my permission. But life never *promised* to be fair.

There were millions of people in this world living with cancer. And thousands of them were survivors too. Cancer had shown me how fragile life was, and how everything could be flipped upside down in a matter of seconds. I was never the type of person who could just sit back and do nothing.

For me, I found comfort in knowing what was going to happen, when, why, and how. But life, as we know it, was unpredictable, and there was no way to plan everything out fully or to prepare me for every single possibility. When I was diagnosed with GBM, I lived every day afterward with unpredictability. Unsure if I would wake up the next morning. Uncertain if I would keep breathing 'til the end of the day. I had no control over my life. And I'd be the first to admit that I liked having control. I only wished I had it.

This was the grim reality of my life. And although I could never predict exactly when that day would come, I'd realized that deciding how to use what little time I *had* left was most important to me now. Cancer transformed us. All of us.

•••

It was morning. I lived to see the sunrise for yet another day. Outside the window, I saw my beloved willow tree. As I gazed into the distance, I saw the bird's nest still resting on one of its branches. It was still there. I smiled.

Mabel entered the room to check on my vitals. She gave me some medication to make me more comfortable.

"Mabel, can you do me a favour?" I asked.

"Of course, dear," Mabel replied.

"Can you keep my curtains open today? I want to introduce myself to Lisa," I said.

"Sure," Mabel said with a smile.

After drawing some more blood, Mabel left the room with the curtained partition pulled up against the wall, exposing myself to my neighbour, Lisa.

"Lisa?" I whispered.

"How you'd know my name?" she asked.

"I'm good at guessing?" I joked.

"I like you. I could use a friend right now. What are you in for sugar?" Lisa asked.

"GBM. Stage IV brain cancer. Terminal," I said bluntly.

"Oh, gosh, honey. Don't make it sound *that* bad. I would trade with you in a heartbeat. This Best's Disease thing is totally *not* the *best*. When all you see is darkness, I no longer *see* the reason to wake up every morning, if you know what I mean," Lisa said sarcastically.

"I know," I said quietly.

"How'd you sleep last night?" Lisa asked.

"Okay, I guess," I replied, surprised with the question.

"I may be blind, but I'm not deaf. People say that when you lose one of your senses, your other ones heighten. I could hear the scratching of pen on paper all night. If the bedbugs were bothering you, then you could have just turned on the television. I would have done that if they offered closed captioning," Lisa joked.

I stared at Lisa awe-stricken. How on earth could Lisa know exactly what was going on without seeing it? There was tremendous potential for the brain to adapt. I'd recalled a scientific research paper that I stumbled upon on Dr. Google. Even in the case of being profoundly blind, the brain was able to rewire itself by making new connections among neurons so we could interact with the environment around us more effectively. It was like Lisa's brain was compensating for blindness.

"Truly amazing," I marvelled.

"Nah, but I did take my disability and turned it into a superpower. Call me Four-sense or whatever you like. Our brains are pretty powerful organs," Lisa insisted.

"I guess there's still hope then," I whispered.

"Always, just have a little faith in your superpowers," Lisa exclaimed.

Lisa and I spent the next few hours sharing our life stories. She told me about her Icelandic adventure in search of the

Aurora Borealis last year. She described the phenomena as bright dancing lights. The shades of green and red set off an eerie glow that illuminated the night sky, like rippling streamers. I would have loved to see something that magnificent. I was glad Lisa had the chance to see it before losing her eyesight. Everyone deserved to have a little *happily ever after*, even if it wasn't for an *infinity.*

•••

I think our closest relationships are our greatest mirrors into ourselves. My relationship with Max was a journey through self-discovery. And by loving him, I'd learned to love myself.

No one wanted to die. For a year, I'd attempted to cope and heal. It was a battle, to say the least, and I had no armour that protected me from the inevitable. The thought of death, but in particular the thought of my own death, was unsettling. And I was certain many felt this way too.

Being in the cancer ward, I'd heard many terminally ill patients ask, 'Am I dying?' only to have someone cut them off with, 'Don't say that, you're going to be just fine.' We defended ourselves against the specter of death by denying its existence. But we all knew that with life comes death. We trusted that by never speaking its name, death would leave us alone. The truth was, we are not immortal, and we could only ignore death's call for so long.

At the time of my diagnosis, I was not able to understand the severity of my cancer. And when my cancer progressed to stage IV, it was a diagnosis that gave no hope. I had my fears and doubts. I turned to my doctors in the hope that with the right medication and treatment, death would be *optional* rather than *inevitable.* I even encouraged myself to go about my everyday routine as I kept fighting in the shadows. But death, of course, was *not* optional. Even the finest medical care could not silence death. I'd realized that I have nothing left to lose now.

Death was a part of life. I had no idea how much longer I could hide from it. Maybe today. Maybe tomorrow. But definitely not a lifetime. Although I expected the worst to come, I had to keep a hopeful heart. I just had to. Because if I'd failed to, my life, as I knew it, would have ended. Although I was tired of running, there was one thing in my heart that was holding me back from truly letting go. Max.

"Emily!" a familiar voice called out from a distance. "Emily! Emily!" the voice yelled again, but this time closer.

I only wished there was more time. But my body continued to deteriorate as my tumour demanded full control. Soon, my brain would ignore my demands, and I would shut down forever. I heard a loud commotion outside of my room, and Mabel's voice consoling the familiar voice. My heartbeat slowed; I could feel death coming to get me.

I turned to the window to seek comfort in the sight of my willow tree. That was when I noticed the bird's nest that I saw this morning now gone. Was I hallucinating?

"Max, where are you?" I cried faintly.

Suddenly, Max bolted into the room. There he froze in front of me. He did not look well, and I had little left in me to greet him.

His emerald eyes were tired. Pained. Fear-ridden. I held out my hand to reach for him, but I could not move further. I could feel my body shutting down; my time was ticking.

"Max? Am I dreaming?" I whispered quietly as my black Moleskine that I was clutching tightly dropped to the floor.

Max snapped out of his trance and ran to my bedside. He clutched my hand tightly, pulling it up to his face. I could feel the warmth of his skin on mine and the tremor in his voice as he spoke. "Emily! I'm so sorry for not coming sooner. I'm here. Please don't leave me. I'm not going to ever let you go. You got to fight this. We can fight this."

I gave him a faint smile as tears welled in my eyes. There was so much I wanted to say to him. I wished for a lifetime together, but it was not what fate prescribed.

I gazed into his emerald green eyes and although the room was far from silent, with the beep of machines and the chatter of doctors rushing down the hallways, it felt like the world just stopped momentarily so I could enjoy the moment just a bit longer.

Softly, I spoke. "Max, we can't always choose the music life plays for us—"

"—But we can choose how to dance to it," Max finished, kissing my hand softly.

"Can we dance together, just one last time?" I whispered.

Chapter Thirty: Epilogue

Two months had passed since Emily's death, and I still mourned her every day. Although she was no longer with us, my love for her continued to grow.

Emily's funeral was organized two weeks after her passing. The mood was solemn. Her coffin was covered with hundreds of white roses, except for one. The one I placed for Emily. I wanted to commemorate my love for her, and a red rose was the only flower that served justice to my everlasting love.

I wished I arrived at *G&C* earlier. I longed to tell Emily about my true heart's desire. I'd seen the best and the worst of her. And honestly, I wouldn't change any of it because I loved all of her.

We don't stop loving someone just because they're sick. And even when she was mad, I still loved her. She was like my coffee, and I was addicted.

•••

That night when I drove home after leaving her on the porch, I told her that I would keep waiting. Whether it was just a couple of hours, days, or a lifetime, my heart always belonged to her. For what it was worth, loving her was totally worth it. I knew there were times when she tried to distance herself from me. She feared to be loved by me because she didn't want to see me hurt.

But the more she tried to distance herself from me, the more my affection grew. Nothing could ever distance what we shared in our hearts. I only wished I could have told her that sooner.

I'd waited for her call. Days passed. And as I waited, I thought to myself if I could have done things differently so that she wouldn't have been so upset. I was confused about why she refused to call. Why she refused to forgive me for hiding the truth. It was unlike Emily to hold a grudge for that long. So, I tried calling her. But to no avail. Perhaps she'd already given up on us.

•••

I had the radio on in my room as I laid in my bed. Then, Ed Sheeran's "Perfect" played in the background, and I suddenly thought of the necklace I gave Emily the night before her audition. I remembered her yanking it off when we fought in the car. I knew I had to find it. I just had to.

I ran out to my car and searched every nook and cranny but came up emptyhanded. I thought I lost it. I sat in the driver's seat with my eyes closed and hung my head in defeat. Then, something sparkled in the corner of my eye. It was Emily's necklace. I lunged forward to grab it. But when I retrieved it, the star pendant broke off in my hands. I'd never been a believer of coincidences, but I did believe in destiny. I knew instantly that something was wrong. Something was wrong with Emily.

I probably broke all speed limits, and ran every red light, as I drove to *G&C* that night. Emily was waiting for me. I could feel it in my heart. And as if my heart was guiding me to her, I entered

G&C and rushed straight to the ICU. Mabel. She would know where I could find Emily. I was certain.

When Mabel caught me rushing down the hallway, she ushered me to room 55. It was like déjà vu as I ran down this hallway. But this time, unlike all the other times, Emily was barely awake. The rhythmic beat of her heart slowed, and I could not bear to see her in such pain. I just stood there, frozen in time. I felt helpless. I almost feared that if I approached her too quickly, I would send her into a never-ending shock. But then I saw it. I saw her hand reaching out to me. So, I ran towards her and held her tightly, not wanting ever to let her go.

This was not how I envisioned spending the rest of my life with Emily would look like. We still had so much to share together. Not just our music. But our lives.

I held Emily in my embrace, and we danced under a million stars by the music in our hearts. She smiled as I kissed her softly on the lips, and I hoped that my kiss would bring her back to life. But it never did. I fell over in a disheveled heap and screamed out in agony. The pain was unimaginable and it felt like a part of me died with her that day.

•••

Emily bequeathed her guitar, Jimi, to me. Jimi sat in the corner of my room beside El, untouched, ever since the funeral. Although I knew that Emily would have wanted me to play Jimi, the flame that burned inside of me was very dim.

It was not until today that I realized why Emily entrusted me with him. I was sipping a cup of coffee when my Mom suddenly entered my room. Since I was deep in thought, her entrance startled me, causing me to spill some of my coffee on the floor. I bent down to clean up the mess when I noticed something colourful inside Jimi.

I approached Jimi cautiously, picked him up, and peered into the soundhole. There I saw a brightly coloured paper that reminded me of the paper airplanes Emily used to like folding with her songs. I shook Jimi lightly to take a closer look. Then, a paper airplane fell out from the hole and onto the floor. Nervously, I picked up the paper airplane and noticed my name written on the wing. I slowly opened the airplane to read the message.

•••

My dearest Max,

> By the time you read this note, I would have already vanished into the perpetual black hole we have come to know as the void of darkness surrounded by stars. Don't think too much about me. I don't want you to be sad.
>
> Isn't it funny how sometimes the lessons we learn are too late? Things that I wished to tell myself many months ago.
>
> A part of me always knew who you were. You are a gift, Max. And in my last moments, you'd help me reconnect with

my Dad. It was like you were a guiding spirit, providing the missing pieces that I needed to make peace. I didn't need you to be my knight in shining armour, though you'd been very good at it most of the time. I don't know if there's such a thing as an afterlife, or even if I'm deserving to go. But meeting you had made me believe that maybe our journey together hasn't ended. Maybe it just begun.

We're like a symphony. And I know that maybe I'm not worthy of you, but I just can't stop loving you. These last few months together have been wonderful for me. I loved every song we played together, and if I could do it all over again, I would in a heartbeat. But maybe this time without the headaches, okay?

Whenever you may feel lost, you can use the stars to help light the way. We are not alone in this universe. Surrounded by stars, each a symbol of hope that brings light to a place that is seemingly only dark. You may wonder where I may go. And I honestly don't know. I guess it is what you want to make of it. I only hope there's coffee.

Dad used to tell me, "where words fail, music speaks." Every song tells a story. Every song has its history. Some have even healed and changed lives. Don't stop sharing your music with the world. The worst that can happen is that you fail, but I doubt someone with your talent could ever go down that path. You owe it to yourself to try. If your music could impact just one person in this world, then I think it's worth it. And for the record, you already did.

Can you promise me something? I know what you're thinking. Emily McGregor, even in her death, she is still making promises. Can you promise me to take care of Jimi? He's pretty easy to handle and makes for a great companion too. He can be as quiet or as loud as you want him to be. He's very obedient. And he deserves a loving home.

I am not sure what led me to you, but I'm happy with the path I'd chosen. May you let my music fill your soul. No strings attached, except for the one to my heart. I promise.

Look after yourself, Max. Stay well and stay hopeful. There is always time for music. May we dance together again someday.

Love you always and forever,

Emily McGregor

•••

Even in loss, we must keep the fight. Life still goes on. My heart shattered into a million pieces without my love, Emily, by my side. I dreamed of being able to touch her again. To hear her sweet voice. And to kiss her endlessly until we were both breathless. I loved her so much. I missed her dearly.

I went through a lot of difficult situations in my life. Death. Failures. Love. And the hardest lesson life taught me was that it was our *job* to continue on. No matter the number of people I'd lost. No matter the number of times I'd failed. And no matter how much I'd loved. I had to face the world as though nothing was wrong, even though my heart was still broken. Life must go on. I must continue writing my song.

Emily taught me a valuable life lesson. We are the promises that we keep. I'd broken a lot of promises in my lifetime. Overpromised plenty. And I even told many sweet lies. But I never understood the importance of promises. My promises. Until I met Emily McGregor. Promises defined who we are. No matter how hard life may get, Emily has shown me that the most important promises in our lives are the ones we make to ourselves.

I believed we have a choice in this world. The choice to decide who we hurt, whose lives we touched, and who we let in. We cannot choose our family and neighbours. But we could choose our friends and our lover. I have chosen Emily. Her love is my song.

To me, the world was like our coffee cup. We all swam inside in circles, endlessly searching for a reason to reach over the rim.

Some liked their coffees hot. Some liked it cold. Some preferred bitter over sweet. Others picked tea over coffee. And that was alright. We often wanted to choose where we go in life, just like drinking our favourite cup of coffee. But Emily has shown me that we really shouldn't be so picky.

We shouldn't be afraid to love the least popular flavour on the menu. Because one day, everyone may be drinking that style. Emily had taught me to love myself and every cup of coffee

I'd ever tried. Frankly, I would have never tried a double-shot espresso if she hadn't introduced it to me. And for the record, I still loved it. And always will.

People come and go in our lives. But the love and memories that we shared together with those people would never fade. As long as we have memories, they lived on. Just like music. One song could change a life.

So, whenever we are on the receiving end of a piping hot cup of coffee, accept it. Embrace it. And maybe even try it. Because we deserved it. We always had.

•••

It was January 13th. Today should have been Emily's 19th birthday. I sat at *Amore* with Emily's favourite, a double-shot espresso with a pinch of cocoa and cinnamon spice. I sat alone in the corner booth, and André gave me a knowing nod.

As I sipped my cup of coffee, I looked at Jimi beside me, wondering if Emily was watching. I felt her presence. Wherever she was, I knew that she was always here with me in my heart. After all, how else could we enjoy a lifetime of coffee dates together? I smiled.

I waved goodbye to André and headed to *G&C.* I haven't entered this hospital since Emily passed. I walked to the cancer ward and invited all the kids to join me under Emily's willow tree. I took a deep breath and strummed Jimi, singing Emily's song of hope to the children.

I sang her song with passion, "That's hope. That's love. That's what I'm thinking of. That's hope. That's love. For me"

As I watched all the kids' faces light up with joy, I knew that Emily was right. And I couldn't help but smile too.

Emily, I don't think our journey together has ended; we are just getting started. From what I see, the possibilities are endless. I promise.

Acknowledgements

I wrote *Hold On Please, Emily* in hopes of opening conversation around challenges in relationships, death, and illnesses for adolescences around the world. Nobody likes to talk about death and illness, even though they are all a part of life. Also, my intention was to reach out to anyone who has or knows someone diagnosed with cancer to help them feel validated, seen, and heard. I hope that my words could bring moments of resonance to my readers so that they can feel less alone and less afraid with whatever challenges they may face in their lives.

I am indebted to the Brain Tumour Foundation of Canada, who shared invaluable information about brain tumours to support the research components of this book. However, I would like to acknowledge that any medical information in *Hold On Please, Emily* should be treated fictitiously as parts were sometimes dramatized to move the story along without impediment.

To the entire team at Self Publishing School, thank you for your support and guidance to launch my authorship career. A special thanks to my two coaches, Ramy Vance and Barbara Hartzler, and my entire launch team.

Thank you to the wonderful people at Cutting Edge Studio, especially Joris van Leeuwen and Marijke van Leeuwen. There were so many moments during the publication process when I felt lost, and Joris pushed me in the right direction every time.

Marijke is the designer behind my professionally-looking book cover; her graphic design skills and knowledge in the literary market are impeccable. If it weren't for Marijke's sound advice, I wouldn't have developed a title with such a powerful hidden meaning. I will have to share the story behind my title one day with my readers. Also, special thanks to Suzanna Chriscoe for going above and beyond in formatting my book. The entire team at Cutting Edge Studio brought my book to life, and I am grateful for all their help.

Hold on please, Emily features lyrics I wrote over several cups of steaming, hot coffee. When writing Emily's songs, I felt compelled to bring them to life. My greatest gratitude goes to Matthew Isaacs, the mastermind behind our accompanying music album, *Hold on please, Emily: Songs of Hope*. Check out our music on Spotify and the music videos on my YouTube channel to see how one song can change the way you dance in life.

Personally, I would like to thank my family for challenging me to reach the finish line. But, especially my son, Lucas, who always loves finding his name in a book. He is my greatest source of inspiration whenever I battle against vexatious writer's block. My husband, Joran, who is my greatest supporter, but also my first and most trusted reader. And my mother-in-law, Priscilla, who made time for me to write whenever I needed it. Thank you for believing in me. To my sister-in-law, Vince, and my parents, brother, and sister, I am grateful for all your support and for celebrating this debut novel with me.

Thank you to all my friends, especially Pamela Boyer, Stephanie Cullen, Shazia Ghafur, Georgiana Roman Sarita, Lynn Slightham, and Seung Hee Yun. I'd been working on this novel for almost two years, and I witnessed so many amazing members of the SPS family launch their books successfully. However, through it all, my finish line always felt unattainable. It was the friendly nudges by these particular individuals who encouraged me to never give up on my dream. My self-publishing journey has been a surreal mix of highs and lows. I would describe it as one of the longest and most epic roller coaster rides I'd ever taken—one with steep slopes, inversions, and tight turns. My friends may not have had all the answers to my problems, but I never had to face any of them alone. Seeing their excitement for my story motivated me to stay on my bumpy roller coaster ride and see it through to the end. Thank you for your continued support and for being a true friend.

Lastly, my readers, thank you for taking the time to read this book. Your support humbles me and drives me to continue writing novels and songs—even creating videos and inspirational material. We all have stories to tell, and I hope my words can resonate awareness, change, and understanding to reach as wide of an audience as possible. Together, we can inspire hope for everyone. Thank you for sharing Emily's message of hope to the world. *Hold on please, Emily*. Hold on.

About the Author

Doris Siu is a Canadian writer and editor based in Toronto with a background in geography and education. *Hold on please, Emily* marks her humble beginnings in authorship and songwriting. As a cancer advocate, her mission is to use realistic fiction, songs, and videos as a medium to connect with patients and families impacted by cancer. Doris does her best writing at 3 a.m. in the morning with, of course, the help of coffee and music. You can learn more about Doris, her writing, and her creative interests at dorissiu.com.

Printed in Great Britain
by Amazon

48523415R00260